Native N

CRITICAL AND CUL͟...VES

Native North America

CRITICAL AND CULTURAL PERSPECTIVES

Essays by
Patricia Monture Angus
Patricia Riley
Gerald Vizenor
Ron Marken
Clifford E. Trafzer
Marianette Jaimes-Guerrero
Hartmut Lutz
Jo-Ann Thom
Armand Garnet Ruffo
Charlotte Hussey
Agnes Grant
Jeanne Perreault
Margery Fee

Edited by Renée Hulan

ECW PRESS

The publication of *Native North America* has been generously supported by The Canada Council, the Ontario Arts Council, and the Government of Canada through the Book Publishing Industry Development Program.

CANADIAN CATALOGUING IN PUBLICATION DATA

Main entry under title:
Native North America : critical and cultural perspectives : essays

ISBN 1-55022-376-3

1. Canadian literature (English) – Indian authors – History and criticism.* 2. American literature – Indian authors – History and criticism. 3. Indian literature – Canada – History and criticism. 4. Indian literature – United States – History and criticism. 5. Indians of North America in literature. 6. Indians of North America.
I. Monture-Angus, Patricia. II. Hulan, Renée, 1965– .

PS8089.5.I6N37 1999   C810.9′897   C99-930556-5

Cover design by Guylaine Régimbald.
Cover: Allen Sapp, "Summer Powwow at Piapot," acrylic on canvas 24" x 36". Reproduced by permission of Allen Sapp Paintings Inc. Imaging by ECW Type & Art, Oakville, Ontario. Printed by AGMV l'Imprimeur, Cap-Saint-Ignace, Québec.

Distributed in Canada by General Distribution Services, 325 Humber College Blvd., Etobicoke, Ontario M9W 7C3.

Distributed in the United States by LPC Group, 1436 West Randolph Street, Chicago, Illinois, U.S.A. 60607.

Published by ECW PRESS,
2120 Queen Street East, Suite 200,
Toronto, Ontario M4E 1E2.

www.ecw.ca/press

PRINTED AND BOUND IN CANADA

Contents

Acknowledgements

Diligent efforts have been made to contact copyright holders; if anyone has been unintentionally omitted, the publisher would be pleased to receive notification and to make acknowledgements in future printings.

Excerpts from Janice Acoose's "Halfbreed: A Revisiting of Maria Campbell's Text from an Indigenous Perspective" from *Looking at the Words of Our People* used by permission of Theytus Books. Excerpts from Jeannette Armstrong's "History Lesson" and "Threads of Old Memory" from *Breath Tracks* (published by Theytus Books) used by permission of the publisher and the author. Excerpts from Marilyn Dumont's "Popular Images of Nativeness" from *Looking at the Words of Our People* (published by Theytus Books) used by permission of the author. Marilyn Dumont's poems "Breakfast of the Spirit," "Half Human/Half Devil Halfbreed Muse," and "The White Judges," from *A Really Good Brown Girl* used by permission of Brick Books. Excerpts from Diane Glancy's *The West Pole* (published by the University of Minnesota Press) used by permission of the author. Excerpts from Louise Halfe's poem "Boarding School," from the collection *Bear Bones and Feathers* used by permission of Coteau Books. Excerpts from Hartmut Lutz's *Contemporary Challenges* used by permission of the author. Material from David McCutcheon's *The Red Record* © 1993 Avery Publishing Group Inc., Garden City Park, New York. Reprinted by permission. Excerpts from Richard Wagamese's *Keeper n' Me* used by permission of Doubleday Canada. Excerpts from Greg Young-Ing's "The Estrangement and Marginalization of Aboriginal Writers in Canada" published in *Paragraph*, used by permission of the author. Excerpts from *She Had Some Horses* by Joy Harjo. Copyright © 1983 by Thunder's Mouth Press. Appears by permission of the publisher, Thunder's Mouth Press.

"Why Native Literature?" by Armand Garnet Ruffo appears by permission of Doug West, editor of *The Proceedings of the Aboriginal Peoples' Conference* held at Lakehead University in 1996.

The editor gratefully acknowledges the support of the Social Sciences and Humanities Research Council of Canada.

Introduction

When Armand Garnet Ruffo suggested changing the working title of this collection to "Native North America," I was immediately convinced. "Native North America" seemed to catch the spirit and intent of the essays collected in these pages, in particular the sense of unity among indigenous peoples on this continent. And yet, this title, haunted as the terms "Native" and "America" are by the history of colonization, reminds us of the history of naming and calls for the careful attention to language and meaning evident in the essays.[1] "Native North America," with all its connotations, is affirmative: it repudiates the borders of nation-states, encircles a community of diverse cultures, and describes something that is geographical, physical, psychological, spiritual.

"Native North America," it seemed to me, also described the commitment to resistance and survival common to the essays. For, what began as a collection devoted to individual reflections on the state of Native literary studies at the present time gradually evolved into a series of statements attesting to the strength and confidence of Native North American literature. In the United States, a number of critical studies of Native American literature have appeared since books such as Vine Deloria's *Custer Died for Your Sins: An Indian Manifesto* (1969) first raised the consciousness of American readers. Anthropological studies by non-Native scholars, such as Karl Kroeber's *Traditional Literatures of the American Indian* (1981), have proliferated while an increasing number of Native American critics have engaged in "defeathering" stereotypes, from the paradoxical "howling" yet "noble" savage remarked by Paula Gunn Allen to the pervasive "dying and disappearing Indian" motif described by Louis Owens and others. Studies of American literature by LaVonne Brown Ruoff, Andrew Wiget, Richard F. Fleck, Gerald Vizenor, and Brian Swann have developed an understanding of "the Native" as cultural sign. Collections such as *Recovering the Word: Essays on Native American Literature* (1987), edited by Arnold Krupat and Brian Swann, bridge the gap between historical revisionism and anthropological inquiry while the work of Kimberly Blaeser,

Alanna Brown, Kate Shanley, Robert Warrior, and others continues to expand the possibilities of literary criticism.

In Canada, such studies as Emma LaRocque's *Defeathering the Indian* (1975) and Howard Adams's *Prison of Grass: Canada from a Native Point of View* (1975) initiated discussion about the cultural position of First Nations in Canada, and critical attention to literature by First Nations has been developing slowly and steadily since the publication of the first book-length critical study, *A Native Heritage: Images of the Indian in English-Canadian Literature* by Leslie Monkman (1981). Penny Petrone's *First People, First Voices* (1983) was soon to follow, as were: *Talking about Ourselves: The Literary Production of Native Women of Canada* (1985), edited by Barbara Godard; *The Native in Literature* (1987), edited by Thomas King, Cheryl Calver, and Helen Hoy; Petrone's *Native Literature in Canada* (1990); *Our Bit of Truth: An Anthology of Canadian Native Literature* (1990), edited by Agnes Grant; and *Writing the Circle: Native Women of Western Canada*, edited by Jeanne Perreault and Sylvia Vance (1990). In 1992, the first anthology devoted to writing by Native people in Canada (now in its second edition), *An Anthology of Canadian Native Literature in English*, edited by Daniel David Moses and Terry Goldie, appeared. Soon after that came the invaluable critical study *Looking at the Words of Our People: First Nations Analysis of Literature* (1993), edited by Jeannette Armstrong, and the Gatherings series published by Theytus.

The field of Native American literary study is broader than this sketch indicates. Native North America, under various names and in various disciplines, has been the focus of serious academic attention for some time. Even so, it may still be new terrain for some, and, although the strength and scope of criticism on Native North American literatures have grown, there is still work to be done. As Agnes Grant remarks in her essay with reference to her national context: "Much has been said about Aboriginals in Canadian literature; much more remains to be said."

For a long time, literature by Native North Americans was read primarily as a source of contemporary anthropological or sociological material. Aware that understanding Native American literature required knowledge of the cultural context of individual works, critics devoted themselves to learning the beliefs and practices within specific Aboriginal cultures. But focusing on this idea of cultural context reveals only part of the world represented in the literature; moreover, as Native American critics point out, the approach risks making literature an artefact of material culture. Another risk of the anthropological reading, as Ron Marken and Margery Fee observe in essays in this collection, is that Native American literature becomes "some kind of rare and exotic growth, to be handled delicately and kept apart" (Marken). Native American scholars have intervened in this current of criticism by calling for "tribal-centred criticism . . . which moves from the culturally centred text outward" (Blaeser 53). As the authors in this collection show, the interpretation of literature by Native North Americans involves the attention to both cultural and literary forms, a method that Arnold Krupat calls "ethnocriticism," because, as Kimberly Blaeser argues, Native American literature reveals the critical methodology appropriate to its study.

To reiterate the importance of reading Native North American literature from the inside out (as Armand Garnet Ruffo argues in his essay) is not to proclaim some natural or essential quality to the writing of Aboriginal people. Neither should references to an Aboriginal Voice by this volume's contributors be construed as essentializing or totalizing gestures. *Native North America* refers to this continent as experienced variously by Native North Americans, not to an abstract "Nativeness"; the term is intended to describe the constant interplay of similarity and difference that gives lived experience meaning.

"There is not an 'Indian' living as an 'Indian' on the planet who is not busy surviving," writes Patricia Monture Angus in the opening essay, "Native America and the Literary Tradition." With this observation, Monture Angus announces a theme traced through several of the essays: the common desire of Native American authors to write resistance. In this effort, the English language helps Native North Americans "to talk out" to other cultures and to educate them about the experience of racism in particular. As an undergraduate student, Monture Angus was told by her English professor that no Aboriginal authors were covered in his course because no work of literature authored by an Aboriginal person was "worthy" of inclusion — even as she read Maria Campbell's *Halfbreed*, the effect of that professor's dismissal endured. "Talking out" is necessary, as Monture Angus observes, because racial prejudice often wears the mask of rational disinterest while academic gatekeeping disguised as evaluation continues the work of colonization. When Aboriginal writers and scholars articulate concerns about identity and authenticity, their work often "stretches the boundaries of accepted academic form in such a way that they are not easily categorized," and acceptance remains difficult. Yet, Monture Angus demonstrates how that work draws on the knowledge of tradition to contribute to the fields of law and literature.

In "Native American Indian Literatures: Narratives of Survivance," Gerald Vizenor celebrates the distinct Native American literatures "eminent in both oral performances and in the imagination of written narratives," arguing that these literatures cannot be properly understood in studies of social science and history. Native American Indian literatures "embrace the memories of creation stories, the tragic wisdom of nature, survivance ceremonies, trickster narratives, and the outcome of chance and other occurrences in the most diverse cultures in the world," and understanding them outside that context means resorting to the imperfect art of translation. Drawing on George Steiner's view that translation is, above all, an act of trust, Vizenor reminds us how often the translation of Native American texts, like the history of Native American relations with the state, has been characterized by betrayal. With an account of American history, Vizenor examines the origins of racism and pays tribute to the continued resistance and renewal of Native America through its literature.

The role traditional stories play in forming the foundation of Native North America as described by both Vizenor and Monture Angus is expanded in Clifford Trafzer's "Spirit and Law in Native American Narratives." Trafzer weaves traditional stories into his argument, demonstrating how these ancient stories "explain the relationship of Native Americans to geographical places, geological formations, and biological features of regions." Trafzer argues that the spiritual beliefs that sustain Native communities and that are necessary to Native American literatures are "best understood through oral narratives," a point reiterated by Charlotte Hussey in her essay. Traditional stories transmit the knowledge, "the spirit and law," that has inspired the survival and the recovery of Native America after the trauma of European contact and colonization.

The relationship between spirituality and survival is also understood to ground literature in Armand Garnet Ruffo's "Why Native Literature?" Writing by Native people, writes Ruffo, "is concerned neither with aesthetic play for the sake of epistemological experimentation, nor with the expression of individual postmodern angst." Founded in a spiritual reality, especially the perception of place that Ruffo's rereading of Frye highlights, literature is a call for "liberation, survival, and beyond . . . to affirmation" — liberation from the stereotypes in the dominant culture, survival of the subjugation these stereotypes entail, affirmation of authentic Native voices. As both individuals and members of a community, Native writers seek to "empower and heal themselves through their own cultural affirmation, as well as to address those in power and give them the real story."

From the critical perspectives of these scholars, the continued survival of Native North America depends in part on the strength of the Native voice in literature, culture, and criticism. "Heard from abroad," observes Hartmut Lutz in "Nations Within as Seen from Without," "the Native Voice from Canada is growing in volume and articulation." Through a comprehensive study of the reception given Native literature in Germany and the history of German fascination with Native North America, Lutz tracks the historical appropriation of Native images by German writers as diverse as the authors of popular fiction and the propagandists of the Third Reich. Although decolonization must take place outside the academy, Lutz argues that Native North America challenges academics. He also warns that, in Canada, the turn to postcolonial studies "dissociate[s] the Canadian cultural discourse from the fundamental Native relationship to the land as source of life and culture," and thus serves to "literarily/literally silence the voices of indigenous cultures."

Tracing the "long, uphill battle for Native writers" to publication and eventual recognition, Agnes Grant, in "'Great Stories Are Told': Canadian Native Novelists," celebrates the achievements of contemporary Native authors and seems to concur with Lutz that understanding Native literature in English requires, above all, respect. Grant describes how discrimination in the Canadian literary industry forced Native literature to develop as an independent genre, parallel to other "Canadian literature." Picking up on the theme of resistance and survivance, Grant notes that Native literature has developed in relation to, and in spite of, the inequalities created by "racist, patriarchal, proselytizing societies," even though the value of the contribution Native writers have made to Canadian literature remains largely unrecognized. In Native communities, Native literature has a role in healing, in "regaining cultural balance," as demonstrated by the work of Richard Wagamese.

In "Aboriginal Writing in Canada and the Anthology as Commodity," Margery Fee considers ideological aspects of the national historical anthology by taking *An Anthology of Canadian Native Literature in English*, edited by Daniel David Moses and Terry Goldie, as an example. Because anthologies are constituted in the reading practices and cultural concepts of particular audiences, the packaging of Native literature in the form of a national historical anthology is suggestive. Fee shows how the convention of placing oral poetry before written suggests that oral poetry constitutes an origin, one that is often appropriated to nationalist ends. By separating Native literature from other literature, an anthology circumvents many questions of comparison, influence, and quality that would help to overturn the assumption that First Nations literature "is inferior because it does not match what [students] are trained to expect in their other literature courses." Those teaching from this anthology should also convey an understanding of the diversity of Native cultures as well as the variety of their relations to the Canadian state; hence, Fee also warns that the concept of pan-Aboriginal culture such an anthology serves may produce a stereotyped "traditional person whose culture is depicted as a mishmash of icons belonging to different groups" when "Aboriginal writers often want to preserve the distinctive practices of their cultures and to pass them on to the next generation."

" 'There Is Nothing but White between the Lines': Parallel Colonial Experiences of the Irish and Aboriginal Canadians" by Ron Marken evokes the author's experience of encountering Native American literature by comparing "coincident events in the histories of Ireland and the Natives of colonized Canada." Marken situates his argument in relation to his experience of teaching Brian Friel's *Translation* to Cree students in La Ronge, Saskatchewan, especially the students' response to the striking contrast between local history and the history retold by Friel. In both contexts of colonization, English settlers invent a language with which to attempt to justify the dispossession of indigenous peoples while denigrating, ridiculing, and outlawing the languages of the colonized. In North America, British colonists would institutionalize the same prejudices: "Whatever tactics the British learned about dealing with the 'savages' in Ireland," concludes Marken, "came with them to British North America, where they were deployed against the Natives."

Patricia Riley's " 'That Murderin' Halfbreed': The Abjectification of the Mixedblood in Mark Twain's *Adventures of Tom Sawyer*" argues that Twain's Injun Joe "functions within the text not only as demonic arch villain, but as a hieroglyph for Euro-America's fear of miscegenation as well." Twain constructs the Mixedblood Joe as a cruel and unredeemable antagonist and as the carrier of an illness (miscegenation) that not only infects others (contact with Joe results in the illness of Tom and Huck), but that also brings about his own destruction. Joe, "the quintessential man without a people," leaves no family or community, no one to mourn his disappearance. Injun Joe stands for the fear of the Mixedblood in nineteenth-century American society, a fear engendered by racism.

Writing as a film critic and as a Native American woman, Marianette Jaimes-Guerrero unearths the entwined roots of racism and sexism that run deep in North American culture in her essay "Savage Erotica Exotica: Media Imagery of Native Women in North America." Throughout film history, from the early cowboy-and-Indian movies to modern-day blockbusters such as *Pocahontas* and *Dances with Wolves*, Native women have served as decorative props or as stand-ins for the European virgin/whore: they are beautiful Indian "princesses"/demeaned Indian "squaws." "Native women in Hollywood cinema are either exotic, erotic objects of lust or mere backdrop if they are not altogether invisible," Jaimes-Guerrero observes. "They are consequently never seen as fully complex human beings in the powerful societal spheres of cinema and other media." Jaimes-Guerrero traces these images of Native women to stereotypes concerning sexuality and miscegenation brought to the Americas by European colonizers and idealized in American nationalist iconography. "Native American women have always rejected both the sexist and racist stereotypes," writes Jaimes-Guerrero, concluding that "only when Native women are able to tell their own stories, as producers and directors, as well as writers, scriptwriters, and actors, will there be a change for the better in authentically positioning our representation and translation to challenge invisibility as well as stereotypes." She cites the work of artists including those involved in the Native Voices Public Television Workshop, the Spider Woman Theater in New York, and *Aboriginal Voices* in Toronto as participating in this challenge. Jaimes-Guerrero concludes by calling on others to resist the commodification that characterizes globalization and to commit to the values learned from indigenous peoples, values that will ensure "a more hopeful egalitarian future."

"When the Good Guys Don't Wear White: Narration, Characterization, and Ideology in Leslie Marmon Silko's *Almanac of the Dead*," by Jo-Ann Thom, studies the role of narrative perspective in developing the novel's distinct ideology. According to Thom, *Almanac*'s ideological agenda "both champions the belief systems of Indigenous peoples and challenges them to adapt and survive." As Thom notes early in her essay, the moral treatise at the heart of this agenda is difficult to ascertain because the distinction between good and evil is often blurred in the novel. Arguing that individual characters represent classes of people and that Silko's moral judgements are aimed at the roles these classes have played in colonizing the Americas, Thom also contextualizes Silko's problematic representation of sexual orientation within a system of life-giving and life-destroying forces. In order to establish this moral dichotomy, Silko highlights the depravity of the upper-class characters. In this reading, the vicious misogyny of the characters who engage in bestial sexual practices is indicative of their role as European colonizers of the Americas. Misogyny, murder, and the wanton destruction of the planet result from a moral corruption that, the novel predicts, will eventually destroy the colonizer's society.

In her essay "Beginner's Mind: Learning to Read the Ghost Dance Songs," Charlotte Hussey approaches the Ghost Dance songs from her own cultural perspective as a poet, teacher, and reader fluent in the language of non-Native literary criticism, yet she respectfully delineates the cultural context of the Ghost Dance by situating the revival of the songs within the historical devastation and disinheritance of the Sioux and Plains peoples. Because the chant rallies members of a group by alluding to, but not describing, shared knowledge, it is less accessible and more challenging to outsiders. Hussey approaches the songs' distinct poetics by describing the "textural differences that might at first perplex a mainstream reader," including "their reliance on synecdoche rather than metaphor," "their grounding in communal ritual, music, and dance, and their close-knit world view of tacit assumptions." In this way, the poetics of the Ghost Dance Songs emphasizes the communal identity of the Plains societies. Like Wovoka's prophecies and the revival he inspired, the Ghost Dance Songs are a form of resistance born out of the assault on the Plains peoples during the late nineteenth century, and, Hussey argues, it is essential to our understanding of Native North American literatures that we first comprehend the nature of that resistance. Other authors in this collection make a similar point.

Like Charlotte Hussey and Ron Marken, Jeanne Perreault writes of her desire for knowledge, remarking: ". . . I realize that the complexity and subtlety of such an integrated intellectual, social, and spiritual context is far from my range of experience." In "Memory Alive: An Inquiry into the Uses of Memory in Marilyn Dumont, Jeannette Armstrong, Louise Halfe, and Joy Harjo," Perreault argues that, while the debate between those who support and those who reject the concept of "memory in the blood" continues, it is inadequate to the task of understanding the role that memory actually plays in poetry by Aboriginal people. In Armstrong's poetic history lessons, for example, blood and memory are clearly linked. In the poetry of Marilyn Dumont, writes Perreault, memory "is the source of nourishment, the site of awakening, and the content of spiritual celebration," while for Halfe, "with memory comes 'voice.'" Memory "as praxis," figured in the spiral Harjo uses, emerges from this mixing of the individual's memories with the collective memories of legends and spirituality. Perreault explicates the complex ways in which these poets work against the crippling effects of cultural, spiritual, and personal amnesia by weaving a tissue of individual and collective memory.

As Patricia Monture Angus remarks in the opening essay, this collection crosses cultures in significant ways. Bringing together scholars from a variety of regions and cultural backgrounds, it demonstrates the diversity of experience and expertise shared by those dedicated to the study of Native North American literature today. By stressing a North American focus, we remind ourselves that the division of the continent into nation-states does not reflect the ancient relationship with the land shared by Aboriginal peoples of the Americas. This focus is intended to help remove, at least psychologically, the traces of colonization that these borders represent. As Hartmut Lutz observes, to Native North Americans, "the U.S.-Canada border, albeit a more penetrable one, is as unnatural as the former Iron Curtain was in Europe," a point that is made by other authors as well.

Although by including essays on writers working within both the United States and Canada we hope to recognize the sharing of experience across national boundaries, the literary critical context that receives literature by Native North Americans has been defined by the national-literature model. For this reason, each essay works within its field by referring to the national literature in question more often than to "North America," indicating the need for further expansion of the critical context. From a literary-critical point of view, "North American" literature has yet to come into being while "American" literature and "Canadian" literature have been institutionalized. A fully realized North American literary study would include literature by Native North Americans written in Aboriginal languages as well as in the other languages of colonization, French and Spanish. Indeed, regrettably absent from the present collection are perspectives on literature produced in Quebec or in Mexico. While this absence signals the obvious dominance of the English language on this continent, it also suggests that, while disciplines tend to "talk in," referring to already defined subject areas, the need to "talk out" is inspiring scholars to stretch the categories they work with — as the dialogue between literature and law in Monture Angus, history and law in Trafzer and Vizenor, or visual media and literature in Jaimes-Guerrero exemplify.

Such dialogues generate knowledge and contribute to the critical and cultural perspectives on Native North America. At the same time, the essays presented here emphatically proclaim both the autonomy and the integrity of Native North American literature and its availability to informed, general critique. In refusing to separate it from general discourses, the authors affirm this strength by maintaining that Native North America should not be subjected to intellectual ghettoization. The strength of Native North America endures in the stories of survival and resistance described and retold by the voices gathered here.

Renée Hulan

NOTE

[1] In this introduction, I use the terms "Aboriginal," "Native," "Native American," "First Nations," "Indian," and "indigenous" in accordance with the individual preferences of the authors.

WORKS CITED

Armstrong, Jeannette, ed. *Looking at the Words of Our People: First Nations Analysis of Literature*. Penticton, BC: Theytus, 1993.
Blaeser, Kimberly. "Native Literature: Seeking a Critical Centre." Armstrong 52-61.
Deloria, Vine, Jr. *Custer Died for Your Sins: An Indian Manifesto*. 1969. Norman: U of Oklahoma P, 1988.
Godard, Barbara. *Talking about Ourselves: The Literary Production of Native Women of Canada*. Ottawa: CRIAW, 1985.
Grant, Agnes, ed. *Our Bit of Truth: An Anthology of Canadian Native Literature*. Winnipeg, MB: Pemmican, 1990.
King, Thomas, Cheryl Calver, and Helen Hoy, eds. *The Native in Literature*. Toronto: ECW, 1987.

Kroeber, Karl. *Traditional Literatures of the American Indian*. Lincoln: U of Nebraska P, 1981.

Krupat, Arnold, and Brian Swann, eds. *Recovering the Word: Essays on Native American Literature*. Berkeley: U California P, 1987.

LaRoque, Emma. *Defeathering the Indian*. Agincourt, AB: Book Society of Canada, 1975.

Monkman, Leslie. *A Native Heritage: Images of the Indian in English-Canadian Literature*. Toronto: U of Toronto P, 1981.

Moses, Daniel David, and Terry Goldie, eds. *An Anthology of Canadian Native Literature in English*. 2nd ed. Toronto: Oxford UP, 1998.

Perreault, Jeanne, and Sylvia Vance, eds. *Writing the Circle: Native Women of Western Canada*. Edmonton: NeWest, 1990.

Petrone, Penny. *First People, First Voices*. Toronto: U of Toronto P, 1983.

———. *Native Literature in Canada*. Toronto: Oxford UP, 1990.

Native America and the Literary Tradition

Patricia Monture Angus

Oh sun, moon, stars, our other relatives peering at us from the inside of god's house walk with us as we climb into the next century naked but for the stories we have of each other. Keep us from giving up in this land of nightmares which is also the land of miracles. We sing our song which we've promised has no beginning or end.

> Joy Harjo (Muscogee)
> (*The Woman Who Fell from the Sky* 1)

For more than a decade now I have read everything by an "Indian" author that I could put my hands on. During this time, I have been both a university student and a professor. My compulsive reading of Native American authors was not just about surviving the loneliness of physical separation from my community while at university. The separation is more significant than mere geography. I was, and continue to be, also spiritually and emotionally separated from my people and our ways. My commitment to further my education, first in sociology and then in law, also removed me from the world of "Indian" thought and knowledge because in the universities I attended there were very few other "Indian" people. This separation is less severe now that I teach Native Studies.[1] To see these experiences as mere cultural separation is to minimize, even trivialize, the experience of postsecondary education for an "Indian" person. I was excited to be included in this volume, but quickly came to the realization that despite my extensive reading of books by "Indian" authors, I knew nothing about Native American[2] literature beyond the gift of survival that it continually gives to me.

In my first year english class, I know that I, like many other Native American students, was frustrated and alienated by the curriculum because no works by Native American authors were included on the course reading list. I now understand this to be a higher standard than including works *about* Native Americans by non-"Indians." The first year english class I took had a section that focused on Canadian literature. I asked the professor why no Aboriginal authors were included and was told curtly that there were no works of literature authored by Aboriginal people worthy of inclusion in a course on Canadian literature. I never returned to an english class in my upper years of university. As a writer now, looking back, I find this regrettable. Although this experience occurred in the early 1980s, I know that it is still occurring at university campuses across the continent. What I was left with, however, was the misunderstanding that there was no such thing as Native American literature. More disturbing is the subtle conclusion that at the time I accepted: Native Americans are inferior writers. This was profound discouragement for an aspiring writer.

Misunderstanding is a gentle description of what occurred in that first year english class (and has been repeated in many other class-rooms). I use this word because I am describing how I felt at the end of that university course. I accepted, at some level, the professor's assessment that if there were Native American works available (I think he thought there were none), then these works were below standard. He acted, thought, and was colonial. I acted colonized and accepted his "expert" opinion. It was at least a decade until I was able to understand that not only had I been misled but I had also internalized that projection of "inferiority" on myself as well as on my own people.

Books by "Indian" authors is a misleading and minimizing cate-gory. Especially in the last twenty years, there has been a rapid increase in the number of books being published by Native American authors.[3] There are novels: *Waterlily*, by Ella Cara Deloria; Jeannette Armstrong's *Slash*; *The Jailing of Cecelia Capture*, by Janet Campbell Hale; James Welch's *The Indian Lawyer*; Beatrice Culleton's *In Search of April Raintree*; and Lee Maracle's *Sundogs*. There are life stories and histories of well-known nations or leaders (generally men who were chiefs): *John Tootoosis: A Biography of a Cree Leader*, by Norma Sluman and Jean Goodwill; and *My Tribe the Crees*, by Joseph F. Dion.[4] There are collections of sacred stories: *Tales of the Iroquois*, by Tehanetorens; and Maria Campbell's *Stories of the Road Allowance People*. There are stories such as Thomas King's *Green Grass, Running Water* and Sherman Alexie's *The Lone Ranger and*

Tonto Fistfight in Heaven. There are plays such as Tomson Highway's *The Rez Sisters* and Drew Hayden Taylor's *Toronto at Dreamer's Rock*. There are books by journalists who have recorded their thoughts for us: Brian Maracle's *Back on the Rez: Finding the Way Home* and Richard Wagamese's *The Terrible Summer*. There are the recorded words of the elders: Arthur Solomon's *Songs for the People*; *Wisdomkeepers: Meetings with Native American Spiritual Elders*, by Steve Wall and Harvey Arden; and *Wisdom's Daughters: Conversations with Women Elders of Native America*, by Steve Wall. I am especially fond of *Stories from Kohkom* by Sylvia Viqc and Darlene Arcand because it also contains Cree syllabics. The work of many Aboriginal academics also stretches the boundaries of accepted academic form in such a way that they are not easily categorized.[5] Of course, the poets cannot be forgotten. There is Joy Harjo's work that was quoted at the beginning of this paper and Chrystos's collection *Not Vanishing*. My favourite is Louise Halfe's *Bear Bones and Feathers*. There is also Beth Brant's early collection, *A Gathering of Spirit*, which has been a friend through many years. (See the works cited, where all these books are listed.)

It is clear that Native authors on both sides of the border are writing and publishing with great frequency.[6] In Canada, this burgeoning of Aboriginal literature coalesced in the early 1980s. However, the growth in the field has not helped me to answer the central question: What is english literature?[7] This is the first broad question I came to. My pondering continued: What is great english literature? Is literature nothing more than a good story? I think most of us know when we have heard or read a good story. If literature is nothing more than a good story, who or what defines "good"? Is literature solely the great stories of Shakespeare, Chaucer, Dickens, the Brontë sisters, Dostoyevsky, and so on to the exclusion of Aboriginal writers such as N. Scott Momaday (Kiowa-Cherokee), Pauline Johnson (Mohawk), Maria Campbell (Métis-Cree), Arthur C. Parker (Seneca), Mourning Dove (Okanogan), or Charles A. (Ohiyesa) Eastman (Sioux)? Is the emergence of a written storytelling tradition among Native Americans part of the literary tradition? Plain and simple, is it literature? This essay is in itself a story. It is a story about how I came to understand the issue of whether or not a broad definition of literature can include both (or either) the written and oral forms of Native American storytelling.

The only answer that has come easily to me is that Native American literature is written by Native American people. It does not matter to me that Native American writers compose primarily in a colonial language, one that we have most recently appropriated to tell things our way, through our own eyes, and in our own voice. Much earlier in my writing career, I noted:

> What is also overlooked is what my people have done with language! We have taken a language that does not speak for us and given it a new life. Perhaps we break all of the structural, style and grammatical rules. But we have learned to use a language which was forced upon us to create powerful messages which convey to you our experience. I do not call this a problem. I call it creativity. It is time my people give themselves credit for the great things we have accomplished against great adversity, rather than continuing to accept and embrace our exclusion. I am proud of my people. (34)

Today, I choose to speak and write in english. It allows me to speak and write to Canadians as well as across the many nation lines and languages of Native America.

The question of Native American storytelling and storymaking is not merely one of exclusion or inclusion in the literary tradition. Michael Dorris (Modoc) notes:

> During the past several thousand years, Native American people have produced literatures rich in diversity and imagery, ancient in tradition, and universal in significance. On the other hand, there is no such thing as "Native American literature," though it may yet, someday, come into being. The roots of this apparent paradox are not difficult to examine or comprehend. "National" literatures, be they French, Sanskrit, Japanese, or whatever, emanate from and are the expressions of coherent aggregations of people. They tend to reflect aspects of a shared consciousness, an inherently identifiable worldview, a collective understanding of custom, language, and tradition. The pool from which both artist and primary audience are culled is generally circumscribed by common linguistics. English literature is expected to be presented initially in English, and to be therefore accessible first and foremost to English-speaking readers. If there had ever been a North American language called "Indian," the mode of communication within a society called "Indian," then there would undoubtedly be something

appropriately labelled "Indian literature." But there was not, and is not. On the contrary, the pre-1492 Western Hemisphere was among the most linguistically and culturally plural areas the world has ever known. The estimated ten to twenty million people who lived in what is today the United States and Canada spoke languages derived from no less than seven different language families, each as distinct from the other as each was distinct from Indo-European. Within each of these families, there existed many separate and mutually unintelligible languages, and within each language, the potential for a variety of diverse regional dialects was high. (232-33)

At the outset, the category "Native American" anything (including literature) must be seen as suspect. The first consequence of inclusion in the english literary tradition affects Native American writers as we become turned into something we are not (that is, from Mohawk, Cree, or Saulteaux into the generic myth of Native American).[8] We become representative of something that does not exist. Nonetheless, I will participate in the paradox as it allows for the opportunity to write across diverse Native American cultures seeking patterns and contradictions. It also allows for the opportunity (which is an opportunity with consequence) to "talk out"[9] to other cultures.

Missing from the discussion of appropriation and authenticity is a sense of both balance and belonging. Non-Aboriginal scholars have held a monopoly on the discourse within the field of english literature, and this has confined the field of literary criticism even further than has being forced to speak and write in a language not one's own. It was not until recently that concerns about appropriation[10] of the Native American voice were raised. The question of appropriation is perhaps the threshold question. At the same time, preoccupation with issues of appropriation obscures more important questions and issues. As time passes, the opportunity to reflect more comprehensively on the styles, voices, forms, themes, and patterns in Native American literature will lead to more complex analyses than are necessary to consider fully the issue of appropriation.

If Native American literature is intended for more than Native American people alone (and I believe it is), then what is its relationship with those outside the culture? Can a non-Native American ever validly critique the writing of an author who is Native American? Julia Emberley offers this consideration:

It remains to be said that the negative critique of resistance writing provokes more than an inkling of resistance on the part of the privileged reader. Though I could mediate on the crisis of the intellectual (in this case the non-Aboriginal academic) and, in so doing, make claims for the representative status of an intellectual vanguard, such a move risks neutralizing the political affects of agency — that is, the active part that subjects play in producing resistance and their specific knowledge of what it is that needs to be resisted. (100)[11]

It is the hierarchy of authenticity and the hierarchy of privilege that causes the problem of closure in a uniquely Native American literature analysis.

The paradox pointed out by Michael Dorris is essential, yet it is not the only grave consequence of the inclusion of Native American voice in the English literary tradition. Robert Allen Warrior (Osage), in his examination of Native American writing and the conventional literary form, comments:

both American Indian and Native Americanist discourse continue to be preoccupied with parochial questions of identity and authenticity. Essentialist categories still reign insofar as more of the focus of scholarship has been to reduce, constrain, and contain American Indian literature and thought and to establish why something or someone is "Indian" than engage the myriad critical issues crucial to an Indian future. As Deloria says in the final chapter of *Custer Died for Your Sins*, " 'Indianness' is in the eye of the beholder." (xix)

This preoccupation with authenticity is one of the clear themes that emerge in a review of the essays on Native American writing. Authenticity is a theme in both the stories themselves and the body of work that critically examines the writing of First People.

This question of authenticity is a complicated one. It is related to concerns about appropriation of voice, but it is not precisely the same issue. It is important to emphasize the difference between a question of authenticity (most often a question raised externally to the Indigenous people telling the stories) and a question (or teaching) of identity (most often a question raised internally, among the Native American authors, in their own writing). Both the external question authenticity and the internal question identity are significant issues that arise as a consequence of colonialism.

Native American authors address directly issues of identity, or, more accurately, the oppression of identity. One of the first published Canadian Aboriginal authors,[12] Pauline Johnson (Mohawk),[13] created a character who had been church married to a white man in "A Red Girl Reasoning" (1906). This work provides an example of how an author directly confronted the notion of non-Indian supremacy:

> ". . . I tell you we are not married. Why should I recognize the rites of your nation when you do not acknowledge the rites of mine? According to your own words, my parents should have gone through your church ceremony as well as through an Indian contract; according to my words, we should go through an Indian contract as well as through a church marriage. If their union is illegal, so is ours. If you think my father is living in dishonour with my mother, my people will think I am living in dishonour with you. How do I know when another nation will come and conquer you as you white men conquered us? And they will have another marriage rite to perform, and they will tell us another truth, that you are not my husband, that you are but disgracing and dishonoring me, that you are keeping me here, not as your wife, but as your — your — squaw." The terrible word had never passed her lips before, and the blood stained her face to her very temples. (33)

It is absolutely clear to me that Ms. Johnson was writing the colonialism (or attacks on her Mohawk identity) she had survived out of her system (a process most Native American writers would be familiar with). It comes as no surprise to me that Native American writing can be organized thematically around the idea of resistance, because Native Americans live resistance.

Identity issues are not always confronted this directly. I borrow this example, an almost poetic passage from *Keeper 'n Me*, from Richard Wagamese:

> What I'm tryin' to say is tradition gives strength to the culture. Makes it alive. Gotta know why you dance steada just how. It's tradition that makes you Indyun. Sing and dance forever but if you're not practicin' tradition day by day you're not really Indyun. Old man told me one time, he said, the very last time you got up in the mornin' and said a quiet prayer of thanks for the day you been given was the very last time you were an

Indyun. Then he said, the very last time you got handed some food and bowed your head and said a prayer of thanks and asked for the strength you got from that food to be used to help someone around you, well, that was the very last time you were an Indyun too. And he told me he said, the very last time you did somethin' for someone without bein' asked, bein' thanked or tellin' about it was the very last time you were an Indyun. See, it's all respect, kindness, honesty and sharin'. Built right in. Do that all the time and boy, you just dance and sing up a real storm next time. Heh, heh, heh. (38)

Similarly, for me, the truth is that you "gotta know why you write steada just how." My writing is very much soul cleansing. I write out the anger and anguish of being an oppressed person. I write until I can live and celebrate my Mohawk identity again. Perhaps this is resistance; it is also survival.

All Native American writers, either directly or indirectly, were and remain repeatedly challenged to respond to the external questioning of others regarding authenticity, as Marilyn Dumont (Métis) exposes:

But what if you are an urban Indian, have always been, or have now spent the greater part of your life living an urban lifestyle? Do you feign the significance of the circle, the number four, the trickster in your life? Do you just disregard these things? *Or do you reconstruct these elements of culture in your life so you can write about them in "the authentic voice," so you can be identified (read "marketed") as a native Artist?*

This is not to argue that an authentic voice does not exist, nor that the artists who do write about/from the "traditional" experience write without the integrity of having that experience. Nor am I arguing that native culture is dying and that these symbols do not exist within the full integrity of the living culture. However, what I am arguing, is that *there is a continuum of exposure to traditional experience in Native culture, some of us have been more exposed to it than others, but this does not mean that those who have been more exposed to it are somehow more Indian, as if we are searching for the last surviving Indian.* (47; emphasis added)

Questions of authenticity (and remember that I earlier asserted this questioning is most frequently external to the culture) are tied to questions of marketability. This conclusion must be related back to my earlier observation that publishing of Native Americans domiciled in Canada burgeoned in the early 1980s. It is impossible to conclude that these Native Americans were not writing before this, that writing is a newfound treasure among us. It is more accurate to assert that Native Americans domiciled in Canada were infrequently published prior to 1980 (and that leads me to point to the fact that publishing houses were exclusively non-Aboriginal prior to this date).[14]

I am not suggesting that the question of authenticity is not also a question for Native American writers. The issue is played out in different ways among us. For example, in an essay entitled "Who Can Speak as an Indian?" Diane Glancy (Cherokee) notes:

> The issue makes me squirm. My great-grandfather was Cherokee. My grandmother probably half. My father a fourth. Me an eighth. I could be more but I'm not sure.
> But what part's Indian? My feet? My hands?
>
> No — I think it's a voice in my chest. I hear it among the other voices. Late at night when the dish scraps is set out back. Under the heavy trees in the distance where we used to drive to Arkansas. Not many times, but enough.
> The Indian voice speaks with my hands. I guess it's my pencil that's Indian. And didn't my red school table say Big Chief?
> It was Sequoyah who made the Cherokee syllabary so the people could write. Working with the alphabet is like driving a car. I get transported to a lot of places. My broken voice rides a broken vehicle. I use a mixed story format. I assimilate "story." The Indian part is a memory I have. An anger over something that's gone. (9)

It is curious that many Native American writers are in fact Mixed-bloods. As Damm remarks, maybe it is the dual position of a Mixedblood that leads us to want to explain the world (18-20).

This brings me to the most important point about the debate over authenticity: authenticity is not really the essential issue. The authenticity debate (or criticism) is no more than colonialism thinly disguised. Authenticity is raised externally, and Native American authors are forced to respond to it. The authenticity debate is premised on the existence of colonizers and those that are colonized. That is a relation of power. There is no question that one of the predominant experiences of being "Indian" in the 1990s still involves the multiple relations of colonialism. There is not an "Indian" living as an "Indian" on the planet who is not busy surviving. Of course, then, colonialism will be a significant subject in any discussion of Native American writing. In the astute words of Janice Acoose (Cree-Métis), writing about Maria Campbell's groundbreaking work *Halfbreed*:

> Maria Campbell's text intervened in a literary tradition that had constructed Indigenous women's lives from within a White-Euro-Canadian-Christian patriarchy. Her text, albeit written in the English colonizer's language and thus seemingly privileging the patriarchal hierarchy, consistently resists conforming to the Christian patriarchy. The author's first act of resistance manifests itself in the construction of her text. As so many previously colonized writers (who are variously cited through this thesis and who have struggled to de-colonize themselves) maintain, *the act of writing is a political act that can encourage de-colonization.* In this context, Campbell is one of the first few Indigenous women who appropriated the colonizer's language to name her oppressors, identify the oppressor's unjust systems, laws, and processes, and subsequently work towards de-colonization. ("Halfbreed" 140; emphasis added)

Colonialism's authenticity disguise is transparent to the majority of us who consider ourselves Native American authors.

In fact, this externally raised authenticity controversy is harmful in that it draws attention away from the "Indian" way to be and subtly reinforces the non-Aboriginal standard of the literary form. For example, my understanding of the Mohawk teachings of life leads me to the conclusion that it is for the individual of mixed blood to choose the path that he or she will walk on — Indian or white.[15] As a person of mixed blood, I am clear in my decision to walk on the Indian (Mohawk) road. This teaching was given to me in a story about the eagles, and in particular the spotted eagle.[16] This member of the eagle family can fly very high, so I was told. It is, therefore, held in high regard. The people with spotted blood who choose to follow the red road should also be held in high regard as they have chosen to follow the more difficult path. This is one of the principal problems that I have found in my research. The critique from outside the culture is a miscritique. It focuses on finding the single authentic Native American voice, as if such a thing could exist among such diversified peoples. This is really the same point (made in another way) that Dorris makes regarding the paradox of Native American anything. In fact, even when we look at a single Native American people, we see that no such authentic voice exists. This search is contrary to the principles of Native American cultures, as these cultures tend to locate knowledge within, not outside, the individual. This means the only thing one can truly know is oneself. The authenticity question turns issues of identity inside out.

A more important question seems to be to examine what advantage accrues to Native American traditions of storytelling by including these traditions fully within the english literary tradition. Granted, to absolutely exclude the Native American traditions as other than literary form, is derogatory. It is an exclusion based at least partially on the troublesome stereotype that "Indian" anything is inferior. This stereotype is one of the ways in which Native American writers are pressured to conform. However, I am not resolved that this single observation about exclusion is sufficient to convince me that Native American writers should fully embrace and aspire to belong to that other literary tradition, particularly if inclusion means turning our Indigenous forms of the literary inside out. It helps to understand more fully what, exactly, literature is before resting this discussion.

Terry Eagleton's discussion of literary theory was most informative to my considerations.[17] He contemplates in his treatise *Literary Theory* the question of whether literature could be defined solely as "creative" or "imaginative" writing (2, 15, 16). If it could, it would make my answer easy; of course Native American contemporary writing is literature. However, Eagleton goes on to make a point that is not dissimilar to the one made by Dorris: "The idea that there is a single 'normal' language, a common currency shared equally by all members of society, is an illusion. Any actual language consists of a highly complex range of discourses, differentiated according to class, region, gender, status and so on, which can by no means be neatly unified into a single homogeneous linguistic community" (5).

Terry Eagleton is not satisfied with his partial definition of literature. He recognizes the literary by its context. He also notes that literature is " 'non-pragmatic' discourse: unlike biology textbooks or notes to the milkman." Literature, he believes, serves no immediate and practical purpose. He concludes his introductory statements "What is literature?" by noting that literature cannot be "objectively" defined (7). I felt not only encouraged but also strengthened by Terry Eagleton's discussion. Perhaps literature is not naturally exclusive of the Native American way.

Equally necessary to this discussion is a second important point that Eagleton's analysis raises: language is an essential consideration. Words are powerful, as they are the reflections and refractions through which culture and thought are transmitted. This recognition is easily attained when one is forced to think and to be in a language not one's own. For me, this is the value of Native American literature. I can surround myself in culture (despite the fact that it is not my language) whenever I choose. Whenever I am in need of comfort.

Thus far in this discussion, I have created a dichotomy, which is misleading. I have presumed that the question must be inclusion in the literary tradition as that tradition is currently defined (that is, before the inclusion of Native American critics or authors). Not only is it misleading, it is probably also demeaning. Why presume that a new tradition of written Native American literature is not appropriate? It is equally difficult to define (and, as Michael Dorris has already noted, perhaps impossible, as the quality "Native American" is really a fiction) what is meant by the term *Native American literature*. Thomas King, in his introduction to *All My Relations: An Anthology of Contemporary Canadian Native Fiction*, demarcates this dichotomy in the following way: "when we talk about contemporary Native literature, we talk as though we already have a definition for this body of literature when, in fact, we do not. And when we talk about Native writers, we talk as though we have a process for determining who is a Native writer and who is not, when, in fact, we don't" (x).

What is common among many Native American writers is our desire to write our resistance. This desire might sometimes be described as "decolonization." As Greg Young-Ing notes, the first wave of Native American literature (typified by the works of Lee Maracle, Harold Cardinal, and, to a lesser degree, Maria Campbell) was "characteristic of protest literature; political in content and angry in tone" (183). More recent writings, particularly those of Native American women, have been characterized as "resistance writing." Julia Emberley advances this definition:

Resistance is itself a process. The process of claiming resisting subject positions Aboriginal woman writers can be interpreted as a practical staging of the deconstructive turn. In a deconstructive analysis, the intolerable hierarchies of race, class, sexuality, and gender contained in binary oppositions such as colonizer/colonized, inferior/superior, Indian/white, woman/man are overturned when these closed oppositions, in which subjects are contained by a revolving motion of being either one or the other are displaced. The point to displacing this opposition, taking an indifferent position toward either side of the opposition, is to re-articulate open, or alternate, subject positions. (102)

After reading this passage, I thought to myself, "I've got it!" This is precisely the difference between the literary tradition and Native American literature. Then I remembered Terry Eagleton. What most people view as the literary tradition also grew out of the resistance and animosity of certain classes towards the Industrial Revolution. Terry Eagleton notes that many early writers, particularly the Romantic poets, were also political activists (17-19). He concludes: "Literature, in the meaning of the word we have inherited, is an ideology" (22). This I both understand and agree with. Although english literature has its roots in resistance, Native American storytelling and storymaking differs. It has become and remains resistance.

This recognition of resistance as a similarity in these two storytelling traditions must be joined to the caution of Elizabeth Cook-Lynn:

Many may understand the complaint that comes from Native American Studies centres about the lack of appropriate curriculum development in both English departments and in the schools of postcolonial studies only because the lack reveals an indifference to changing peoples lives and is, therefore, irrelevant. More appropriately, the complaints should be understood in terms of wanting to strive for the formation of a Native American literary canon, not for the reform of the Western canon. (14-15)

When I was asked to participate in the project of this text, I readily agreed because I thought that it was long past the time that academics (as I certainly am a better academic than I ever was a lawyer) should have begun to commit themselves seriously to breaking down the boundaries between disciplines. I am committed to engaging and encouraging an academic discourse that shatters existing presumptions and boundaries (as this is one of the mainstays of our continued colonialism). What is also interesting to me is that, of the Native

Americans who have aspired to be academics, a great majority of us have ended up in disciplines involving storytelling, such as law, history, or english. As an Indian person, I was taught to watch the patterns of life that are represented to us because patterns carry teachings. Therefore, noting that Aboriginal academics often end up in disciplines that involve storytelling is worth noting.[18]

The first of my objectives in writing this paper (that is, to consider the idea of literature and the way in which the writing of Native Americans can be, or cannot be, embraced by that tradition) has been accomplished. I move along now to the second objective, which is to compare the idea of voice against several storytelling traditions. This might also be described as examining the patterns in different storytelling traditions. These two objectives are not exclusive categories, and there are overlaps between the ideas. For example, the first question is really a question about forms of telling stories. It is interesting to note that several of the novels I read as I contemplated the question "What is literature?" were stories about Indian lawyers, including *The Jailing of Cecelia Capture* by Janet Campbell Hale and *The Indian Lawyer* by James Welch. Perhaps this is simply because I am educated in the law.

Here is an example of a legal story, randomly picked. It is a little lengthy, as well as a little confusing (neither of which I make an apology for):

> The plaintiff brings this action for the alleged unlawful taking by the defendants of the plaintiff's vehicle, a 1985 Ford (hereinafter "the Vehicle").[19] There does not appear to be any dispute that the Vehicle was owned by the plaintiff. The motor vehicle permit for the Vehicle indicting the plaintiff is the owner was filed as Exhibit 2.
>
> Indeed, there does not appear to be a great deal in dispute in terms of the relevant facts. The plaintiff was, at all material times, married to one Terry Lynn Syrette, (hereinafter "Ms. Syrette"), from whom he separated in the fall of 1994. Ms. Syrette brought an Application in Ontario Court (General Division) and an Order was made in that Application on September 29th, 1994 by the Honourable Madam Justice G. Pardu, (hereinafter "the Order"), a copy of which was filed as Exhibit 1 in this proceeding. Pursuant to para. 5 of the Order, Ms. Syrette was to have interim exclusive possession of the Vehicle.

All the defendants are police officers[20] within the meaning of the Police Services Act, R.S.O. 1990, c.P.15 and at all material times were attempting in good faith to carry out their duties as such.

On either October 4th or 6th of 1994, (the exact date is not of importance to any of the parties), the defendant Douglas Sewell was attended by Ms. Syrette, who had with her a copy of the Order. She asked for assistance in getting the Vehicle and showed the Defendant Douglas Sewell the copy of the Order. The defendant[21] Douglas Sewell requested the defendant Noel Syrette to come to the office and the defendants Noel Syrette and Albert Williams responded to this request.

The defendants Noel Syrette and Albert Williams, having reviewed the Order, accompanied Ms. Syrette (who travelled with another gentleman in another vehicle), to the location of the Vehicle at the home of the plaintiff's brother and sister-in-law, Brad and Peggy Syrette, at 483 Gran Street on the Rankin Reserve. It is common ground that the Rankin Reserve is a "reserve" within the meaning of the Indian Act, R.S.C. 1985, c.I-5.

Ms. Syrette went to the Vehicle and found that it was locked. Having no keys to the Vehicle, and suspecting that the plaintiff's mother may have such keys, Ms. Syrette went to the home of the plaintiff's mother, again accompanied by the defendants Noel Syrette and Albert Williams in their separate vehicle.

The plaintiff's mother said that she had no such keys and, while Ms. Syrette and the defendants Noel Syrette and Albert Williams were still at her home, called the plaintiff's sister-in-law Peggy Syrette at her place of employment and advised her of the situation, following which Peggy Syrette spoke on the telephone with the defendant Noel Syrette, with whom she was acquainted. She asked him whether she had any right to keep the Vehicle at her home until her husband and the plaintiff returned home, because she did not feel that the Vehicle should be removed in their absence. The defendant Noel Syrette responded that Ms. Syrette had a court order.

Thereafter, since no keys were forthcoming, one of the defendants called a tow truck and the vehicle was towed away as directed by Ms. Syrette.

The plaintiff claims that this taking of the Vehicle was a wrongful taking to which the defendants were parties, and that they are accordingly liable for all the damages flowing from it. Counsel have asked that I not assess the damages, as they are confident that they can agree on that issue, so I am to direct myself only to the question of the liability of the defendants (Syrette v. Sewell, Syrette, and Williams).[22]

Lawyers call these the facts. This is the form that a legal story is presented in, although it is not presented as a story. In fact, in the legal realm, the idea of good storytelling probably has negative connotations, as the profession prides itself on objective assessment. Law does not deal with creative and imaginative thought. Law presumes to deal only with what is. Law presumes to be objective (a value that I believe can only be asserted narrowly among specified groups, such as men or women, Indian or not, and so on). Objectivity is culture- and gender-specific reality, if it exists at all. Facts, separated from the larger context of the story, are the commodity of law. The story is not important just because it is a story. It is important because it embodies a dispute. This is the fundamental problem with the law as a storytelling vehicle: it is not the people or the message in the story that are important. Spend a moment considering how a good storyteller would tell this same story about Ms. Syrette's experience of marital breakup.

The form and style of the legal story are also noteworthy, especially since my objective is to compare the idea of voice in several traditions. In the legal story I chose to share with you, the people are objectified; a woman becomes merely "the plaintiff." She loses not only her name, but also her character and her feelings. This is all "no never mind" to one who is legally trained.[23] Perhaps it was my dissatisfaction with stories of, and in, law that led me to study literature instead. This tells me something about myself that is important. I did not go into law because I was solely interested in the process of how disputes were resolved. I went into law because I carried a message about the way "Indians" were erased from the legal story. I thought the presence of "Indian" people in legal institutions would somehow fundamentally change the story of Canadian law. I stopped teaching law several years ago because whatever change I could facilitate at a single law school came at too great a personal consequence.

When I became dissatisfied with the descriptions of myself as "lawyer," "professor," and "academic,"[24] I turned to the culture and settled on the culturally significant image of storyteller. The story for many Native Americans is much more than just a good book. It is how the culture is passed. It is how history is shared. It is how the sacred is taught. When I picked up this image, I did not intend to suggest that I was a storyteller in the old way. Perhaps a better image is "storymaker." I have never been trained in the old storytelling tradition, although I have learned from the old ones who have earned those story ways. I am not a community (tribal) historian, nor would I retell or reproduce a sacred story without instruction and permission. This is not because I think unconditionally that the stories should not be reproduced. I simply do not think that, as someone who is not fluent in the original language, I can ever assume this role. I am not saying it is wrong to share sacred stories in print (though of course the proper cultural traditions and protocols must be honoured). I am just saying that sharing those stories is not my "job." I mean no disrespect when I borrow this image, storyteller, to describe who I am and what I do. This is the continual problem I face as an academic: Just where do I fit in?

For Native Americans, and in the english literary tradition, stories have different forms. There are the sacred stories, there is oral history (the stories passed down from generation to generation), there is the oral tradition (the process of sharing lessons across generations), and then there are the stories told for enjoyment.

I do not remember in which of my university courses Maria Campbell's autobiographical *Halfbreed* was required reading.[25] It might have been the single anthropology course I took before I was discouraged from continuing in that discipline. Even while reading and cherishing this autobiography, I was not convinced that I should question the presumption implanted by that first year english professor about the lack of Native American literature.[26] Years later, I learned that Maria's book was not, in fact, a first; her work was predated by the writings of Pauline Johnson in what is now known as Canada and by the writings of many others on the other side of the border.[27]

In her introduction to her most recent work, *Stories of the Road Allowance People*, Campbell talks about both the process of storytelling and the manner in which the storyteller earns his or her credentials:

> I remember a warm kitchen on a stormy winter night. I am sitting on the floor with my Cheechum and the old ladies. The room is full of grandpas, mammas and papas, aunties, uncles

and cousins. There is laughter, hot sweet tea and the smell of red willow tobacco. "Hahaa kiyas mana kisayano kahkee achimoot . . . Long ago the old man told us this story," my uncle would begin and my Cheechum and the old ladies would puff their clay pipes and nod. "Tapwe anima, Tapwe . . . Yes, yes it is true." This was the first snowfall and the first night of storytelling in the little road allowance village where I grew up. If someone knocked on our door, my papa would call out: "Tawow, pay peetiqwak . . . come in, there is room." My mamma would pour another cup of hot tea and people would make room for the visitor, who would lean forward and become a part of our circle. Today, the stories I heard then, I have learned, and I have been given permission to share them with you. They are old men's stories. I had hoped when I became a student of storytelling that I would get old women teachers, but that was not meant to be. The old women were kind, made me pots of tea, cooked me soup and bannock, made me starblankets and moccasins, then sent me off to the old men who became my teachers. I am a very young and inexperienced storyteller compared to the people who teach me. And although I speak my language I have had to relearn it, to decolonize it or at least begin the process of decolonization. This has not been an easy task and the journey has taken me eighteen years. I have paid for the stories by re-learning and re-thinking my language and by being a helper or servant to the teachers. I have also paid for the stories with gifts of blankets, tobacco and even a prize Arab stallion. With the stories, I have had lifetimes of "stuff" put into my memory. I am not even sure what it all is but the teachers say, "Don't worry about it, just think that your brain is the computer you use and we are the people typing it in. When you need it, or you have had the experience to understand it, your spirit will give it to you." I have learned to trust them. It is in this spirit that I share these stories with you. I give them to you in the dialect and rhythm of my village and my father's generation. I am responsible for the mistakes. (2)

I want to make sure that we are hearing the same things in the words of Dr. Campbell.[28] The culture that I know, which comes from the ancient ways, is very gentle. It is subtle. Things are not said bluntly but are left in the story for each listener to pick up. However, as

I know this book crosses cultures, the cultural translation I give (although in no way complete) gives but one example of the vast complexities and subtleties in Native American cultures; here it is Métis culture.[29]

First, Maria tells us that the process of storytelling is a family process. She introduces the people in the room with her as relations. As I understand a little about traditional ways of being, I also understand that noting these relationships is a way of making a circle to draw everyone in. The old ways are largely about relationships. A blunt parallel would be to point out that sharing the stories around the fire is one way of sharing Aboriginal laws. (Quite different from the judgement shared earlier.) Maria, as storyteller, begins her book by introducing, in the right way, her relations. In this, her first paragraph, Dr. Campbell also notes that the stories told by the men are affirmed by the women when they say "Yes it is true" (which is not to say that women were not, and are not, the storytellers). In my experience, the storytelling is a gentle way of teaching. Each story is a combination of elements, from entertainment to law. We pick the different things we need from the stories on the occasions we hear them. It is not the theme, plot, or setting that is most important, contrary to what those within the literary tradition might claim. In her introduction, as well as in the stories, Dr. Campbell shares with us, among other things, the Indigenous rules of "copyright" of her people and their stories.

Storytelling is more than just a form. It involves different beliefs about both truth and learning. These differences are made clear by Richard Wagamese in his novel *Keeper 'n Me*:

> *them missionaries when they came here saw all these Indyuns ev'rywhere prayin' real strange. Strange to them anyway. Had big pipes they were passin' aroun' and sittin' there passin' smoke over themselves offa burnin' grass, moss and partsa trees. Some were goin' into sweat lodges. Prob'ly looked like little smokin' tents to them missionaries. Guess they couldn't figure out what was goin' on so they decided we all needed helpin' in a big way. Called us savages, heathens, pagans. Said we needed direction. Said our way of prayin' was wrong.*

> *See, them they came ashore with what they called The Great Book of Truth. Us we never knew truth to be somethin' had to be spelled out. Always figured was somethin' we each carried around inside. True human bein's got that. Truth inside.*

You see it in the way they move around the world. Always
kind, respectful, honest. That kinda way. You learn that from
watchin' nature. The world'll teach you everything if you look
long enough. Natchrel law's true for everything. Anyways, they
come here with their Great Book, lookin' strange at our ways,
not takin' time to learn about it, not askin' for a guide, judgin'.
Guess when your truth's all spelled out for you you got no need
to learn no more. I don't know. (74–75)

Keeper 'n Me is more than just a novel. It is the sharing of oral
tradition (or Ojibway culture). The definition of truth — that which
we all carry inside — contrasts sharply with western ideas of truth.
Fiction is probably not, for this reason, a good description of a lot of
Native American literature. In the same way, categories such as
history, literature, and law are not very useful in understanding
Native American ways of being.

In the second paragraph of the introduction to *Stories of the Road
Allowance People*, we learn that winter is the time for storytelling.
We learn that the culture is a welcoming one, and that all those who
come to the door are invited in. There is always room for another
listener or another storyteller. In the next paragraph, we learn about
the belief that things are as they are "meant to be." This is the
knowledge, a knowledge that is fundamental in the old ways: there
is a natural order to life — all life, not just human life. The reader
also receives a clue about the way gender is structured in original
cultures. There are men's stories and women's stories; but this is not
absolute, as Maria is to learn from the men. This is just a small clue
that a rigid structuring of gender[30] relationships does not exist in
Native American cultures.[31] In the third paragraph, we are also given
an important lesson: permission is necessary before you can go
around telling these sacred stories yourself. What I have shared with
you is just a little information about the differences. It is not enough
information for anyone who absorbs it to conclude that they understand the place or process of story in Native American traditions.

I remain hesitant about including Native American storytelling
traditions, whether written or oral, within what is understood commonly as the english literary tradition. Inclusion feels too much like
being boxed in, forced to conform to ways that we do not share. It
feels like cutting the heart out of an ancient way of being. It is certain
that Native America will continue to write, to tell, to share. I borrow
the words of Kateri Damm to conclude:

Through the power of words we can counteract the negative images of Indigenous peoples. We can fight words with words. Then, with the weakening of colonial attitudes we can move together towards greater cultural, artistic and creative forms of expression that reflect the changing faces of who we are. Along the way, our identity as Indigenous writers, whether mixed-blood or fullblood, will continue to inform our work and strengthen us spiritually and politically. We will look with two sets of eyes and hear with two sets of ears and we will speak from the place where we stand with full confidence in the power of our voices. Indigenous literatures will resist the boundaries and boxes. In reality, more of our varied voices will be raised in art, literature and music and the definitions of who we are will be forced to change. Our different voices will create a new harmony. More importantly we will open the borders to each other. ("Says Who?" 24)

NOTES

[1] I started my teaching career on 1 July 1989 and spent the first five years in two Canadian law schools.

[2] I do not usually refer to First Peoples as "Native American." When I write about law or politics I adopt, with both hesitation and regret, the language of the Canadian legal system. The term I use in that context is "Aboriginal" people or peoples. This is not most appropriate to this paper. Here I refer to "Native Americans," as I wish to focus on the northern area of what I understand in the ancient way as Turtle Island (others would understand North America).

[3] I have added a bibliography to this paper to demonstrate the wealth of Native American writing that presently exists. This bibliography in no way includes all Native American works of fiction, poetry, or literary criticism. The length of the bibliography demonstrates the rapid growth in the area.

[4] There are other biographies of great Native American leaders that I have chosen not to list, as they were not even coauthored by a Native American writer. On this basis alone, I find them less credible and have excluded them from this discussion. Generally, the subtleties of Native American cultures are lost in the writing of outsiders.

[5] Probably the best-known example is the work of Vine Deloria Jr. (Standing Rock Sioux), but I would also include that of Robert Allen Warrior (Osage).

[6] For example, Greg Young-Ing (Cree), in his article "Aboriginal Peoples' Estrangement: Marginalization in the Publishing Industry," notes: "In the

1990s all books by Aboriginal peoples were published through small and independent presses. Not one Aboriginal author has been published by a large Canadian publishing house; while over a hundred books *about* Aboriginal peoples have been published by large Canadian houses. . ." (185).

[7] I had great difficulty deciding on an adjective to precede "literature." To use "literature" without adding the silent cultural prefix contributes to the marginalization of great works of writing by Native Americans. Not acknowledging the culturally specific roots of a concept such as (english) literature contributes to the invisibility of privileged cultures and therefore reinforces cultural exclusions of those labelled "other" (that is, non-privileged). I settled on "english," but I am still not fully content that this covers all I wish to communicate.

[8] This is the reason I have noted the national identity in parentheses after the names of the scholars and authors.

[9] Please see Monture, Thornhill, and Williams, "After Words" (224). "Talking out" is there explained as the act of educating those external to a culture about experiences of racism. It is much less usual for people of colour or Aboriginal people to have the chance to "talk in" — that is, to talk to each other about those experiences. This is a problem, because it is the "talking in" conversation that tends to be sustaining. It takes a lot of energy to constantly explain racism (or colonialism) or sexism or (homo)sexuality to those who do not share that experience.

[10] Appropriation of voice is the taking of voice from the dispossessed or less powerful, in this case Native Americans, and taking it as your own. Examples include works by W.P. Kinsella and Anne Cameron. Appropriation is a concern because it tends to reinforce and perpetuate negative stereotypes of Native American peoples as well as to exclude authentic writers from the field.

[11] There are two specific reasons I am content to quote Emberley: her consideration of her own role in this discourse as a non-Aboriginal scholar, and her recognition that academia is a robe of privilege. Academic credentials alone cannot, and do not, prepare or authorize any person to study Native America.

[12] Greg Young-Ing notes: "The late Mohawk author Pauline Johnson was the first Aboriginal author to be published in Canada. Johnson published three books in the early 1900s and was one of the most prominent poets of her time. To this day, she still holds the distinction of being the Aboriginal author who gained the highest level of notoriety in the literary world and sold the most books in Canada. However, the 'Pauline Johnson phenomenon' was not to be a catalyst that would open up the Canadian publishing industry to Aboriginal literature" (182).

[13] There is a controversy that follows Pauline and her work. This controversy flows almost exclusively from the pens of non-Aboriginal

academics. Is she really an "Indian" (her mother was white)? In other words, is she authentic? I have already noted that the discussion of authenticity supports colonialism. For a fuller discussion of authenticity and how it impacts on the Mixedblood writer, please see Kateri Damm (Chippewa).

[14] Pemmican Publications in Winnipeg and Theytus Books in Penticton were both founded in 1980 (see Young-Ing 185).

[15] It is not quite this simple for Haudeenausonee people. If you are born to a non-Indian mother, you are born clanless.

[16] Nia:wen Kevin Deere. Any error in the presentation of this teaching is my own.

[17] I have consciously tried to focus my comments on the critique of Native American literature by Native American people. In trying to come to terms with "What is literature," out of necessity I relied on one non-Indigenous scholar: Terry Eagleton. Julia Emberley, the second non-Indigenous scholar cited, is present as she reflects on the way she places her non-Indigenous voice into a dialogue that really belongs to Native Americans. This is one of the points I made earlier about authenticity. Relying on non-Indigenous scholars cannot help me make sense of Indigenous writing and the patterns present in our traditions.

[18] For example, four is the seasons, the directions, the person (body, mind, spirit, and emotions). Four is important because it is a pattern of life.

[19] Note the capitalization of "vehicle," an inanimate object, and the failure to capitalize "plaintiff," the person. This is a profound notation on importance (property over people) and perspective.

[20] The fact that Ms. Syrette chose to be accompanied by the police indicates at minimum that relations between these people were not amicable. It is also highly possible that Ms. Syrette had left a physically violent or otherwise abusive relationship. However, this is not apparent on the face of the text. Law has the power to make invisible any facts lawyers do not think are significant (remember that until quite recently women were overwhelmingly excluded the legal profession).

[21] Irregularity in capitalization is in the original text.

[22] For the curious, I want to describe how this case ended. Despite the fact that the defendants were acting on a court order that gave the vehicle to Ms. Syrette, the seizure took place on a reserve. The provisions of the Indian Act were interpreted to protect the husband's property from seizure. For discussion of the gender discrimination in the law of matrimonial property located on the reserve, please see Martha Montour and Mary Ellen Turpel.

[23] The consequences of this phenomenon are not usually discussed by lawyers in any public way. Clients are the commodities of cases. For example, in perhaps the most famous Aboriginal rights case, R. v. Sparrow, legal academics have not generally noted the overwhelming responsibility

Mr. Sparrow undertook when he became the first individual to approach the Supreme Court of Canada to define Aboriginal rights.

[24] Please see Monture Angus 44–52.

[25] Dr. Campbell's writings have been much discussed. Please see Acoose, *Iskwewak-Kah' Ki Yaw Ni Wahkomakanak*, and "Halfbreed"; Damn, "Dispelling."

[26] He was also careful to point out to me that I could not write.

[27] I am dancing around this idea of a border between the United States and Canada. It is problematic for me as a Mohawk person (as it is for other Native Americans). It draws a line through traditional Mohawk territories that are located principally in what are now known as Ontario, Quebec, and New York State. This is a symbolic example of the degree of separation one lives as an "Indian" person.

[28] The name "Dr. Campbell" looks funny to me as it sits there on the page. That's no put-down of Maria and the credits she has been honoured with by academia. It looks funny because it denies the relationship that I feel, which means I think and feel of this woman as "auntie," although there is no biological relationship or even cultural affiliation (she is Cree-Métis and I am Mohawk). I also want to note that I respect the sacredness of the stories Maria shares with us in print. Just because they are shared in a form outside our traditions does not change their sacred character. In adopting her book as a class text, I sought permission and offered my gift.

[29] As I am not a Métis person, I run the risk of transposing my Mohawk beliefs on those of the Métis people. This is dangerously close to an appropriation. I am not attempting to offend anyone.

[30] In the Native American languages that I am familiar with, you cannot say "he" or "she." Traditional-language speakers usually use only "he" when speaking english (but note that this is not a gendered decision). Consider the ramifications of a language with no gender: in my mind, it is a reflection of the degree of equality that exists between the genders; the distinction was unimportant in everyday language.

[31] Dr. Campbell and I had lunch recently and came to talking about just this. She shared with me her understanding of why her teachers were men. I cannot share that with you, as it is her personal story. I do want to point out that her understanding is much different and clearly more profound than my own. As it is her story, I leave it to her to choose the way she will share it.

WORKS CITED

Acoose, Janice. "Halfbreed: A Revisiting of Maria Campbell's Text from an Indigenous Perspective." Armstrong, ed. 137–50.

———. *Iskwewak-Kah' Ki Yaw Ni Wahkomakanak: Neither Indian Princesses nor Easy Squaws*. Toronto: Women's Press, 1995.

Alexie, Sherman, *The Lone Ranger and Tonto Fistfight in Heaven*. New York: Atlantic Monthly, 1993.

Armstrong, Jeannette. *Slash*. Penticton, BC: Theytus, 1985.

——, ed. *Looking at the Words of Our People: First Nations Analysis of Literature*. Penticton, BC: Theytus, 1993.

Brant, Beth. *A Gathering of Spirit: A Collection by North American Indian Women*. Toronto: Women's Press, 1984.

Campbell, Maria. *Halfbreed*. Toronto: McClelland, 1973.

——. *Stories of the Road Allowance People*. Penticton, BC: Theytus, 1995.

Chrystos. *Not Vanishing*. Vancouver: Press Gang, 1988.

Cook-Lynn, Elizabeth. "Who Stole Native American Studies?" *wicazo sa review* 12.1 (1997): 9–28.

Cornplanter, J.J. *Legends of the Longhouse*. Ohsweken, ON: Iroqrafts, 1986.

Culleton, Beatrice. *In Search of April Raintree*. Winnipeg: Pemmican, 1983.

Damm, Kateri. "Dispelling and Telling: Speaking Native Realities in Maria Campbell's *Halfbreed* and Beatrice Culleton's *In Search of April Raintree*." Armstrong, ed. 93–155.

——. "Says Who? Colonialism, Identity and Defining Indigenous Literature." Armstrong, ed. 11–26.

Deloria, Ella Cara. *Waterlily*. Lincoln: U of Nebraska P, 1988.

Deloria, Vine. *Custer Died for Your Sins: An American Indian Manifesto*. New York: Macmillan, 1969.

——. *God Is Red*. New York: Grosset, 1973.

——, and Clifford M. Lytle. *American Indians, American Justice*. Austin: U of Texas P, 1983.

Dion, Joseph F. *My Tribe the Crees*. Calgary: Glenbow Museum, 1993.

Dorris, Michael. "Native American Literature in an Ethnohistorical Context." *Paper Trails: Essays*. New York: HarperCollins, 1995. 232-33.

Dumont, Marilyn. "Popular Images of Nativeness." *Looking at the Words of Our People: First Nations Analysis of Literature*. Ed. Jeannette Armstrong. Penticton, BC: Theytus, 1993. 45-50.

Eagleton, Terry. *Literary Theory: An Introduction*. 1983. Minneapolis: U of Minnesota P, 1996.

Eastman, Charles A. (Ohiyesa). *Old Indian Days*. Lincoln: U of Nebraska P, 1991.

Emberley, Julia. "Aboriginal Women's Writing and the Cultural Politics of Representation." Miller et al., eds., 97–112.

Glancy, Diane. "Who Can Speak as an Indian?" *The West Pole*. Minneapolis: U of Minnesota P, 1997.

Gunn Allen, Paula. *Studies in American Indian Literature: Critical Essays and Course Designs*. New York: MLA, 1983.

Hale, Janet Campbell. *The Jailing of Cecelia Capture*. Albuquerque: U of New Mexico P, 1993.

Halfe, Louise. *Bear Bones and Feathers*. Regina: Coteau, 1994.

Harjo, Joy. *The Woman Who Fell from the Sky*. New York: Norton, 1994.

Highway, Tomson. *The Rez Sisters*. Saskatoon: Fifth House, 1988.

Hill, Barbara-Helen. *Shaking the Rattle: Healing the Trauma of Colonization*. Penticton, BC: Theytus, 1995.

Johnson, E. Pauline. *The Moccasin Maker*. Tuscon: U of Arizona P, 1987.

———. "A Red Girl Reasoning." *Voice of the Turtle: American Indian Literature, 1900–1970*. Ed. Paula Gunn Allen. New York: Ballantine, 1994. 20–40.

King, Thomas. *All My Relations: An Anthology of Contemporary Canadian Native Fiction*. Toronto: McClelland, 1991.

———. *Green Grass, Running Water*. Toronto: HarperCollins, 1993.

Maracle, Brian. *Back on the Rez: Finding the Way Home*. Toronto: Penguin, 1996.

Maracle, Lee. *Sojourner's Truth and Other Stories*. Vancouver: Press Gang, 1990.

———. *Sundogs*. Penticton, BC: Theytus, 1992.

Miller, Christine. "Aboriginal Women's Writing and the Cultural Politics of Representation." Miller, et al., eds.

Miller, Christine (Blackfoot) and Patricia Chuchryk, eds., with Marie Smallface Marule (Blood), Brenda Manyfingers (Cree), and Cheryl Deering. *Women of the First Nations: Power, Wisdom, and Strength*. Winnipeg: U of Manitoba P, 1996.

Momaday, N. Scott. *House Made of Dawn*. New York: Harper, 1968.

Montour, Martha. "Iroquois Women's Rights with Respect to Matrimonial Property on Indian Reserves." *Canadian Native Law Reporter* 4 (1987): 3–18.

Monture, Patricia, Esmeralda Thornhill, and Toni Williams. "After Words." *Canadian Journal of Women and the Law* 6.1 (1993): 224–47.

Monture Angus, Patricia. *Thunder in My Soul: A Mohawk Woman Speaks*. Halifax: Fernwood, 1995.

Mourning Dove (Humishuma, Christine Quintasket). *Cogewea, the Halfblood: A Depiction of the Great Montana Cattle Range*. Lincoln: U of Nebraska P, 1981.

Native Women's Writing Circle, and Lenore Keeshig-Tobias, eds. *Into the Moon: Heart, Mind, Body, Soul*. Toronto: Sister Vision, 1996.

Parker, Arthur C. *Seneca Myths and Folk Tales*. Lincoln: U of Nebraska P, 1989.

Perreault, Jeanne, and Sylvia Vance, eds. *Writing the Circle: Native Women of Western Canada*. Edmonton: NeWest, 1990.

Ruoff, LaVonne Brown, and Donald B. Smith, eds. *Life, Letters and Speeches: George Copway (Kahgegagahbowh)*. Lincoln: U of Nebraska P, 1997.

Sluman, Norma, and Jean Goodwill. *John Tootoosis: A Biography of a Cree Leader*. Ottawa: Golden Dog, 1982.

Solomon, Arthur. *Eating Bitterness: A Vision beyond the Prison Walls, Poems and Essays*. Toronto: NC, 1994.

———. *Songs for the People: Teachings on the Natural Way*. Toronto: NC, 1990.

Syrette v. Sewell, Syrette, and Williams. *Canadian Native Law Reporter* 1 (1997): 207–13.

Taylor, Drew Hayden. Toronto at Dreamer's Rock *and* Education Is Our Right: *Two One Act Plays*. Saskatoon: Fifth House, 1990.

Tehanetorens. *Tales of the Iroquois*. Akwesasne: Akwesasne Notes, n.d.

Turpel, Mary Ellen. "Home/Land." *Canadian Journal of Family Law* 32.1 (1991): 17–40.

Viqc, Sylvia, ed. *Stories from Kohkom*. Trans. Darlene Arcand. Saskatoon: READ Saskatoon, 1995.

Wagamese, Richard. *Keeper 'n Me*. Toronto: Doubleday, 1994.

———. *The Terrible Summer*. Toronto: Warwick, 1996.

Wall, Steve. *Wisdom's Daughters: Conversations with Women Elders of Native America*. New York: Harper-Perennial, 1993.

———, and Harvey Arden. *Wisdomkeepers: Meetings with Native American Spiritual Elders*. Hillsboro, OR: Beyond Words, 1990.

Walters, Anna Lee. *Talking Indian*. Ithaca, NY: Firebrand, 1992.

Warrior, Robert Allen. *Tribal Secrets: Recovering American Indian Intellectual Traditions*. Minneapolis: U Minnesota P, 1995.

Welch, James. *The Indian Lawyer*. New York: Norton, 1990.

Young-Ing, Greg. "Aboriginal Peoples' Estrangement: Marginalization in the Publishing Industry." Armstrong, ed. 177–87.

Native American Indian Literatures: Narratives of Survivance

Gerald Vizenor

Native American Indian literatures embrace the memories of creation stories, the tragic wisdom of nature, survivance ceremonies, trickster narratives, and the outcome of chance and other occurrences in the most diverse cultures in the world. These distinctive literatures, eminent in both oral performances and in the imagination of written narratives, cannot be discovered in causal expositions and reductive social science translations, nor can they be altogether understood in the historical constructions of cultures in one common name.

The name "Indian" is a convenient one, to be sure, but it is an invented term that does not come from any Native language, and it does not describe or contain any aspect of traditional Native experience or literature. *Indian*, the noun, is a simulation of racialism, an undesirable separation of race in the political and cultural interests of discovery and colonial settlement of new nations; the noun does not reveal the experiences of diverse Native communities. The name is unbidden, and the Native heirs must bear an unnatural burden to be so christened in their own land.

The term *American Indian* has come to mean "Indianness," the set of conditions that indicates the once despised tribes and, at the same time, the extreme notions of an exotic outsider; these conditions are advocated as real cultures in the world. The simulations of the outsider as the Other serve racial and cultural dominance. Race is an invention, not a noticeable genetic presence, and cultural traits are the brute concoction of the social sciences.

"The origins of racism" are obscure, but the consequences "are more tangible," writes Richard Drinnon in *Facing West*. "Racism defined natives as nonpersons within the settlement culture and was in a real sense the enabling experience of the rising American empire: Indian-hating identified the dark others that white settlers were not and must not under any circumstances become, and it helped them wrest a continent and more from the hands of these native caretakers of the lands" (xvii–xviii).

Naturally, there were many distinct names for other tribes, names that were used in the course of trade relations, war, and other situations, but there were no common, ethnic, racial, or national names for the estimated hundred million Natives who lived in thousands of tribal communities in the Americas. The third edition of *The American Heritage Dictionary of the English Language* notes that the "term Indian has always been a misnomer for the earliest inhabitants of the Americas. Many people now prefer Native American both as a corrective to Columbus's mistaken appellation and as a means of avoiding the romantic and generally offensive stereotypes associated with phrases such as wild Indian or cowboys and Indians." The term *Native American Indian* distinguishes the esteem of Natives from that of both the native-born and the inhabitants of India.

Some historians have underestimated the Native presence before colonization by millions, and conservative reductions have sanctioned the notion that colonialism and settlement dislocated a tribal population of no significance in such a vast and "unused" hemisphere. Indeed, the opposite was true. "The Americas were densely populated at the time Europeans found their way to this New World," writes Henry F. Dobyns in *Native American Historical Demography*. He points out that recent estimates place the Native hemispheric population at more than one hundred million in about 1490 (1). Perhaps thirty million of that total lived in what is now Mexico and ten million in what is now Canada and the United States.

Old World diseases decimated tribal communities. "Smallpox became the single most lethal disease Europeans carried to the New World," writes Dobyns. "This contagion repeatedly spread through Native American peoples, killing a high proportion of susceptible individuals not immunized by surviving a previous epidemic" (2). Malaria, yellow fever, plague, typhus, and influenza decimated the survivors of other diseases and became the pernicious relations of colonialism.

The epidemics "weakened the Indian economic systems and dispirited the people, whose world order seemed to have collapsed in the face of unknown forces," writes Francis Paul Prucha in *The Indians in American Society*. "Many Indians and their white friends maintained that the proper status of the Indian tribes was as small independent nations under the protection of the United States" (33). The Native economies, once based on mythic associations with nature, were weakened by racism, nationalism, and the politics of colonial dominance.

"Historians of Indian-white relations face the special problem of dealing with two diverse cultures," observes Prucha, "for we must understand two others, quite diverse in themselves" (5). These "others" are the tribes and the "past white societies." The policies that defined the relations between the two others wavered between sovereignty, assimilation, and termination of Native communities on federal reservations, established in hundreds of treaties with the tribes. These capricious policies have maintained a federal dominance over the tribes for more than a century.

"Indian Affairs were at first seen as a domestic problem, equal to and linked with the problems of war debts, western land claims, orderly expansion, and so on," writes Dorothy Jones in *License for Empire*. "It was only after the repeated failure of attempts to handle Indian affairs as a domestic problem that United States officials were forced to consider relations with the Indians, rather than a unilateral policy for the Indians" (147). The basis of the relations with tribes shifted from the "domestic to the diplomatic," and the treaty system became a new social order. "Outright land-grabbing was not nearly so widespread as is commonly believed. There was no need. The treaty system itself was the primary vehicle of transfer" (147). The treaties were mentioned more often in histories than Native resistance to colonial settlement and dominance.

Jones notes that when the English trader Alexander Henry arrived at the post of Michilimackinac in the fall of 1761, he was lectured by the Chippewa leader Minivavana: "Englishman, although you have conquered the French, you have not yet conquered us. We are not your slaves. These lakes, these woods and mountains, were left to us by our ancestors. They are our inheritance; and we will part with them to none" (71). The treaty system was not a course of action that honoured similar or equal diplomatic powers. Native rights to the land were inherent and not given to the tribes in treaties, but the dominance of the government could not be overthrown in the absence of inseparable tribal power.

"Declining from a position of prosperity and of considerable political and economic power at the beginning of the national history of the United States," writes Prucha, "the Indian tribes by the early decades of the twentieth century had become politically subordinate to and almost completely dominated by the federal government; they were economically dependent, too, upon white goods and services" (*Indians*, 29).

The Indian Citizenship Act of 1924 was a cruel irony of assimilation policies; Native communities were hardly protected by the patent promises of a constitutional democracy. "Previously, Indians in the United States had received citizenship through a variety of haphazard means: by receipt of an allotment, by separation from one's tribe, by special permission of the Secretary of the Interior, or by service in World War I, to name a few of the more common routes taken," writes John Wunder in *Retained by the People*. Federal citizenship, however, "did not change many things. Citizenship status theoretically gave Indians the right to vote. But this right was not protected by force or federal statutes, and it was not fully attained until several decades later." Several states prevented tribal citizens from voting. The Fifteenth Amendment, which provides that the right of citizens to vote shall not be denied or abridged by any state, "could be overcome," some states argued, "because Indians did not pay state taxes; they were still wards of the federal government, which precluded them from voting; or they were residing on lands that were not a part of the state for voting purposes" (Wunder 50).

Native American Indian authors have presented some of these issues of inherent Native rights, the duplicities of federal policies, and the burdens of racial identities in their autobiographies, short stories, poetry, and novels. D'Arcy McNickle, for instance, an established scholar and literary artist, asserts in *Native American Tribalism* that the tribes have not accepted oblivion. "Caught up in succeeding waves of devastating epidemics and border wars as settlement moved westward, the Indians retreated, protecting what they could, and managing to be at hand to fight another day when necessity required it. They lost, but were never defeated" (4).

McNickle's first novel, *The Surrounded*, was published in 1936, two years after the Indian Reorganization Act was passed near the end of the Great Depression in the United States. This new policy ended the federal allotment of communal land to individuals, and provided for the establishment of representative governments on reservations. The dire conditions in remote Native communities, however, were exacerbated by the economic devastation in the nation as a whole. President Franklin Delano Roosevelt announced at the time that "the only thing we have to fear is fear itself." The New Deal legislation created the Works Progress Administration and employment for millions of people in various national programs.

The "baneful effects" of the economic depression were "crushing blows to the Indian economy," writes William T. Hagan in *American*

Indians. "The depression shook the faith of many Americans in the nineteenth-century version of individualism. The hordes of unemployed seemed to demonstrate that we already had too many factory workers and too many farmers. And if the government was forced to succour college-trained white Americans, it was patently absurd to continue to talk of the average reservation Indian moving into a free, competitive society" (154).

McNickle writes in *Native American Tribalism* that the "opportunities offered in the Indian Reorganization Act brought into use the capacity for social action which had never died in the Indian people, though it had been obscured. The start was slow in many instances, since the written constitutions introduced ideas and procedures which had not been part of customary practice" (94-95).

Archilde, the main character in McNickle's novel *The Surrounded*, returns to the reservation and there encounters the mistrust of his father, who is himself an outsider, the silence of his tribal mother, and the complex burdens of his identities. He has been away at boarding school and is coming back to the reservation at the end of the Depression, a clever Mixedblood in a white shirt and blue suit. Archilde tells his mother that he had a job playing fiddle in a show house. Caught in the heart of family loyalties, burdened with the contradictions of federal policies of assimilation, and touched by tragic wisdom, he is displaced by the author in the transcendence of Native reason on the reservation.

Two years earlier, F. Scott Fitzgerald published *Tender Is the Night*, a novel of tragic dissolution and hedonism in a culture at a great distance from the poverty on reservations. At the same time, the government was sponsoring authors and arts programs; the themes of discovery, regionalism, and tourism were new forms of literary dominance over Native American Indians.

The memories of Native creation, the humour of trickster stories, survivance, and Native constancy were heard as the promise of an enlightenment at the end of the last century. That enlightenment, a Native performance, was associated with the first generation of students who returned from federal and mission boarding schools to reservations and outbraved the cultural extortion of the federal government. The next generation of Native scholars, artists, and bureaucrats endured in their time the poverty of the nation. The Indian Reorganization Act provided for democratic governments, ended the allotment program, and established a new policy that favoured the employment of Natives in the Bureau of Indian Affairs.

These new routines, policies, and economies on reservations created new Native connections and identities, and these identities were causes of Native contention at the end of the Great Depression.

John Joseph Mathews, a prominent historian and novelist who, like his characters, was born in Indian Territory, Oklahoma, published *Sundown* in 1934. Challenge Windzer, the main character in the novel, is an educated Mixedblood. His mother is traditional Osage. The sense of the novel, which is set in the 1920s, is both traditional and historical, and the burdens of the protagonist are ancestral, personal, and economic; the oil discovered on tribal land was in this era a dangerous source of family wealth. Virginia Mathews writes in her introduction to *Sundown* that the author of the novel, her father, was in the "vanguard of American Indian writers who brought their education, their sophistication, and their considered pondering on a dual cultural heritage to the service of their tribes and of Indian people collectively. As a result, for more than fifty years now, Indians have been speaking on equal terms — and often on terms of significant advantage — with bureaucrats and politicians, with historians, philosophers, and other intellectuals" (xiv). Mathews created Challenge "out of what he had expunged from his own life — despair, dichotomies, the aimlessness, the uncertainties he knew when he was young — to become valuable and uniquely himself, triumphantly white and Indian" (xiv). At the end of *Sundown* Mathews writes, "mixedblood families came back to the old Agency from their homes in the mountains, in California, and elsewhere. They dropped their golf clubs and lost their homes and came back to wander aimlessly along the familiar streets. They asked with the other citizens of the town, 'S'pose it'll come back?' All agreed that it would, but they wondered just the same" (304).

McNickle, Mathews, and other authors cannot be separated from the enlightenment of their Native traditions and experiences on reservations, or from the national political and economic conditions of their times. McNickle attended a boarding school in Oregon. Later, he studied at the University of Montana and Oxford University. Mathews also studied at Oxford and he attended the School of International Relations in Geneva, Switzerland. These Native authors endured *real* tragedy, not mere victimry, and they earned a tragic wisdom that has not been envisioned in the unceremonious themes of aesthetic heroism in other novels written during the Great Depression. Thomas Wolfe published his second novel, *Of Time and the River*, in 1935. John Steinbeck's *Tortilla Flat* appeared the same year, and his proletarian novel *The Grapes of Wrath* was published four years later. *Gone with the Wind* by Margaret Mitchell was published in 1936.

Native American Indian survivance is a sentiment heard in creation stories and read in the tragic wisdom of Native literature; this common sentiment of survivance is more than a survival reaction in the face of violence and dominance. Tragic wisdom is the source of Native reason, the common sense gained from the adverse experiences of discovery, colonialism, and cultural domination. Tragic wisdom is a pro-Native voice of liberation and survivance, a condition in Native stories and literature that denies victimry.

Native survivance is heard in creation and trickster stories, dream songs, visions, and other presentations in thousands of Native oral languages in North, Central, and South America. Some of these diverse oral narratives have been translated and published in various forms, for untold reasons, as social scientific evidence. The problem, of course, is that written translation, even when the languages involved are similar, is not a representation of oral performance, and even the best translations are scriptural reductions of rich oral nuances.

How, for instance, can a word heard or a scene imagined in an oral story or performance have the same meaning in a written language? Moreover, how can personal dream songs or the performance of creation stories in tribal communities be understood as poems or short stories in published translations? The stories that are heard are not the same as the silence of the written word.

The many existing anthologies of tribal songs, dreams, and stories contain beautiful translated images, to be sure, but the original communal context of performance and other circumstances of oral expression are seldom understood in translation. "Anthropologists and folklorists, whose disciplines are not directed toward appreciation of superior artistry, usually play down, or ignore, the individual distinction of creative accomplishment in ethnographic material," Karl Kroeber points out in *Traditional American Indian Literatures* (17). The causal theories of the social sciences and the concerns of evidence have unnerved the memories of tribal stories. Too often the rich sources of Native imagination and oral literary styles have been reduced in ethnographic studies to the mere evidence of culture.

The fragments of songs and oral stories published in anthologies of tribal literatures seldom have anything in common but the language of dominance. The metaphors in oral stories are mundane, abstruse, mysterious, unnameable, and more, but few collections in translation reveal the rich context of the songs and stories. For instance, is a song sacred or secular, public or private, and is that song an individual dream or a communal ceremony? How, then, can translations of distinct tribal expressions ever be definitive or representational in another language?

The first "hermeneutical motion" of translation is "initiative trust, an investment of belief, underwritten by previous experience," George Steiner writes in *After Babel*, his study of translation. The "demonstrative statement of understanding which is translation, starts with an act of trust" (296). Native American Indian literatures have endured "acts of trust," manifest manners, and the dominance of translation for more than three centuries. Brian Swann, who edited *On the Translation of Native American Literatures*, writes that "Given the history of this hemisphere, to settle for the dignity of mystery is far preferable to any claims of definitiveness" (xvii).

Some translations, however, simulate nuances, and that "initiative trust" overcasts the practice and assumes that other cultures can be represented in musical scores, registers, and scriptures. "If culture depends on the transmission of meaning across time," Steiner writes, "it depends also on the transfer of meaning in space" (*After Babel* 31). The translations of tribal stories by social scientists in search of cultural evidence can be misinterpretations of tribal time, space, and the rights of consciousness. "Almost at every moment in time," Steiner observes, "notably in the sphere of American Indian speech, some ancient and rich expression of articulate being is lapsing into irretrievable silence" (*After Babel* 51).

The translations of tribal stories are obscure manoeuvres of dominance that contribute to the simulations of Indianness over distinct tribal memories and stories. Moreover, translations are scriptural, and the sudden closure of oral literatures favours written texts over heard stories; the eternal sorrow of lost sound haunts the scriptural translation of tribal stories.

Larzer Ziff, for instance, argues in *Writing in the New Nation* that literary "annihilation, in which the representation offers itself as the only aspect of the represented that is still extant, is not, of course, physical extermination." Thomas Jefferson, James Fenimore Cooper, and thousands of others who have written about tribal cultures have "sincerely regarded their writings as efforts at preservation." Moreover, the "process of literary annihilation would be checked only when Indian writers began representing their own culture" (172, 173).

Henry Rowe Schoolcraft was one of the most recognized interpreters of tribal cultures in the early nineteenth century. His translations of Anishinaabe (Chippewa or Ojibway) songs and stories were published in *Algic Researches*. Henry Wadsworth Longfellow was influenced by this material and based his *Song of Hiawatha* on the translations of oral narratives from one tribal culture to name another. This dubious tribal epic was a very popular poem at the time. "Hiawatha elegiacally counsels his people to abandon the old ways and adapt themselves to the coming of 'civilization,' but he does so in a verse form which only 'civilization' can provide," writes Arnold Krupat in *For Those Who Come After*. "Longfellow derived Hiawatha's trochaic meter from the Finnish epic, Kalevala" (55). There is no evidence of an "act of trust" in either the translations or the uses of tribal literature in this instance.

"Great translators," Steiner argues in *Language and Silence*, "act as a kind of living mirror. They offer to the original not an equivalence, for there can be none, but a vital counterpoise, an echo, faithful yet autonomous, as we find in the dialogue of human love. An act of translation is an act of love. Where it fails, through immodesty or blurred perception, it traduces. Where it succeeds, it incarnates" (270-71). Most anthologies of translated tribal literatures are "blurred perceptions" that serve dominance rather than the independence of Native imagination. The inclusion of translations in anthologies of Native literature without critical mention of context, texture, and the oral nuances of performance contributes to literary dominance.

"The Indian, becoming the province of learned groups especially organized to study him, soon was a scholarly field in himself, just like a dead language," observes Roy Harvey Pearce in *Savagism and Civilization* (129). The American Ethnological Society, organized in 1842, encouraged the scientific study of Indians. The Smithsonian Institution was organized four years later and "its scientists were specifically bidden to gather information on the Indian." However, as "scientists moved towards the modern study of the Indian as a normally complex and difficult human who possessed a tolerably respectable civilization of his own, they continued to think of him literally as a primitive, as one whose way of life was somehow earlier than their own" (Pearce 129, 130).

Native American Indians have published their own books since the beginning of the nineteenth century. For example, *A Son of the Forest* by William Apess, published in 1829, could be the first autobiography written by a tribal person. Professor LaVonne Brown Ruoff, the distinguished literary historian, points out in *American Indian Literatures* that Apess was an orphan and that the "whites" he lived with "as a child taught him to be terrified of his own people. If he disobeyed, they threatened to punish him by sending him to the forest" (53). Apess was a minister, an activist for tribal rights, and a Mixedblood who traced his descent to the Pequot. "His own birth and death are not documented," Barry O'Connell observes in *On Our Own Ground* (xxiv). "Born to a nation despised and outcast and perhaps, to add to the stigma, not only white, a 'mulatto' or 'mixed breed,' but also part African American, a child with William Apess's history who simply made it to adulthood would be doing well" (xxxix).

Luther Standing Bear was one of the first tribal students at the new government school at Carlisle, Pennsylvania. "One day when we came to school there was a lot of writing on one of the blackboards," he writes in *My People the Sioux*. "We did not know what it meant, but our interpreter came into the room and said, 'Do you see all these marks on the blackboard? Well, each word is a white man. They are going to give each one of you one of these names by which you will hereafter be known'" (136-37).

John Rogers was born at the turn of the last century on the White Earth Reservation in Minnesota and attended the federal boarding school at Flandreau, South Dakota. "At school, if we brought in a nest or a pretty leaf, we were given much credit, and we thought we would also please Mother by bringing some to her," he writes in *Red World and White*. "But she did not like our doing this. She would scold and correct us and tell us we were destroying something" (39). Rogers writes with a sense of adventure, peace, and Native responsibility in spite of the adversities arising from assimilationist policies that he experienced on reservations. He praises his boarding-school education and, at the same time, he is critical of the government.

Captain Richard Pratt, the first superintendent of the federal industrial school at Carlisle, told an annual meeting of educators three years after the massacre at Wounded Knee, South Dakota, that

> the Indian has learned by long experience to believe somewhat that the only good white man is a dead white man, and he is just as right about it as any of us are in thinking the same of the Indian. It is only the Indian in them that ought to be killed; and it is the bad influences of the bad white man that ought to be killed too. How are these hindering, hurtful sentiments

and conditions on both sides to be ended? Certainly, never by continuing the segregating policy, which gives the Indian no chance to see, know, and participate in our affairs and industries, and thus prove to himself and us that he has better stuff in him, and which prevents his learning how wrong is his conception of the truly civilized white man. (Prucha, *Americanizing* 279)

Luther Standing Bear, John Rogers, and others of their generation were the last to hear the oral stories of natural reason in their Native families before the stories were recorded and translated, and they were the first to learn how to write about their memories and experiences.

Charles Alexander Eastman was raised with a tribal name in the traditions of the Santee Sioux. He graduated with distinction from Dartmouth College and earned a degree from the Boston University medical school. He was determined to serve Native communities and became the government physician at the Pine Ridge Reservation. A few months later, he treated the few survivors of the 29 December 1890 Wounded Knee Massacre in which the Seventh Cavalry murdered hundreds of ghost dancers and their families.

Eastman was raised to be a traditional Native leader, but that natural event would not be honoured in the course of national histories. Many Lightnings, his father, was imprisoned for three years in connection with the violent conflict between settlers and the Minnesota Sioux in 1862. President Abraham Lincoln commuted the death sentence. Christianity touched Many Lightnings and he chose the name Jacob Eastman.

Charles was about twelve years old when he and his relatives escaped the retribution of the military. His sense of a traditional Native world was never the same, and his new surname, education, and marriage were revolutions in tribal and personal identities at the time. Elaine Goodale, his wife, was a teacher on the Pine Ridge Reservation. She was from Massachusetts. Together, they were forever burdened with the remembrance of that horror, the massacre at Wounded Knee.

Eastman and others of his generation, the first to be educated at federal and mission boarding schools, must have been haunted in their dreams by the atrocities of the cavalry soldiers. Wounded Knee has had post-traumatic effects on several generations because the stories of the survivors were seldom honoured in the literature and histories of dominance. *The American Heritage Dictionary of the English Language*, for instance, notes in the geographic entries that Wounded Knee was the "site of the last major battle of the Indian Wars." Indeed, the massacre of unarmed men, women, and children is not the "last major battle." The murder of Native dancers could be the end of civilization.

"Those soldiers had been sent to protect these men, women, and children who had not joined the ghost dancers, but they had shot them down without even a chance to defend themselves," writes Luther Standing Bear in *My People the Sioux*. He was one of the graduates of a federal school and returned to the reservation as a teacher. "The very people I was following — and getting my people to follow — had no respect for motherhood, old age, or babyhood. Where was all their civilized training?" (224).

Eastman found and treated two wounded survivors in the snow at Wounded Knee. His composure would later turn to outrage. "Trying to save the survivors of Wounded Knee had called upon all of Eastman's medical training and skill, but trauma management had not been the goal of his long preparation," writes Frances Karttunen in *Between Worlds*. "He had intended to serve the Sioux in positive ways, especially in the field of public health" (148).

Luther Standing Bear was educated in a new Native enlightenment that would outbrave dominance; he never lost his sense of humour and tragic wisdom at boarding school or on the reservation. Clearly, he was never the hostage of an education, and he never reduced his various experiences to mere victimhood. The simulations of academic remorse and substitutional victimization serve the literature of dominance, not survivance.

"I always wanted to please my father in every way possible," Standing Bear writes in *My People the Sioux*:

> All of his instructions to me had been along this line: "Son, be brave and get killed." This expression has been moulded into my brain to such an extent that I knew nothing else. My father had made a mistake. He should have told me, upon leaving home, to go and learn all I could of the white man's ways, and be like them. . . . When I thought of my father, and how he had smoked the pipe of peace, and was not fighting any more, it occurred to me that this chance to go East would prove that I was brave if I were to accept it. . . . Now, after having had my hair cut, a new thought came into my head. I felt that I was

no more Indian, but would be an imitation of a white man. And we are still imitations of white men, and the white men are imitations of the Americans. (141)

Standing Bear graduated and worked in a department store owned by John Wanamaker in Philadelphia. He read in the newspaper that Sitting Bull, the Lakota healer, was scheduled to lecture in the city. "The paper stated that he was the Indian who killed General Custer! The chief and his people had been held prisoners of war, and now here they were to appear" in a theatre (184-85).

Standing Bear visited Sitting Bull at his hotel. "He wanted his children educated in the white man's way, because there was nothing left for the Indian." The interpreter was in the room, so "I did not get a chance to tell Sitting Bull how the white man had lied about him on the stage. And that was the last time I ever saw Sitting Bull alive" (184-85). Standing Bear, to be sure, "was more fortunate" than most of the students who returned to the reservation. Some had "only a superficial education and a trade that was usually of no value," Richard Ellis writes in *Indian Lives*. Standing Bear "had a recommendation from Pratt which led to immediate employment as an assistant teacher at a salary of three hundred dollars a year" (147).

Standing Bear returned to teach at the government school on the Rosebud Reservation and heard the horror stories of the massacre at Wounded Knee. Later, he toured with Buffalo Bill's Wild West Show in Europe. He was active in tribal rights movements, acted in several motion pictures, and wrote several books about his experiences.

"Native Americans who attended boarding schools are living archives, storehouses of memory and experience. Their memories and experiences, shaped into spoken narratives, continue to shape families, communities, and educational endeavours," writes K. Tsianina Lomawaima in *They Called It Prairie Light: The Story of Chilocco Indian School*. "The fact that schools often strengthened rather than dissolved tribal identity is not the only surprise tucked within alumni reminiscence. The idealized school society envisioned in federal policy often bore little resemblance to reality." Oral and "documentary sources build an image of a boarding school culture that was created and sustained by students much more than by teachers or staff. Ironically, the practical realities of adapting to institutional life did foster self-sufficiency in many students" (xii).

No one in our time has the right of consciousness to renounce the courage and humour of Native students in boarding schools at the turn of the century; no one has the right to erase the virtues and reason of their parents, or the ardent manners of certain teachers. The government created the conditions that menaced Native traditions, and to shame the spirit, nerve, and bravery of the students would be to recant their memories. To invoke that shame would also be to make those students aesthetic scapegoats, and the many personal letters they wrote to and received from their teachers at boarding school would be nothing more than coerced remembrance.

Native American Indians have published thousands of books, stories, and poems since the nineteenth century. George Copway and Sarah Winnemucca were followed by Charles Eastman, Francis La Flesche, Gertrude Bonnin, and countless others who wrote and published their life stories, autobiographies, short stories, and novels in the twentieth century. Christine Quintasket, for instance, was a notable author from the Colville Confederated Tribes of eastern Washington State. She was born in a canoe on the Kootenay River in Idaho. She assumed the pen name Mourning Dove and published her romantic novel, *Cogewea: The Half-Blood*, in 1927. "There are two things I am most grateful for in my life," she writes in her autobiography:

> The first is that I was born a descendant of the genuine Americans, the Indians; the second, that my birth happened in the year 1888. In that year the Indians of my tribe, the Colville, were well into the cycle of history involving their readjustment in living conditions. They were in a pathetic state of turmoil caused by trying to learn how to till the soil for a living, which was being done on a very small and crude scale. It was not an easy matter for members of this aboriginal stock, accustomed to making a different livelihood, to handle the plow and sow seed for food. Yet I was born long enough ago to have known people who lived in the ancient way before everything started to change. (3)

Janet Campbell Hale has also published novels and an autobiography. She was born in Los Angeles in 1947 and is a member of the Coeur d'Alene tribe of northern Idaho. *The Jailing of Cecelia Capture*, published in 1985, is a novel that turns on the burdens of separation and racial renunciation. "I first saw the light of day in California, but the first place I remember is our home in Idaho," Hale writes in *Bloodlines: Odyssey of a Native Daughter*. "For an Indian, home is the place where your tribe began. . . . I have never heard a creation myth from my own tribe, probably because of their early conversion to Catholicism" (xviii).

Wynema, by Sophia Alice Callahan, the first novel attributed to a Native author, was published in 1891. *Queen of the Woods*, by Simon Pokagon, was published eight years later, but the actual writer of the novel may be someone other than Pokagon. LaVonne Brown Ruoff has uncovered and studied *Wynema*. Callahan, a Mixedblood Creek, was aware of such tribal issues and instances of resistance as federal policies, the Ghost Dance, and Wounded Knee. She "devotes most of the novel to Indian issues," Ruoff writes in "Justice for Indians and Women: The Protest Fiction of Alice Callaghan and Pauline Johnson." Callahan "also includes some strong statements about equality for women" (251). She was born in 1868. She studied at the Wesleyan Female Institute in Virginia and taught at Muskogee's Harrell International Institute and the Wealaka School. Callahan died three years after the publication of her novel.

Since then, many novels by distinguished Native authors have been published and reviewed in national newspapers and journals. Some of these novels have been awarded national literary prizes. Native American Indian authors have earned considerable recognition for dozens of novels published in the past few years. *The Surrounded* by D'Arcy McNickle was published two years after *Sundown* by John Joseph Mathews. These novels, and other books by Native authors, were important literary events in their time. Mathews's *Wah'Kon-Tah*, for instance, was a selection of the Book of the Month Club in 1932. Novels by McNickle, Mathews, John Milton Oskison, Todd Downing, and many others have been reissued in the past few years by university presses.

Louis Owens points out in *Other Destinies*, his study of Native American Indian novelists, that *The Surrounded* was first entitled "The Hungry Generations," a "version almost twice as long as the published manuscript, and very different in its implications" (60). In the earlier version, Archilde, the tribal protagonist, is "allowed to travel to Paris and to experience the heady atmosphere" and milieu of the Lost Generation. He falls in love and returns to Montana. Publisher Harcourt, Brace returned "The Hungry Generation" in 1929 with a rejection letter that said the story of an Indian "wandering between two generations, two cultures," was excellent. "A new territory to be explored: ancient material used for a different end. Perhaps the beginning of a new Indian literature to rival that of

Harlem" (62). *The Surrounded*, with a more tragic closure, was published by Dodd, Mead.

N. Scott Momaday won the Pulitzer Prize for his first novel, *House Made of Dawn*, published in 1968. *Ceremony*, by Leslie Marmon Silko, *Winter in the Blood*, by James Welch, and many other novels followed, receiving favourable reviews. *Love Medicine*, by Louise Erdrich, won the National Book Critics Circle Award. Wendy Rose, Maurice Kenny, Erdrich, and Gerald Vizenor have received the American Book Award sponsored by the Before Columbus Foundation. Momaday, Paula Gunn Allen, and Welch have received the Native American Indian Literature Prize. The American Indian Literature and Critical Studies Series at the University of Oklahoma Press, established in 1990, has published more than thirty books, including several first novels: *The Light People*, by Gordon Henry, *From the Glittering World*, by Irvin Morris, and *Eye Killers*, by A.A. Carr.

WORKS CITED

The American Heritage Dictionary of the English Language. 3rd ed. 1992.

Dobyns, Henry F. *Native American Historical Demography*. Bloomington: Indiana UP, 1976.

Drinnon, Richard. *Facing West*. Minneapolis: U of Minnesota P, 1980.

Ellis, Richard. "Luther Standing Bear." *Indian Lives*. Ed. L.G. Moses and Raymond Wilson. Albuquerque: U of New Mexico P, 1985.

Hagan, William T. *American Indians*. Chicago: U of Chicago P, 1961.

Hale, Janet Campbell. *Bloodlines: Odyssey of a Native Daughter*. New York: Random House, 1993.

Jones, Dorothy. *License for Empire*. Chicago: U of Chicago P, 1982.

Karttunen, Frances. *Between Worlds: Interpreters, Guides, and Survivors*. New Brunswick: Rutgers UP, 1994.

Kroeber, Karl. *Traditional American Indian Literatures*. Lincoln: U of Nebraska P, 1981.

Krupat, Arnold. *For Those Who Come After*. Berkeley: U of California P, 1985.

Lomawaima, K. Tsianina. *They Called It Prairie Light: The Story of Chilocco Indian School*. Lincoln: U of Nebraska P, 1994.

Mathews, John Joseph. *Sundown*. Norman: U of Oklahoma P, 1988.

Mathews, Virginia. Introduction. John Joseph Matthews v–xiv.

McNickle, D'Arcy. *Native American Tribalism: Indian Survivals and Renewals*. New York: Oxford UP, 1973.

———. *The Surrounded*. Albuquerque: U of New Mexico P, 1978.

Mourning Dove. *Cogewea: The Half-Blood*. Lincoln: U of Nebraska P, 1981.

——. *Mourning Dove: A Salishan Autobiography*. Ed. Jay Miller. Lincoln: U of Nebraska P, 1990.

O'Connell, Barry, ed. Introduction. *On Our Own Ground: The Complete Writings of William Apess, a Pequot*. Amherst: U of Massachusetts P, 1992. xiii–lxxvii.

Owens, Louis. *Other Destinies*. Norman: U of Oklahoma P, 1992.

Pearce, Roy Harvey. *Savagism and Civilization: A Study of the Indian and the American Mind*. Baltimore: Johns Hopkins UP, 1967.

Prucha, Francis Paul. *Americanizing the American Indians*. Lincoln: U Nebraska P, 1973.

——. *The Indians in American Society*. Berkeley: U of California P, 1985.

Rogers, John. *Red World and White*. Norman: U of Oklahoma P, 1996.

Ruoff, LaVonne Brown. *American Indian Literatures*. New York: MLA, 1980.

——. "Justice for Indians and Women: The Protest Fiction of Alice Callaghan and Pauline Johnson." *World Literature Today* 66.2 (1992): 249-55.

Standing Bear, Luther. *My People the Sioux*. Lincoln: U of Nebraska P, 1975.

Steiner, George. *After Babel: Aspects of Language and Translation*. New York: Oxford UP, 1975.

——. *Language and Silence*. New York: Atheneum, 1982.

Swann, Brian. Introduction. Swann, ed. xiii–xx.

——, ed. *On the Translation of Native American Literatures*. Washington: Smithsonian Institution, 1992.

Wunder, John. *Retained by the People*. New York: Oxford UP, 1994.

Ziff, Larzer. *Writing in the New Nation: Prose, Print, and Politics in the Early United States*. New Haven: Yale UP, 1991.

Spirit and Law in
Native American Narratives

CLIFFORD E. TRAFZER

At certain times and for all times, creative forces put the Earth into motion. Wind stirred the world into creation, breathing life into the Earth. Movement set the world into motion, expanded that which was first created, and contributed to the continuance of the creative power. Clouds, fog, and water developed when the Earth was young, providing elements of the creative process. Beings of many names and sorts, some familiar and some unfamiliar, some seen and some unseen, interacted with each other in great drama. Animate and inanimate presences within the sky, land, and air joined together in this drama to create laws by which all life was to function. Creative forces differed from place to place, just as laws differed from group to group. Dualities emerged on Earth. There was night and day, male and female, good and evil, love and hate, cooperation and murder. The world contained much that was good and beautiful, but it also had its problems and perils. Monsters and evil forces emerged at the beginning of time as a counter to positive forces. Tension and confusion developed at the beginning of time along with the ability to counter these forces to create calm resolutions. Through stories filled with meaning and symbolism, Native Americans tell of the creation that is at once historical and contemporary, a process that continues to this day.[1]

* * *

Wolf walked through the woods, bumping into trees as he moved along. Not far away, a tiny grey mouse ambled along until he spotted Wolf. Mouse hid behind the trunk of a great oak tree and watched Wolf. The great animal continued to have problems as he moved forward, running headlong into a tree trunk, then backing up and moving forward until he ran into another tree. Courageously, the small grey mouse walked in front of Wolf, who sniffed the air.

"I see you have a problem," Mouse announced.

"Yes, I do," Wolf responded. "I have gone blind and can see nothing, and so I will die. I can no longer hunt, and without my eyes, I will perish."

Without a word, Mouse moved his tiny forepaws to his own eyes and removed them. Mouse then reached up to Wolf and gave him his eyes. With Mouse's eyes, Wolf could see. Wolf wept with joy at the magnanimous gift and thanked Mouse profusely.

"But what of you, Little Brother," Wolf said, suddenly realizing that Mouse would now be blind. "You cannot see and must have eyes in order to live."

"You are a great and wonderful animal, and you should live," Mouse replied. "As for me, well, I am a small and insignificant animal. There are many like me, but you are a large and powerful creature that must live."

Wolf thanked Mouse again and again for the gift of sight, and told Mouse they would be brothers. Wolf placed Mouse on the back of his neck and explained that from that day forward and forever they would be friends. They travelled that way through life, hunting together and eating together. In fact, for years Wolf and Mouse camped, sang, prayed, and sweated together as brothers. One day as they travelled along, Mouse felt a change come over him. His tiny nose elongated and became hard like a beak, while his forearms spread out and became great feathered wings. His hind legs straightened out and talons formed where his toes had been. And his eyes — his eyes grew back into his noble head and he could see again. Mouse became Eagle, the all-seeing one, and he flew from Wolf's back directly into the sun, becoming like Eagle from the Light. Elders say that the Master of Life saw the good that Mouse had done and returned the gift of sight that he had so unselfishly shared with Wolf.

Native Americans offer their eyes to the great Wolf through their stories. The Wolf in this case is the institutionalized study of history, literature, political science, sociology, biology, and many other disciplines. Like Mouse, Native people have been marginalized by the dominant society, particularly that element forming colleges and universities, where the Wolf has wandered aimlessly in his understanding and representation of Native Americans. Oral narratives provide a vehicle through which the Wolf may see better and survive through friendship and cooperation with Mouse and his many brothers and sisters. And, through reciprocity, Mouse may benefit as well, gaining greater insight into areas of study so well known in Wolf's world. Seeing anew, moving from darkness to light, and comprehending the processes involved in the transformations that may come are well worth the journey that Mouse and Wolf take together. Rather than separating as they naturally would do, Mouse and Wolf come together out of mutual respect and gain from their union. And so it is with the use of oral narratives: both peoples grow and develop from knowing something of Native cultures through stories. The story illustrates a small portion of Native American history that began in these creative times.

Native American history did not begin with the arrival of the Vikings or Spaniards. According to tribal historians, Native American history began with creation, a time when the first movement took place and set creative powers afoot on this land. Archaeologists maintain that Native Americans did not originate in this land but moved across the frozen tundra via a land bridge linking Siberia with Alaska. Native American traditionalists look to their oral narratives for their origins. For tribal elders and young people who think in the old way, traditional Native stories are sacred texts filled with meaning for the past and present. They tie the people to the natural world as well as to certain places that have meaning to Native peoples. Such places are marked by rivers, hills, forests, swamps, prairies, mountains, valleys, deserts, and rock formations. They contain specific varieties of plants and animals that are part of the Native American community. The redwoods of northern California have no place in the oral texts of Plains Indians, and the buffalo of the plains are not a part of the sacred narratives of California's Native people. The places of Native America are distinguished by certain weather patterns and natural phenomena such as earthquakes, hurricanes, tornadoes, thunderstorms, lightning, drought, floods, and fires. Oral narratives are the cultural foundations of Native people, providing life's lessons and explaining who the people are and what they are obligated to do in this life.

Native American history began before humans, when plants, animals, and places of nature interacted with each other to make the world ready for humans. Stories weave this time together, establishing laws by which all things should function. Such laws include those detailing which foods can be eaten or used for medicine and those prescribing times and methods for their use. Laws include songs of thanksgiving and prescribe ceremonies that have to be conducted in specific ways to ensure the success of the ceremony and the continuance of the community. In many stories, animal people, plant people, mountain people, or spirit people act out a drama that teaches the law. Among the Yakama of present-day Washington State, there is a story about Mount Adams and the other volcanoes of the region, including Mount Hood, Mount Saint Helens, and Mount Rainier. According to the story, Sun married five great Mountain Women in the Northwest, and each day when he chose to appear he embraced his wives with his light. The wives grew jealous of Mount Adams because she received her husband's embrace earlier than the others, so they plotted against her. They caused this beautiful Mountain Woman to explode and disfigure herself. But the Creator saw this jealousy and caused her to re-create herself. It took years, but Mount Adams received a new face and her beauty was restored. She is still a favourite wife who receives her husband's embrace early in the morning.

Among the Chinook, Clatsop, Kickitat, Wasco, Yakama, and other people of the Northwest, it is against the law to dam rivers. The Creator established this law long before the arrival of whites at a time when the five giant monster women known as the Tah Tah Kleah blocked the flow of the Columbia River to create a fish dam. When the salmon made their annual run up the Columbia, they could not break through the fish dam, so the Tah Tah Kleah could take as many as they wanted. The story is about greed taking over the minds of the monsters; the Tah Tah Kleah were more concerned about themselves than others who lived upstream and depended on the salmon. It is also about a hero who worked for the benefit of the people rather than for his own glorification, although he could not help but bask in his own glory. He had a right to do so, since he had reestablished the law broken by the five monster women who were shortsighted. By establishing the fish dam, they would destroy the salmon runs altogether within a few years: the salmon could no longer travel up the river to spawn.

Of course, animal people living upstream from the fish dam knew that the dam was against the law, but no one wanted to go down the river and challenge the dangerous monsters. But Coyote agreed to challenge the monsters and, to this end, he dressed like a baby, climbed into a basket, and floated down the Columbia to the fish dam. In this story, Coyote is a hero, a being who works on behalf of the community and teaches people an important lesson that has not been forgotten. When he arrived at the lake created by the dam, the five Tah Tah Kleah saw him and thought he was a baby. Enamoured with the baby, the four oldest sisters wanted to fish Coyote from the water and raise him as their own child, but the youngest sister sensed danger in the situation. She warned her older sisters not to adopt Coyote, but her older sisters did not heed her warning. They adopted Coyote as their own baby and took care of him. Each day, while the monsters went forth to fish, hunt, and gather great quantities of food — because they had voracious appetites — they tethered Coyote to a pole with a rope tied around his waist so that he would not fall into the river and drown. Each day, Coyote untied himself and used five digging sticks to dig out the dam. The first day, he made five digging sticks and five ladles from the horns of bighorn sheep. He set the ladles aside and worked furiously digging out the dam for five days.

On the fifth day, the monsters left the village as usual after tying their baby with the rope. Then Coyote went to work on the dam. During the course of the day, a digging stick being used by a Tah Tah Kleah broke, which was a sign to them all that something was wrong. They hurried back to camp early to check on the baby, only to find that the child was Coyote and he was digging out their dam. Coyote had almost finished digging out the dam and could not stop, so he kept at it while the monsters beat his head with great clubs. Coyote used a ladle as a helmet to protect his head and continued digging. When the first ladle broke, he used another one and kept digging. The monsters kept beating him on the head, which is why Coyote is still a little crazy, but the hero continued his work until the monsters broke the last ladle with their heavy clubs. By this time, Coyote had broken through the dam. The waters of the Columbia rushed out to the Pacific and the salmon raced inland in great numbers, travelling up the river, following their new chief. Coyote led the salmon people up the river systems of the inland Northwest, allowing the fish to swim near those villages where the people would generously give him wives and food. He prohibited salmon from going by the village of stingy people, forcing them to travel some distance in order to get salmon at their fisheries. According to the law, no one could place dams on the river.

Like many others, Coyote is an unusual hero. In this story, he acts when no other person wants to face the Tah Tah Kleah. And he faces his challenge in an innovative, if not provocative, manner, dressing as a baby and floating down the Columbia River. Although other animal people think him a fool, he uses this method to disarm his adversaries. Coyote demonstrates great courage in going down the river to face five monsters, and he is wise to dress as a baby in order to get the monsters to take him in as their own. Certainly, babies are disarming, and each monster succumbs except for the youngest, who warns her sisters that something is not right about the baby. Often, older siblings scoff at the ideas of the younger members of the family, even when they would do well to consider their opinions. Once Coyote is accepted by the monsters, he plans ahead by making five digging sticks and five helmets. He has the forethought to create these items and takes the time to do so before he launches into his job. As for the monsters, they heed the sign of the broken digging stick, returning to the village early and finding their baby busy busting their dam. By breaking the dam, Coyote frees the waters of the river, allows the salmon to enter the river to spawn, and corrects the law that the Creator has established. For many Native people, dams violate ancient tribal laws and are built by monsters bent on disturbing the Earth to benefit themselves. Such selfishness is still a violation of Native laws, since people are supposed to act in the common interest of communities.

Iroquoian peoples of the Northeast believe in a Sky World above the Earth, a place where life began while the Earth was filled with seawater. Before there was land on Earth, great sea animals inhabited the endless ocean and birds lived in the sky. Many people lived in the Sky World, including a selfish woman who was pregnant and demanded that her husband provide her with a variety of foods and medicines. In the middle of the Sky World, a huge and unusual sacred tree grew. It was against the law for anyone to disturb the sacred tree in any manner. But the woman did not care, for she wanted bark from the roots of the tree for herself and ordered her husband to bring her some bark. He dug around the base of the tree, exposing some of its roots. Much to his surprise, he opened a hole in the sky and could look down upon the endless sea on Earth. Without disturbing the great tree, he went home to tell his wife about the great hole in the Sky World. His curious wife went to the tree, peered down at the earth, and fell through the opening. In her hand, she grasped plants and parts of the sacred tree.

As she fell towards the ocean the birds in the sky used their wings to catch her. The birds arranged with Sea Turtle to set the Woman Who Fell from the Sky on his back. Muskrat dove to the bottom of the ocean and brought up soil, which the woman used to create Earth on Turtle's back. Endlessly, the woman walked sunwise around Turtle's back, which made the earth expand out and form into valleys, mountains, lakes, and prairies. With the plants and debris she had brought down from the Sky World, the woman created the first plants on Earth. One day, she gave birth to a girl who walked with her mother upon Turtle's back, helping the Earth grow and prosper. When the girl was older, a man appeared to her, a man likely from the Sky World, and the sight of him made her faint. While she was asleep, the man placed two arrows on her chest, a blunt arrow and sharp one. When she awoke, she was pregnant with twin boys who quarrelled endlessly with each other in utero. One of her sons, the right-handed one, was straight minded, but his brother, the left-handed one, was of a crooked mind. The right-handed son, called Sapling, was born in the normal fashion, but the left-handed son, called Flint, came out of his mother under her left arm, which killed her.

The boys buried their mother and from her head came corn, squash, and beans — the Three Sisters. From her heart grew tobacco, a sacred plant used in sending prayers into the sky. The boys continued their feud with each other outside of their mother's body, creating tensions between positive and negative powers, and their competition was manifested through the creation of different plants and animals. At this time, Sapling created the first humans, moulding them from clay and baking them in a fire. Flint may have helped him, because the forces of both characters are in all people. The boys duelled with each other until Sapling defeated Flint and tossed his body off the edge of the world, where he began to control the night; his brother sustains the daylight. Their grandmother had always favoured Flint, perhaps because she was of a selfish nature, and when she learned that Sapling had killed Flint she became enraged. In his own anger against his grandmother, Sapling killed her, cut off her head, and tossed it into the sky. At night she looks over her beloved Flint in the form of the moon. Both Sapling and Flint influence life on Earth to this day, but they do not live on the same plane of being as humans. Iroquois refer to Sapling as the Master of Life, Creator, or He Holds Up The Skies, and they call Flint the Devious One, Old Worty, or One Covered With Boils. Both are important figures in Iroquois history as well as contemporary society. The people pray, sing, dance, and burn tobacco in remembrance of creation, ritual acts that tie the past to the present and ensure the future.

Some years ago, Maidu Indian elder Dalbert Castro of northern California related a portion of the Maidu creation story. In a shortened version of a complex narrative, there was a time when a great ocean enveloped the entire Earth. Earthmaker and Coyote floated on a raft on an endless sea. For an extended period of time, they were content with this life. Then Earthmaker had a vision of solid ground with an Earth made of mountains, rivers, valleys, forests, and meadows. In his vision, Earthmaker saw clouds, rain, thunder, lightning, plants, and animals. So he sang his song of creation, calling on his mountains and valleys, his fog and rain to appear.

> Little world,
> Where are you?
> Little world,
> Where are you?
>
> My world of great mountains,
> Where are you?
> My foggy mountains,
> Where are you?
>
> My world,
> Where one will travel
> By the valley's edge,
> By great foggy mountains,
> By the zigzag paths
> Through mountain ranges
> After mountain ranges.
>
> I sing of the country
> I will travel in.
> In this world,
> I will wander.

Earthmaker sang day and night until he became tired. He asked Coyote to continue his song. And so Coyote sang until he became tired. Earthmaker then resumed the song of creation until one day he heard Robin singing, and he saw a round nest bobbing in the water. Earthmaker told Coyote that he would make his Little World from the nest. He took ropes and stretched them out from the nest in many directions. Earthmaker brought mud from the bottom of the ocean and packed it on the nest and ropes, forming the earth and sculpting mountains, valleys, prairies, and meadows. Coyote helped, painting some of the Earth red, the colour of blood.

All Native Americans enjoy a rich oral tradition detailing the creation of the Earth, plants, animals, sky, sun, moon, stars, and other elements of the universe. The story of people, places, leadership, migrations, settlements, warfare, and times of peace are chronicled in these accounts. Ancestors of contemporary Lenape people kept their history and spiritual accounts in an oral document known as the Wallam Olum. There are many versions of this poetic record preserved in symbolic pictographs and remembered in the Lenape language. Native Americans disagree about various words and translations of the Lenape text, but most agree that the Wallam Olum is a sacred document, preserved so that there may be some understanding of important cultural ideas and events in Lenape history. In 1989, David McCutchen provided this version of the opening episodes of the account in *The Red Record: The Wallam Olum.*

Sayewitalli	At the beginning,
Wemiguma	The sea everywhere
Wokgetaki	Covered the earth.
Hackung-kwelik	Above extended
Owanaku	A swirling cloud,
Wak yutali	And within it,
Kitanitowit-essop	The Great Spirit moved.
Sayewis	Primordial,
Hallemewis	Everlasting,
Nolemewi	Invisible,
Elemamik	Omnipresent —
Kitanitowit-essop	The Great Spirit moved. (52)

The creative movement brought forth the sky, Earth, clouds, and heavens. Movement was central to creation, and the continuation of activity keeps the creation alive. The Great Spirit did not put all things in motion in seven days, but set things in motion at different times — for all time — establishing a process that moves and continues today. According to the Lenape, the Creator ignited the universe into being, making the day, night, planets, and stars. The Creator made the sky, releasing various kinds of wind into the atmosphere. Light cool and warm breezes sometimes caress the Earth, while at other times strong winds topple trees or turn into tornadoes that drop from the sky, creating havoc on Earth. The Master of Life made the rivers of clear waters that rush over rocks, sometimes forming raging torrents and other times torpid trickles. The Creator made many kinds of snow and brought ice, wind, and winter to many parts of the great island. Originally, all things in nature were good, placed there by the Great Spirit that created all things. When the time was appropriate, the Creator continued the process.

Lappinup	Again,
Kitanitowit	The Great Spirit
Manito	Created:
Manitoak	The creator spirits,
Owiniwak	Living beings,
Angelatawiwak	Immortals,
Chichankwak	The Souls [for]
Werniwak	Everything
Wtenkmanito	Then the Spirit
Jinwis	Ancestor,
Lennowak	Grandfather
Mukom	Of Men,
Milap	Gave
Netami-gaho	The First Mother
Owini-gaho	Mother of Life
Namesik milap	[Who] gave the fish,
Tulpewik milap	Gave the turtles,
Awesik milap	Gave the beasts,
Cholensak milap	Gave the birds.

With the positive creation came husbands, wives, children, food, helpful spirits, and a carefree life. But in the wake of the positive creation came the negative, including bad spirits, snakes, sea monsters, flies, and mosquitoes. An evil snake came upon the Earth, spreading havoc, wickedness, bad weather, sickness, death, floods, and wrong deeds among all beings. All things in the universe became infused with the positive and negative, including human beings, who all have the ability to use their creative power to do good for their communities or evil for their own selfish ends. Negative forces may manifest themselves in a number of ways, depending on the tribe, but they are always powerful and harmful. Among the Hupa of northern

California there is a belief that people who wish to gain prominence and power can use their creative abilities to transform themselves into bear people and do great harm to others, including murder. Diné (Navajo) people believe that destructive and greedy individuals can use their power to become "witches" who can turn themselves into coyote people or skin walkers. Hopis believe that there are people within their communities who become part of the negative forces that kill others or do great harm in order to live longer. They call such people Two Hearts. Most Native peoples — if not all — have traditional beliefs about individuals who use negative power to benefit themselves, a dangerous power that emerged at the time of creation.

Several traditional stories deal with the issue of negative power and the misuse of power to benefit oneself over communal good. An old Wyandot story tells of a boy who grew up in a village along the Saint Lawrence River. Elders greatly admired this young man because he was courteous, athletic, generous, smart, and eager to learn from them. He knew how to listen and learn. As the years passed, the elders often told other young people that they should be more like this young man, which created tension between the boy and his peers. When the boy was in his early teens, the other boys of the village hatched a plan to kill him and be done with him forever. They invited the boy to join them in a great hunt on the river between Hochelaga and Lake Ontario, and the boy naïvely accepted. They canoed a great distance to a large island in the river, an island inhabited by numerous wildcats, bears, and other animals. As they had gone there to prove themselves great hunters of the most dangerous beasts, the boys split up and set off in several directions, agreeing to meet back at the river's edge to make camp for the night. The boy they had brought with them walked off alone with his bow and arrow, but found no scat, no sign of animals. As the sun began dropping quickly in the west, he returned to camp. The other boys had taken the canoes and abandoned him on the island.

By this time, the sun had set and night had begun to fall. So the boy climbed an old tree and slept in the crook of a large branch. He slept well until he awoke feeling someone breathing on his neck. It was the time of grey morning light. As the boy opened his eyes, he saw steam in the air and still felt the heavy breath upon his neck. He slowly turned to see what was there. Wildcat was beside him with his right paw raised as if to strike. The boy turned his head and waited for the blow, but it did not come. He waited and turned again to look.

74

Some storytellers say that the small wind in his ear spoke to him, telling him to look again. And so he did. Wildcat's paw was still raised, and his fully extended claws gleamed in the morning light. This time, the boy did not turn away but studied the great paw and saw a thorn stuck deep in the furry place between the pads.

Again, he heard the small wind in his ear, this time telling him to pull out the splinter, and so he did. Bravely, he reached up. Carefully, he took hold of the paw with one hand and grasped the thorn with the fingers of his other hand. With a mighty tug, he pulled out the thorn. Wildcat spoke to him. "Thank you, grandson," Wildcat said. "I have tried for four days to pull the thorn out with my teeth and paw, but I could not. You have saved my life, for the splinter would have turned my paw bad and poisoned me. You have been very brave and kind to help me, so I wish to give you something in return. From this time forward, you will have my power as a hunter. You will always do well hunting, and your family and friends will never be without meat because you will have my power as a hunter." The boy thanked Wildcat for his gift, a lifelong gift that he would use to feed his family and village.

The boy and Wildcat spoke for some time, getting to know each other. Then Wildcat gave the boy another gift. "I know that the other boys brought you here and left," Wildcat announced. "I watched you leave on the hunt and saw all of the boys get back into the canoes and leave you here. I know they wanted you dead, so I watched. They have returned to your village to announce your death to your parents and the elders. Don't be afraid. The elders do not believe you are dead, and they are already on their way back here to find you."

Wildcat paused momentarily to lick his sore paw and allow his cold words to melt in the boy's mind. He knew that the boy was angry at the treachery of the other boys. He wanted revenge, so Wildcat gave the boy time to think about what he had said. "When the villagers return to this island, the boys will be with them," Wildcat continued. "But you should not set your mind on them and the harm they intended for you. Rather, you should train your mind on the gift I have given you, the ability to hunt and provide. Whenever your mind turns to revenge, push those thoughts aside and remember the good that has come of our meeting. If you do this, you will do well. If you allow yourself to dwell on the jealousy and hate they have for you, then you will harm yourself and never be well."

Wildcat and the boy came down out of the tree and Bear jumped up on her hind legs to attack the boy. Wildcat jumped between Bear and the boy, threatening Bear if she attacked. When Bear learned that Wildcat was a friend of the boy, she withdrew. Wildcat turned to the boy. "They are coming for you now," he said. "They will be here soon and I will watch from the trees. Remember my words but do not tell them that we have met or the things I have told you. These things are between us. Carry my words in your heart."

And so it was that the villagers canoed to the island where they found the boy patiently waiting for them. His parents were overjoyed to find him safe, but not the other boys. They fully expected the young man to tell his story, but he did not have to say a word. Some of the people understood what had happened, while others did not think about it. The boy said nothing against the others. They all returned to their village and, over the years, the boy grew to become a hunting leader, a man respected by many people for many abilities. He never told his story until he was dying. Before he left this world, he summoned his children, grandchildren, and great-grandchildren and told them his story of Wildcat and the lessons this grandfather had taught. They listened to the story and remembered. They told their children and grandchildren who, in turn, told their children and grandchildren. And so the story of Wildcat is still alive, a small part of Wyandot history that lives with each telling, a reminder to keep one's mind focused on the positive things of life, not the negative, even when life or limb is at stake. This is the law, taught through story.

When Native storytellers share these stories, their accounts are filled with colourful descriptions and minute details that have been handed down from generation to generation. Often, storytellers will make animal sounds or sounds of thunder, thrashings, waterfalls, winds, and the wild excitement that comes of presenting stories orally. Stories of creation often last several nights, and storytellers may vary them, emphasizing a particular episode at the first telling and another episode another night. Some stories originated thousands of years ago and have been kept alive with each telling, while other stories are more recent. Stories have life, and Native people consider them a part of their history. Traditional stories lay the foundation for understanding particular Native nations, tribes, bands, villages, and people. The stories are interdisciplinary, offering information about religion, medicine, economics, literature, politics, psychology, biology, and many other fields of study. Stories explain the relationship of Native Americans to geographical places, geological formations, and biological features of regions. Within a body of stories there are actions and reactions, transitions and continuances, and, always, instances of survival. And survival is a theme found in contemporary Native American communities and within ancient stories. Native Americans embarked on a long and dangerous journey that began with their first contact with Europeans; they survived and recovered from the American holocaust. This survival theme is much like one found in an ancient story shared by many tribes of the Columbia Plateau.

During the time of the Wah-tee-tash, or animal people, the five Cold North Wind Brothers invaded the Pacific Northwest from Alaska to California. They froze the entire region, all the lakes and rivers, with cold winds, snow, and sleet. In the springtime, the Cold North Wind Brothers fought off the warm chinook winds from the ocean and would not allow them to enter the region. When the salmon attempted to travel up the Columbia River to spawn, the great fish could not pass through its frozen waters. Salmon Chief challenged the five Lalawish (Wolf Brothers) to a wrestling match: if the Salmon Chief won, the Cold North Wind Brothers would melt the snow and ice and return to their original home. The Wolf Brothers agreed, but added that if the Salmon Chief lost a match, Coyote would slit his throat. Salmon Chief accepted this condition and wrestled the Wolf Brothers. He defeated the first and second brother, but he lost to the third. When the third Wolf Brother threw Salmon Chief to the ground, Coyote raced over to kill him.

When Coyote slit Salmon Chief's throat, a great bloodletting began. The allies of the Wolf Brothers and the Cold North Wind Brothers killed all the salmon people. They cut open the stomachs of all the females, including the wife of Salmon Chief, and ripped out their eggs. The Wolf Brothers and their friends tried to smash every one of the eggs in order to stamp out the salmon people. But the Wolf Brothers and their allies missed an egg belonging to Salmon Chief's wife. It had fallen between some rocks and could not be reached easily. They knew where the egg was lodged, and they tried long and hard to dislodge it. They could not, and they left the area believing that the sun and wind would dry up the egg. The Creator had watched the entire scene and sent a warm rain to wash the egg into the water at the point where the river began to freeze. The egg attached itself to the sand, and semen floating in the water fertilized it. A salmon was born, and when it became a smolt it swam back to the ocean, all the while moving backwards with its head upstream. When Young Chinook Salmon reached the Pacific, his paternal grandmother embraced him and took care of him.

Grandmother Salmon did not at first tell Young Chinook Salmon what had happened to his parents, but she began training him to face future challenges. She put him on a strict diet to make him healthy and had him train himself to wrestle. She made him lift heavy weights, such as trees and rocks, to build his muscles and stamina. When he was a little older, Grandmother Salmon told Young Chinook Salmon stories about his mother, father, and people. She told him how the Cold North Wind Brothers had broken the law by freezing the inland Northwest, which prevented the salmon from spawning. She told him how his father had fought the Wolf Brothers and lost. She told him that Coyote had slit his father's throat and helped kill all of the salmon people. Grandmother Salmon explained to him how he had been born through a holy act of the Creator. Listening to this story, Young Chinook Salmon realized what he had to do and why his grandmother had expected so much of him. He trained for another year, and when he was prepared, Young Chinook Salmon led the people up the Columbia River to challenge the five Wolf Brothers.

Young Chinook Salmon faced the five Wolf Brothers in a wrestling match, just as his father had a few years before. Two women who had been forced into slavery spilled fish oil on the ice to help Young Chinook Salmon. He wrestled the five Wolf Brothers, throwing each one in succession to the ice where Coyote killed them with his knife. After enduring years of ice and snow, Coyote had changed sides and now supported the salmon people. When Young Chinook Salmon threw the last Wolf Brother, the chinook wind began to blow into the Northwest, melting the snow and ice. The sister of the Wolf Brothers then ran off to the north. From that day forward, there has been a time of winter and a time of spring during which the warm chinook wind comes from the west to melt the snow and ice. Each year, She Wolf returns to the Northwest, but only for a few months. Since the time of the Wah-tee-tash, She Wolf returns with the winter cold, but she is unable to freeze the entire region for lengthy periods as her brothers had done.

This story is a metaphor for Native American peoples, who faced years of near death resulting from the successive invasions, conquests, wars, epidemics, and government policies brought to Turtle Island by Europeans and non-Native Americans. In large part, the history of early America is a history of a holocaust, a tragic era in which non-Native peoples overran most Native American lands, forcing many Native people to move, and stole valuable resources. However, Native people survived, and during the twentieth century many Native nations, tribes, bands, villages, *rancherias*, groups, and individuals recovered their interest in preserving portions of their cultures, including languages, songs, stories, music, dance, and ceremonies. Like the small salmon egg, Native people have survived and sustained themselves, growing in number during the twentieth century with the help of elders such as the grandmother of Young Chinook Salmon. This is an important era of Native American history. It is also an era that consists of many changes and important transitions.

Native American narratives often emphasize the relationship of Native people to place and the biological elements of their homes. Narratives offer a way of knowing place and time, the relationship of humans to the larger community, which to Native peoples includes trees, rocks, rivers, mountains, hills, valleys, and other elements of the natural world. These relationships are described in detail in oral narratives. The relationship between humans and their environments have historical, spiritual, sociological, biological, and philosophical meanings that are generally not well understood. Stories often tell of the important relationship of humans to the Earth, particularly the soil that holds the remains of ancestors. In addition to the tie between American Indians and the things of nature, there is an ongoing relationship between Native North Americans and the bones of their people. This remains an issue among several tribes from the East that presently live in Oklahoma and Kansas. As remains are unearthed in Ohio, Kentucky, Pennsylvania, and other eastern states, tribes that once lived in these areas express their wish to have a say in their disposition. The same is true of Native American remains stored in boxes by various museums and universities in the East. Tribal members and elders have spiritual relationships with the dead and tribal laws dealing with the dead that are not generally understood by non-Indians. These and other spiritual factors are powerful elements in Native American literature, past and present, and are best understood through oral narratives.

Although anthropologists, folklorists, and linguists have collected and published a large number of oral narratives, the stories still belong to the tribes in which they originated. Most of these stories are not "owned" by individuals but are part of the collective knowledge and memory of the people. The people have shared these stories with one another, not only within one tribe but among many tribes. Often, storytellers know different versions of stories and tell these versions to one another, but no one person owns most stories, particularly those of animal people or places of nature. However, women "own" birthing stories while men "own" war stories. In such cases, the teller may forbid others to relate his or her story without permission. Nez Perce warrior Yellow Wolf fought throughout the Nez Perce War of 1877 and lived to tell his stories about the war. On one occasion, he scolded his son, Bill, for telling war stories that did not belong to him. Only Yellow Wolf and those to whom he granted permission could tell his war stories. Yellow Wolf told all of his war stories to Lucullus Virgil McWhorter, who used them to compose *Yellow Wolf: His Own Story*. The great warrior also told McWhorter a number of traditional narratives that no one person owned but were told throughout the Northwest Plateau, particularly among the bands of Nee Me Poo.

Numerous Native Americans from the Northwest Plateau shared stories with McWhorter, who planned to publish them one day in an anthology of oral literature. He never did because his work as a historian and advocate of Indian rights claimed all of his time and energy, but Michigan State University Press published these stories in a collection entitled *Grandmother, Grandfather, and Old Wolf* in 1998. The collection acknowledges that all of the stories it contains belong to the storytellers, although permission from McWhorter's family and Manuscripts, Archives, and Special Collections of the Holland Library at Washington State University was obtained. In addition, all proceeds from the sale of the collection were to be donated to the Yakama Nation Tribal Library in Toppenish in recognition of the fact that most of the stories were told to McWhorter by Yakama people or storytellers associated with the reservation. Donating royalties is one way in which editors and users of the Native American oral tradition can contribute to the community from which stories are taken. It is a way of returning the gift of the stories, which many Native people would argue "belong" to the tribe and have been appropriated by non-Indians or people from outside their communities.

Not all traditional stories are derived from published accounts or unpublished manuscripts. In fact, a rich oral tradition exists among several contemporary Native American tribes. If scholars choose to enter into the lives of these people, they must do so with honesty and integrity, informing the Native storytellers from the outset about the nature of their projects and the possibility that their words will be published. It is also important to ask tribal elders for their permission to use stories. Among Native peoples, it was once common practice to ask such permission orally, but, more and more, people are requesting permission in writing; this way, fewer misunderstandings emerge. At a meeting with the Twenty-Nine Palms band of Mission Indians in August 1997, one Native scholar told the tribe that any oral histories or narratives collected in the course of the Chemehuevi and Cahuilla Oral History Project were the property of the storytellers and tribe. The researcher advised the tribe to permit no one to use the oral narratives without written permission from the tribe and the storyteller in order to protect the rights of both. Most of the stories used in this paper were told to me by friends and family and are used with their permission. Other stories have appeared in published and unpublished sources that are named in the text; these are also used with permission. Most storytellers are pleased to share their stories with those whom they trust, but editors have the obligation to be forthright and inform elders orally and in writing if they plan to publish any portion of what is shared.

The purpose of traditional narratives was to inform and educate, to transmit to successive generations the spirit and the law. Elders intended the stories to be told, assessed, interpreted, and used. Ancient Native American stories provide a voice for Native peoples and offer interpretive frameworks that all scholars may use in their works. Every Native American community contains tribal historians, men and women who enjoy the past and act to preserve elements of tribal memory. These people use oral narratives in their explanations of the past and present. They are the real Native American intellectuals, and scholars have much to learn from them. Like Quechan historian Lee Emerson, many storytellers received the calling to be a historian and storyteller through their dreams. Cahuilla scholar and historian Katherine Saubel received her training from her father and father-in-law, and she has preserved portions of her tribe's history through her writings, stories, and songs. Some of her knowledge is too sacred to be shared outside of the Cahuilla community, and since no one has asked her to teach them the sacred songs that she learned as a young woman they will die with her. As she says, "The book will close on that chapter of Cahuilla history when I pass away."

The book has been closed on many aspects of Native history, but other chapters are waiting to be preserved and written whenever it is appropriate to do so. Many chapters can be found in the teachings of elders all across Indian country, among the men and women who know the stories of past generations of their families, clans, tribes, and nations. Other chapters will be found in the written documents that provide another voice for Native people. Native American oral traditions not only provide portholes through which to see and understand Native peoples, but they also offer opportunities for further research, analysis, and interpretation. There is much work yet to be done.

NOTE

[1] Research for this essay was made possible by grants from the Ford Foundation, the National Endowment for the Humanities, and the Western Center for Archaeology and Paleontology; research was also made possible by a University of California intercampus research grant. Earl Henry, Mary Lou Henry Trafzer, Dean Mike, Theresa Mike, Joe Benitez, Henry Rodriguez, Lee Emerson, Mary Jim, and Emily Peone provided oral interviews based on their tribal experiences.

WORKS CITED

McCutchen, David, trans. *The Red Record: The Wallam Olum.* Garden City Park, NY: Avery, 1993.

McWhorter, Lucullus Virgil. *Yellow Wolf: His Own Story.* Caldwell, ID: Caxton, 1948.

Nashone. *Grandmother Stories of the Northwest.* Newcastle, CA: Sierra Oaks, 1987.

Sioui, Eleanore. Interview with the author. Mar. 1998.

Trafzer, Clifford E., ed. *Grandmother, Grandfather, and Old Wolf: Tamán-wit Ku Súkat and Traditional Native American Narratives from the Columbia Plateau.* East Lansing: Michigan State UP, 1997.

Nations within as Seen from Without: Ten Theses on German Perspectives on the Literature of Canada's First Nations

Hartmut Lutz

1. Nation *and* Nationalism *Are Uneasy Terms in the German Experience*[1]

My own concept of *nation* and *nationalism* has always been very apprehensive, to say the least. This has to do with recent German history. The concept of a German nation in terms of a national state is a rather later-nineteenth-century development. In fact, the German national state is younger than Canada, being founded under Prussian hegemony in 1871 at the end of the French and German war. Only at the beginning of the nineteenth century, with the impact of Napoleonic rule, did German Romantic intellectuals begin campaigning for a united German national state in an attempt to overcome *Kleinstaaterei*, or the existence of over thirty small sovereign states ruled by diverse kings, dukes, counts, and other feudal rulers. Such attempts were largely unsuccessful, but the Romantic construction of a German national and ethnic culture was on its way. Indeed, German Romanticism's search for a national ethnicity based on a body of traditional narratives provides an illuminating case study in "the invention of ethnicity" as described by Werner Sollors, and it seems to be precisely the constructedness of German ethnicity that makes it easy for Germans today to identify with Indians because some of the parallels are striking, albeit ideologically structured, inventions. In brief, the Romantic infatuation with the historical past led to the construction of Germanness out of the *Germania*, an idealizing ethnographic account of the "wild and savage" (*silvatici*, or "dwellers of the woods," which later became "sauvage" in French and "sa(l)vage" in English) Germanic tribespeoples written by the conservative Roman historian Publius Cornelius Tacitus (AD 55–

116), and out of the *Nibelungenlied*, a Middle High German saga (written down circa 1200–05) presenting the life and death through treachery of Siegfried the dragonslayer and the revenge for his death taken by his wife, Kriemhild. Since then, Germans are prone to seeing their origins in the wood-dwelling tribespeople who successfully fought the Roman conquerors and to identifying with the virtues of Siegfried, the superhero, who could not be defeated in open combat but was stabbed in his vulnerable back by Hagen von Tronje, the pagan. Both texts were forgotten for centuries and then rediscovered and finally popularized into national myths in the late eighteenth century. To this day, there is no clearly definable German nation. Whenever Germans, whoever and wherever they were or are, try to define themselves as a nation and act collectively on that premise, they tend to overreact in a paranoid, aggressive, and disastrous manner. And we still do.

As with other categories defining people as members of groups such as culture, ethnicity, race, sex, gender, and, most prominently, class, the overall question of hegemony in terms of economic and political power has to be addressed and reflected simultaneously whenever we speak of nation. The concept of nation is neither universal nor neutral.

2. Approaches to Canada: Impostors, Imperialists, and Courageous Women

The first impressions I received of Canada as a child came from books. Before my brother and I were even ten years old, my mother read some of Grey Owl's beaver stories to us, I believe from *Das einsame Blockhaus*.[2] We were fascinated and moved to tears by the stories of perhaps the most famous environmentalist and Indian impostor, the Englishman Archibald Stansfeld Belaney (1888–1938), whose Anishnabe Indian identity we never came to doubt.[3] Later, when I must have been about thirteen years old, I read *Häuptling Büffelkind Langspeer erzählt sein Leben*, the autobiography of Chief Buffalo Child Long Lance, alias Sylvester Long, another celebrated impostor, who was of African American, Catawba Cherokee, and European American background but claimed a Canadian Blackfoot identity.[4] At about the same age, I was given a book of stories about the Canadian Mounties and their adventures entitled *Männer im roten Rock* (*Men in Red Coats*). A year or two later, I read a book that fascinated me immensely: *Ein Mädchen reitet durch Kanada* (*A Girl Rides through Canada*), the autobiographical account of a young woman's transcontinental horseback ride.

Typically for a German reader, my first exposure to aspects of Canada came via Indians. The books I read were the accounts of famous impostors, people who had emulated a Native lifestyle and "gone Indian." In other words, I first received an ersatz Indian image created for the European and European Canadian market by people who had appropriated an Indian voice but were really of British or American background. Those "Indians" were taken for real Native people; their texts were read as authentic Native literature.

The second aspect of my first impression of Canada involved the imperial penetration and appropriation of the Canadian landscape and Aboriginal societies and the struggle between what Roy Harvey Pearce called, in the American context, "civilization and savagery." In the Canadian context, it was the struggle between the RCMP and the wilderness arising from the imperial perspective of the British colonizer and his movement between garrison and bush. Only *Ein Mädchen reitet durch Kanada* offered a different reading — that of a young woman. In hindsight, it seems almost as if the text prepared me for my later reception of CanLit as women's lit.[5]

The first text I consciously read *as* a Canadian book was Bobbi Lee's, or rather Lee Maracle's, autobiography, *Bobbi Lee: Indian Rebel*, published in German as a paperback by a small alternative press in 1977, two years after its publication in Canada. It was not until 1983 that I began to read CanLit more systematically as a new or emerging national literature. Again, like so many other Canadianists in Scandinavia and Germany, I came to CanLit as a reader of women's literature when I stumbled across the works of Margaret Atwood.

3. A German Approach to First Nations People: Indianertümelei

There is a curious phenomenon I call *"Indianertümelei"* in German. *Indianertümelei* might be translated as "craze for all things Indian," "Indian-hood-ness," "exaggerated interest in Indians," "romanticizing of Indians," or — for want of a translation that better catches the ironic ambiguity of the German term — "Indianthusiasm." When using the terms *Indian* or *Indianer*, I am referring solely to the image or the idea that non-Natives, and, in the latter case, Germans, have of North American Aboriginal people. Almost two decades after Robert F. Berkhofer's *The White Man's Indian* (1979) and twelve years after my own German study *"Indianer" und "Native Americans"* (1985), such linguistic practice in scholarly usage seems standard, although for various reasons many First Nations individuals or Native Americans may still or again prefer *Indian* as a term for themselves. I hope they will not be offended.

Indianthusiasm or *Indianertümelei* is the remarkable interest in Indians shared by most Germans. The interest is generally ahistorical, in that it refers to Indianness as an ethnic identity independent of historical contexts. At the same time, Indians are often seen as exclusively historical figures, implying that Indianness is something from the past and that anybody who is truly Indian will follow cultural practices and even resemble, in lifestyle and physiognomy, First Nations peoples before contact. Relatively seldom is the German concept of *Indianertum* (Indianness) focused on contemporary Native American life.

Indianertümelei is deeply ingrained in German everyday culture. It is also found in the cultures of several of our neighbours. In some European countries, there are hobbyist clubs with thousands of members who like to dress up, with painstaking attention to detail, like old-time Indians and to live in tepees on weekends and holidays. They try to emulate as best they can the lifestyles, artefacts, and often the *Weltanschauungen* of the Native peoples of North America. Much of this initially Romantic infatuation with all things Indian goes back to authors such as Chateaubriand, Cooper, or Longfellow, and to painters such as Catlin, Bodmer, Kane, and Kurtz.

In Germany, the most influential writer of Indian books was and still is Karl May (1842–1912), and hence our most popular "Indian" is Winnetou, a fictitious character, supposedly a Mescalero Apache chief, who, much like Natty Bumppo's Chingachgook or the Lone Ranger's Tonto, faithfully follows his white German friend, Old Shatterhand, through the Wild West, fighting for law and order. Throughout his life, the impostor Karl May strove to be identified with his fictional Saxon superhero, Old Shatterhand, and he claimed blood brotherhood with Winnetou, who is really a typical apple Indian, or, rather, a German petit-bourgeois Christian in Indian guise. German readers willingly identified with Old Shatterhand, a nineteenth-century rendering of our mythological hero Siegfried, and they came to share his love for the beautiful Winnetou and his *Indianer*.

For example, in 1929, at the height of the Depression and at the dawn of Nazi fascism in Germany, the editor Hans Rudolf Rieder wrote in his introduction to a German translation of Buffalo Child Long Lance's "autobiography":

The Indian is closer to the German than to any other European. This is perhaps due to our partiality to the world of nature. Blacks, Eskimos, peoples of the South Seas do not possess the human qualities necessary to win our friendship and arouse our sympathy. As young lads, however, we find in the Indian an example and a brother; later he remains one of our favourite memories and images of those years. (author's translation)

Rieder's racist comments express, in a nutshell, an irrational German belief in a close affinity between Germans and Indians. While this affinity exists in ideology only, that is, between Germanics and Indians and not between Native Americans and citizens of a German state, this ideological construct of Germanic-Indian ethnocultural relatedness was consciously utilized propagandistically in the so-called Third Reich (Haible 22–77, Lutz, *"Indianer"* 357–410).[6]

Given the lasting prevalence of Karl May's hero, it is certainly no historical coincidence that Adolf Hitler once confessed to being an ardent believer in Karl May's Indian world.[7] In Nazi times, propagandists utilized the Indian image and presented Indians as a chosen race with individuals such as Sitting Bull and, most prominently, Tecumseh as ideal Führer figures, uniting all First Nations and forming the "red race" into an alliance against foreign encroachment and conquest — and this was a posture Germans identified with after the Treaty of Versailles.

The fascist appropriation of the Indian image is a German phenomenon. Historically, Germany as a national state never had any dealings or relations with First Nations at all, and that is the most important basis for our infatuation, I am sure. The romantic idealization of German-Indian relations seems to me to be one side of a coin; the other side is imprinted with racism and German anti-Semitism.

To expound this curious infatuation is beyond the scope of this paper. Suffice it to say that varying degrees of *Indianertümelei* have influenced the approaches to North America of millions of people in Scandinavia, Poland, Hungary, Austria, Czechoslovakia, and Germany — and, I believe, in France as well. Today, still, in Germany as in North America, a romantic and idealizing Indian image is often used in advertising and popular appeals.[8] For whatever ideological (exc)uses the stereotype is employed, Indians loom large in the German imagination, and generally in a positive way.[9]

In the political context, First Nations are respected as the first and indigenous Americans on whose continents all non-Native new-comers are illegal squatters. They are seen as Fourth World peoples who are internally colonized within their own territories, much like the Maori in New Zealand/Aotearoa or the Sami people in Northern Scandinavia, the Frisians along the North Sea coast. In general, little distinction is made in Europe between Canadian or American Native peoples. Rather, they are seen as members of tribes or Indian nations, independent of modern nation-states on the American continent, which is increasingly known as Turtle Island.

4. *Aboriginal Peoples as* First Nations *and "Nations First!"*

In November 1978, after an NGO conference in Geneva, a large Native American delegation from Canada, the United States, Mexico, Bolivia, and Peru undertook a speaking and consciousness-raising tour through Sweden, the Netherlands, Switzerland, and Germany. Clyde Bellecourt, speaker of the American Indian Movement, addressed a large audience in Bremen and earned much applause when he explained: "To be a nation, you need three things: your own land, your own language, and your own culture. The USA is not a nation. They stole our land, they speak the language of the English, and they have no culture of their own except McDonald's hamburgers and Coca-Cola."[10] Land, language, and culture (both material and ideological) are indeed crucial to ethnic identity as a nation. Most German listeners obviously sympathized with this notion and were happy to laugh about the implied lack of culture of their all-powerful big brother across the Atlantic. They also sympathized with the defiance of colonial power encoded in Bellecourt's words. But, by implication, his statement is also true of Canada as a settler culture.

It is no coincidence that Bellecourt used the three categories of land, language, and culture, because in these areas ethnocidal colonial practices have had the most devastating effects on First Nations in North America. Land, in its physical and spiritual aspects, is crucial to Native cultural identity, and so are language, religion, and everyday-life practices. The deliberate removal of many First Nations from their ancestral territories and the enforced linguistic and religious de-Indianization that went on in residential schools for three consecutive generations have indeed taken their toll. No wonder that today it is over these issues that First Nations people are fighting the hardest, attempting to retain/regain their status as distinct and self-determining — and self-respecting — nations within North America.

Their struggle is reflected in prominent texts by contemporary Native authors. "Land" and "language," "earth" and "voice" are central concepts. Several First Nations authors from Canada have stated in public that, in their writing, they are expressing the "Voice of the Mother." The ties of modern Native literature to the oral tradition generally seem to be stronger in Canada than in the United States. Jeannette Armstrong, Maria Campbell, Ruby Slipperjack, Lenore Keeshig-Tobias, Beth Cuthand, Lee Maracle, and Tomson Highway have stressed repeatedly in interviews that the oral tradition is tied to land (see the interviews in Lutz, *Contemporary Challenges*). But how can Western literary criticism honour this relationship? How will critical theory accommodate a Native elder's statement, as quoted by Maria Campbell, that English lost its Mother a long time ago and that Campbell, as a modern Native writer, has to put the Mother back in the language (Lutz, *Contemporary Challenges* 41–65; 49)?

Unless such a comment is brushed aside as "nonacademic" in a gesture of colonial arrogance and/or academic provincialism, it posits a serious challenge to contemporary academia. It would require some cross-cultural learning on the part of non-Natives, which could seriously question (and thereby "impede") the rapid progress of literary theory development in mainstream academia. The Caribbean critic Barbara Christian and Chicana critic and writer Gloria Anzaldúa, like other writers of colour, have stated that, in concerns and diction, literary scholarship and literary scholars have removed themselves further and further from the texts and the voices, the intentions, the social conditions, and the history of authors — particularly authors of colour. Instead, critic now writes to critic, scholar to scholar. Such criticism is pertinent to non-Native approaches to Native literature as well. It is time to stop and listen to the discourse of Native critics.

At a Canadian Studies conference at Aarhus, Denmark, in November 1992, Lenore Keeshig-Tobias, the Anishnabe storyteller, writer, critic, and cultural activist from Ontario, took up the definition of

Native literature as the Voice of the Mother: since mothers give birth to children and raise them, since most children hear the voices of their mothers first, singing to them, talking to them, telling them stories, and teaching them, the Voice of the Mother encodes the first and most important exposure of a Native child to the oral tradition. Thus, in Native literature, the Voice of the Mother carries the earliest and most often heard expressions of Aboriginal history and *Weltanschauung* as passed for generations from the grandmothers to the mothers, daughters, and granddaughters. The Voice of the Mother, then, is also a voice of lineage, as Lee Maracle has stressed (Lutz, *Contemporary Challenges* 172; 176). That this is so has to do with traditional gender roles and modes of childrearing as well as with the importance of women as carriers of cultures and bearers of life.

If much of Native literature today is deliberately encoded in the Voice of the Mother, the voice of the land, and the history or stories of its people and all their relations, then First Nations literature would be the most fundamental, most deeply rooted voice of the North American continent, exploding/transcending the boundaries of all present nation-states in terms of space and time.[11]

5. Native Literature and European Needs for Spiritual Escape

First Nations writers and critics in Canada are fully aware of the special role of their literature as opposed to, or as seen within, the literary mainstream. In his conversation with Terry Goldie, which forms the introduction to their jointly edited *Anthology of Canadian Native Literature in English*, Daniel David Moses, the Delaware poet, playwright, editor, and critic from Toronto, explains ". . . I think the ideas presented by Native people are particularly important. I think Native people have a sense of a larger responsibility to the planet, whether we come at it just from the idea that Native traditions honour the environment as a mother, or whether we come at it from the idea that we're looked at as people who should have those ideas and therefore we're allowed to have them" (xii). And referring to the relationship between Native literature and the mainstream and the dangers of absorption and appropriation or tokenization and ghettoization, Moses says: "My image of that mainstream is that it is pretty wide but it's spiritually shallow. I don't think we are worried about being 'subsumed.' If we become part of that mainstream we're going to be the deep currents" (xiv). This is a proud assertion that Native literature is not shallow but possesses an inherent spiritual value, which carries, as literary scholar and critic Arnold Krupat puts it, "an ecosystemic, nonanthropocentric perspective on the world" (55).

In the early 1970s, relations were more openly political. The warriors of the American Indian Movement (AIM) were the political heroes of young German AIM Support Group members and anti-bourgeois revolutionaries or ecologically oriented socialists. In the 1980s, the antinuclear deployment movement and ecological concerns overcame anticapitalist campaigns and opened the way for a more spiritually oriented gesture of appropriation. The haunting moral lament of Chief Seattle's plagiarized speech[12] seemed best to encode the general feeling aroused by the destruction of Mother Earth, and it encouraged those environmentalists who actively fought that destruction. Today, there is a wide selection of "instant medicine men," "plastic shamans," or "Indian ersatz gurus" promising initiation and immediate escape from reality for those who can pay for the trip.[13]

Many people in Europe and elsewhere understand the importance and urgency of the Native Voice of the Mother. They see the gradual, daily erosion of stone sculptures and the silent, slow death of our forests from acid rain; they are faced with the fact that the next nuclear catastrophe is building up around us. For many Europeans, the concluding stanzas of Jeannette Armstrong's complex poem "Rocks" carry a very immediate, concrete, and vitally pertinent global message delivered in a traditional tribal or national Okanagan voice and setting:

> as old stone worked churches dissolve ever so minutely
> in the sad rain
> while in the distance
> one tiny grain waits
> to flower into blazing white
>
> I study the rocks
> I have set into a circle
> opening to the east
> on this mountaintop (24)

For many Europeans, the attractiveness of Native philosophy and literature lies exclusively in its spiritual aspects, which, in that narrower, functionalizing, and appropriatory perception, become disconnected from the land, the voice, and the material aspects of First Nations political reality in the world of today. Hungry for a new age beyond the nightmares of our multiple, self-created dilemmas, looking for an ecology so deep it will transcend all obstacles of class, race, or gender, Europeans in increasing numbers flock to read and hear the words of Indian sages willing to lead them on their transcendental flights. And they pay, and pay, and pay.

6. Canadian Culture/Literature and Native Voice

Given the state of Native/non-Native relations in Canada, it seems ironic, and at the same time reflective of an exploitative hegemonic relationship, that Canadians utilize an Indian iconography in many official or private public-relations activities outside of the country. In their glossy brochures and large advertisements, the Canadian tourist industry, as well as provincial governments seeking to attract foreign investors, appropriate the Indian as image, thus helping to confirm the idea of Canada as Indian country.

Things are quite different, however, when we look at the promotion and perception of modern Canadian literature and the establishment of a Canadian literary canon (see Lutz, " 'Is the Canon Color-blind?' "). Until recently, contemporary Native literature was almost totally absent from CanLit (see Lutz, "Canadian Native Literature and the Sixties"). In Carl F. Klinck's 1976 edition of the *Literary History of Canada* it was relegated to the section titled "Children's Literature"; one page was devoted to Indian and Eskimo legends (Egoff 205). Or the works of prominent authors were dismissed as "protest literature," as in the 1983 *Oxford Companion to Canadian Literature*, where Penny Petrone saw *Prison of Grass, The Rebirth of Canada's Indians, Halfbreed*, and *We Are Métis* as "written by militant patriots and couched in strident, sloganistic language" (387). Even Robert Lecker's 1991 anthology *Canadian Canons: Essays in Literary Value* contains only a single reference: it mentions Tomson Highway as being from a "non-white culture" (Knowles 106).

In recent years, however, this has begun to change. The new interest in Native literature is documented by the appearance of new anthologies of Native writing; by an increasing number of critical articles in literary journals, such as the special issue of *Canadian Literature* published in 1990; by the inclusion of Native authors in collections of interviews and critical statements; and by a first book-length study of literary theory related to Native literature in Canada, Julia Emberley's *Thresholds of Difference.*

Most authors of colour I asked tended to see the new outburst of literary activity as a result of the summer of 1990, when Elijah Harper in the Manitoba Assembly and the Mohawk Warriors in Kahnesatake and Kahnawake put Native issues on the national agenda. Others, mainly scholars and teachers of Canadian literature, explained it as the result of changes in the academy, that is, as the result of a more perceptive and open discourse about postcolonial literatures, about the voice of the Other, about liminality, and about writers from the borderlands.

Undoubtedly, both levels of discourse — the political struggles in the streets or, rather, on the bridges, and the theoretical debate in academia about postcolonial writing — have helped to foreground Native Voice as never before in Canada. And yet much is left to be desired, as the Aboriginal poet, photographer, publisher, editor, teacher, and critic Greg Young-Ing has explained, most recently in an article entitled "The Estrangement and Marginalization of Aboriginal Writers in Canada":

> In the 1990s, nearly all books by Aboriginal peoples have been published through small and independent presses; yet over a hundred books about Aboriginal peoples have been published by large Canadian houses already in the twentieth century. Typically, a so-called Native Studies section in a high-volume bookstore in Canada will have books by non-Aboriginal authors prominently displayed. If they are lucky, Aboriginal authors will have their books at the bottom of the Native Studies section and not in the literature section, as if their books were not legitimate literature. [Kimberly M.] Blaeser has sarcastically commented on this particular phenomenon, saying, "No, I'm not a poet, I just write Indian stuff." (23)

Within the academic and publishing establishment, at present, there are definite signs of tokenism, that is, the foregrounding of a few selected "pet" authors — usually male, though Native literature in Canada is a predominantly female domain — whose works may be more amenable to established literary tastes and perhaps more manageable in postmodern theories. This foregrounding happens at the expense of Aboriginal authors who are less concerned with innovative form than with the articulation in English of traditional as well as current social concerns in a contemporary setting.

Besides, there are traditions within the discussion of CanLit that are structured to obliterate and silence the presence of First Nations in Canada through established and systematic theoretical discourses in which Canada is thematized as struggling to overcome an Atwoodian victim position. These discourses are the rejection of continentalism and an anti-American, nationalist bias in Canadian literature and literary criticism; and the postcolonial debate itself, and its inherent bias, which causes it to view Canada as a settler culture struggling for national identity.

7. Canadian Literature Asserts Itself as National Literature against American Literature

With her seminal, albeit controversial, study, *Survival*, Margaret Atwood focused international attention on the colonial victim position of Canadian culture. In it, she advocates the notion of nation against American continentalism and British imperialism. In her novel *Surfacing*, also published in 1972, she personifies the enemy as "the Americans," whose influence can no longer be externalized from Canadian cultural identity. In that sense, we are drawn to conclude, Canadians are even less of a nation — in Bellecourt's definition — than Americans.

Seen from a European perspective, Atwood's ideological construct seems very outdated in light of the international respect Canada is enjoying in the world today. However, much of Atwood's influence as *the* representative of CanLit is still felt, and her notion of Canada as struggling against victimization is shared by most Canadian intellectuals I have talked to.

Many Europeans may sympathize with some of the reservations Canadians have about the influence of an all-powerful, globally dominating United States. However, since both European Canadians and European Americans — the socioculturally dominant groups — share the same continent, since many of their mutual historical experiences and many aspects of their cultures are informed by this "Turtle Island,"[14] to neglect the commonalities may also lead to intellectual isolationism and a certain type of nationalist provincialism, adversely affecting the status of Aboriginal peoples and their literary voices. This danger becomes more obvious when we look at First Nations cultures and Canadians from abroad. It should be remembered that many Europeans still see North America as essentially Indian country. The division of Turtle Island along the forty-ninth parallel is as artificial and unnatural as the imperial surveyor's grid system.

For First Nations such as the Haudenosaunee (or Six Nations), the Anishnabeg (or Ojibway/Chippewa), the Lakota, Dakota, and Nakota (Sioux), the Okanagan, or the Blood, Blackfeet, Peigan, and Siksika, and for many other nations from Passamaquoddy Bay to the Strait of Juan de Fuca, the United States-Canada border, albeit a more penetrable one, is as unnatural as the former Iron Curtain was in Europe for Finns and Russians in Karelia, for Sami people in the Soviet Union, Finland, Sweden, and Norway, or for Hungarians and Austrians or the Germans on either side. To perceive Canadian culture as separated from American culture and as more closely linked to that of other postcolonial settler societies on other continents is to dissociate the Canadian cultural discourse from the fundamental Native relationship to the land as source of life and culture.

8. Canadian Literature as Postcolonial Settler Literature

The ongoing discourse on postcolonial literatures outside of Britain and the United States draws attention to political and cultural hegemonies and the necessity of deconstructing them. This discourse focuses mainly on settler cultures such as Aotearoa/New Zealand, Australia, or Canada, which use various englishes to write their own identities against imperial English (see Ashcroft et al.). While some studies are careful to at least mention the fact that besides English — and French in Canada — there are the languages and literatures of the indigenous nations within or alongside these settler nations, others seem happily oblivious to internal colonization. Thus, the postcolonial discourse may, in effect, tend and in some cases has tended to neglect and literarily/literally silence the voices of indigenous cultures.[15] The notion of overcoming one's own victimization as members of Euro-Canadian, anglophone, or francophone settler societies in effect displaces the languages and literatures of the Fourth World nations on whose territories the settler societies squat. Again, the overall context of hegemony, of unequal economic and political access and power according to lines of class and ethnic or gender categories, needs to be addressed within the settler colonies at the same time as their victimization by the former empire is discussed.

And there are encouraging beginnings. While neglect or displacement may happen in many cases, there are, at the same time, some courageous and self-critical attempts in settler cultures to come to terms with guilt-ridden historical legacies.[16]

It may be an Atwoodian stereotype, but discourses reading CanLit as colonized/decolonizing/postcolonial literature seem to run the danger of luxuriously wallowing in feelings of victimhood. CanLit, when foregrounded as one literature of colonization and decolonization, tends to occupy a place that within an internal Canadian or even a continentalist approach would really be occupied first and foremost by the literatures of indigenous nations, and then by texts written by other writers of colour and nonanglophone or nonfrancophone ethnic writers, as internally colonized groups. Special attention would focus on the triple or even fourfold oppression of women writers belonging to such internally colonized "minority" groups (see Herms).

Ultimately, the process of understanding CanLit vis-à-vis Native literatures would have to involve, in terms of class, gender, ethnicity, race, and national policies, a fundamental renegotatiation of the intercultural positionings of First Nations and settler cultures, thus necessitating the radically postcolonial deconstruction of established hegemonic relations extending far beyond the academic arena.

9. Appropriation and Respect are the Crucial Issues

Within the internal (post)colonial hegemony in Canada, relations are never quite easy between authors, literary critics, scholars, and publishers in the mainstream and Aboriginal publishers, scholars, and writers. Their dialogue is overcoded with a load of historical legacies and discourses inherited from the past, which often obstruct and slant communication. While there are no patent solutions with which to untangle the various strands in this Gordian knot, and while a forceful means to cut through all intricacies would be far from expedient, respect may be the best and only basis for a new dialogue. Respect for the Other, respect for, and awareness of, the past, the patience that has to go with it, and the openness and the empathy that were missing from crucial communications in the past.

While Canada is a relatively young and very dynamic nation, a culture in flux without closure, First Nations are ancient, and while the flexibility and adaptability of Aboriginal cultures is astounding, these cultures also manifest an awareness of traditions and history that is equally strong in determining the present. Without going into the issue of appropriation of Native Voice any further in this paper (see Lutz, "Cultural Appropriation"; and "Confronting Cultural Imperialism"), we must remember that this timely debate about respect, not censorship, is the central and the most crucial issue between First Nations writers and non-Native writers and critics. Seen from abroad, a lot of credit must be given, and is given, to Canadians for addressing the issue so widely; this is so unlike the American debate of about fifteen years ago over "whiteshamanism" (see Lutz, "Regional Cultures"). I wish we in Germany had only a fraction of the kind of intercultural awareness this debate has engendered among Canadians.

In Europe, the American Voice of the Mother poses no threat to cultural, ethnic, or national identities. Maybe, therefore, it is at times easier from across the Atlantic to accept and understand the importance of Native Voice (see Lutz, "'O Canada!'"; "Contemporary Native Literature"; and "First Nations Literature"). Besides, in densely populated Europe, the effects of the neglect of a discourse with nature that Aboriginal peoples have pursued for millennia are much more visible and seemingly more urgent than they might be on the giant North American continent. But when we look at the international networking of North American First Nations with other indigenous and tribal peoples all over the globe, with Fourth World nations, with environmentalist groups, and even with the academic world abroad, then we see that the global village has arrived, and there is a direct path from the tribal to the global, bypassing or transcending nation-states.

10. Natives and Europeans Interact and Network

While open lines of communication may run from First Nations to individuals and groups throughout the world, nation-states often present real impediments. As a recent example, in December 1991, German customs officers and border patrols refused to honour the Aboriginal passports presented by a delegation of Western Shoshone people from Nevada intending to travel through Germany on a speaking tour en route to Stockholm, where they were scheduled to receive the alternative Nobel prize for their engagement against the nuclear radiation pollution in a Nevada test-site area, their unceded tribal territory. In the past, Swiss, Swedish, Dutch, Austrian, and German customs officials have respected Aboriginal passports, sometimes after much negotiation and intervention by support groups. Mohawks, Anishnabe, and others have entered and left the Federal Republic with their own travel documents, issued on behalf of their nations by their tribal governments.

In 1983, a pan-Indian peace delegation headed by Mohawk and Onondaga clan mothers visited the University of Osnabrück, where I was then teaching, on a solidarity trip to lend support to our struggle to halt the deployment of more American and Russian nuclear warheads in West and East Germany. A few years later, an international delegation of Fourth World peoples affected by uranium mining and nuclear testing spoke to a large audience in our main auditorium in the castle, welcomed and introduced by the university's president. Two of the delegates were Métis women from Wollaston Lake, Saskatchewan. At the opening of the university's interdisciplinary research centre for North American studies in 1992, Jeannette Armstrong, novelist, poet, activist, and director of the En'Owkin School of International First Nations Writing, delivered the opening address with Cree poet Barbara Frazer. A few months later, on 12 October 1992, again in the castle's main auditorium, Don Fiddler, a Métis from Saskatchewan and director of the En'Owkin Centre, addressed a large audience on Columbus and his aftereffects. That, we felt, was a very historic occasion indeed: after five hundred years of one-way communication, we now had a Native person speaking to us from the rostrum. And there have been many similar events within a period of over twenty years, including art exhibitions; individual lectures by scholars, among them Jack Forbes, Howard Adams, and Eddie Benton Banai; and readings by other authors and artists, such as Beatrice Culleton, Shirley Cheechoo, Ray Thomas, Drew Hayden Taylor, Allen Ahmoo Angeconeb, Daniel David Moses, Chrystos, and Blake Debassige. Many of these guests travelled to, and spoke at, several universities. Meanwhile, I have taught in the former East Germany for four years at the University of Greifswald, and many First Nations writers, artists, and scholars have visited us here as well.

In academia, more and more scholars and students are turning to Native studies, each in their own field.[17] Scholars such as Brigitte Georgi-Findlay, Konrad Gross, Wolfgang Hochbruck, Hartwig Isernhagen, Rudolf Kaiser, and Bernd Peyer have established themselves as experts on Native Literature in the United States and Canada. The most substantial study by far of the presentation of the Canadian Métis people and their leader Louis Riel in English Canadian literature, a most excellent book by Wolfgang Klooss entitled *Geschichte und Mythos in der Literatur Kanadas: Die englischsprachige Métis- und Riel-Rezeption*, appeared in Germany. In geography, a large research project is being conducted by Dieter Soyez, a geography professor at the University of Cologne who is the former head of the Canadian Studies Association in the German-speaking countries — the largest outside of Canada. Soyez is investigating the networking among environmentalist groups in Canada and the United States in support of the Cree Nation's struggle to halt the La Grande Baleine hydroelectric project in Quebec. This has given rise to multiple investigations and inquiries from Hydro Québec.

In October 1993, the University of Marburg and the Canadian Embassy in Bonn cohosted the first of a series of symposia in which graduate students could present papers based on their ongoing research in Canadian Native studies. Papers ranged from environmental studies and research on Indian law and Indian rights to ethnographic investigations and a large variety of doctoral dissertations and MA theses on Native writing, both fiction and autobiography.[18] Research on womanist poetry by First Nations writers was presented as well as a thesis exploring the background and text of the only existing German version of the diary of a Labrador Inuit. The 1995 annual convention of the German Canadian Studies Association focused on First Nations peoples and hosted a number of Native speakers.

Translating Native authors and disseminating their voices is one of the prime endeavours we in Germany are engaged in. In 1989, we founded OBEMA (*Osnabrück Bilingual Editions of Minority Authors*, later renamed *Marginalized Authors*) at the University of Osnabrück, in which we publish twice a year, in German and English, works by Fourth World authors or writers who are marginalized on account of class, gender, or ethnicity.[19] We translate most of the issues and prepare them for desktop publishing with the assistance of our students. For them, it is a good exercise in translation and a chance to learn about cultures removed from their own experiences, to exchange letters with authors, to prepare manuscripts for publication, and to network inside and outside the ivory tower. Occasionally, we are also successful in launching translations of First Nations authors through commercial publishing houses. In 1994, Beatrice

Culleton's *April Raintree* (1983) came out in a German translation, and the fall of 1997 saw the publication in German of Jeannette Armstrong's *Slash* (1984) and Chrystos's *Wild Rice*, both translated by Audrey Huntley, a graduate of Marburg University.

This list of activities could be added to ad infinitum. While only ten or fifteen years ago some colleagues gave war whoops to an academic involved in Native studies, or jokingly referred to him as "The Last of the Mohicans" or "Winnetou," this attitude is changing. Right now, Native studies is undoubtedly in as an area for graduate research — and some will still pursue it when it is out again. While much of the motivation may initially come from *Indianertümelei*, and while some of it may acquire forms of appropriation, students and scholars seem to be growing increasingly aware of these mine-fields and mirrors, and to be trying in their research to address the intricacies of their approaches. In a society that is wracked by immense internal social tensions resulting in gruesome acts of open racism, a heightened awareness of intercultural relations is long overdue.

Heard from abroad, the Native Voice from Canada is growing in volume and articulation. More and more of our students are trying to study at Canadian universities, hoping to be able to pursue Canadian literature *and* Native studies in situ. Credit is given and interest is focused on Canadian mainstream institutions that actively engage in a mutual process of learning with the First Nations of North America. In the national context of Canada, it may seem surprising that in order to fill a professorial position in Native literature in 1990, the English Department of the Saskatchewan Indian Federated College, part of the University of Regina, had to hire someone with a PhD from Europe, but in the international context it is not surprising. By now, however, there may be some Native scholars in Canada with PhDs in literature, and these people will speak for themselves.

In this vein, let me finish with a long quotation from Greg Young-Ing's article. This passage will also explain why it is high time, indeed, for me to shut up:

> Even today the patterns set by Cooper and Leacock are continued by Canadian writers like W. P. Kinsella and Anne Cameron, and the ghosts of Grey Owl and Long Lance live on through "plastic shaman" writers like Lynn Andrews and Adolf Hungry Wolf.

A more recent development has been a wave of writing by non-Aboriginal academics, such as Frank Cassidy, Boyce Richardson, Thomas Berger, Sally Weaver, Menno Boldt, and Anthony Long. Many of these authors are involved with higher-level academic institutions, and have established themselves in the mind of the Canadian public as authoritative "Native studies experts." The majority of these writers are knowledgeable and supportive of Aboriginal peoples' political aspirations, and they must also be credited with some of the increased public awareness in recent years. However, these academics do not promote the Aboriginal Voice nor do they speak for Aboriginal peoples' unique perspectives on the issues.

Albeit well-intentioned, this body of work tends to reduce emotionally, historically, and culturally charged issues to dry, information-laden legalese and/or academic jargon. Furthermore, by creating a recognized school of experts, who are a relative "low risk" to publishers, and by saturating the market with books about Aboriginal peoples, this wave of academic writing has the effect of ultimately blocking out the Aboriginal Voice. (24)

NOTES

[1] These ten theses are from the revised and updated version of one of six papers read at the Canada through Foreign Eyes Symposium, organized by the Humanities Centre, University of Victoria, 21–22 January 1994. Other speakers from various backgrounds and continents were: Homi Bhabha, Karen Gould, Shirin Kudchedkar, Jean-Michel Lacroix, and Kateryne Longley.

[2] *Das einsame Blockhaus* appeared in 1938. Other works by Grey Owl appeared in German in 1954 (*Männer der letzten Grenze*), 1958 (*Sajo und ihre Biber*), and 1960 (*Kleiner Bruder*).

[3] The most fascinating recent text dealing with Archie Belaney is *Grey Owl: The Mystery of Archie Belaney*, a book-length cycle of lyrical poems that reconstruct and explore the life of Grey Owl, created by the Ojibway poet and critic Armand Garnet Ruffo, whose first book of poetry, *Opening in the Sky*, came out in 1994. Some of Ruffo's family members interacted closely with Grey Owl in their time. See also Lovat Dickason, *Wilderness Man: The Strange Story of Grey Owl*; Hartmut Lutz, *"Indianer" und "Native Americans": Zur sozial-und literarhistorischen Vermittlung eines Streotyps* (especially 375); Donald B. Smith, *From the Land of Shadows: The Making of Grey Owl*; Daniel Francis, *The Imaginary Indian:*

The Image of the Indian in Canadian Culture (especially 131–41).

4 See Dempsey (196–203); Lutz, *"Indianer"* (375); and Smith, *Long Lance*.

5 See Lutz, "Von den Ladies im Busch zu den Heldinnen der Prärie: Anglokanadische Erzählerinnen und das Land," and "Anglocanadian Women Writers and Canadian Female Identity."

6 A German doctoral dissertation, Barbara Haible's *Indianer im Dienste der NS-Ideologie: Untersuchungen zur Funktion von Jugendbüchern über-nordamerikanische Indianer im Nationalsozialismus* ("Indians Serving Nazi-Ideology: Analyses of the Function of Juvenile Literature about North American Indians under National Socialism"), provides the first substantial historical analysis of how German Indianthusiasm was functionalized in the production of Nazi literature for the young. After 1933, there was a brief but heated debate about whether Karl May should be utilized for Nazi propaganda and whether the "effeminate enthusiasm for colored people" (*"weibische Farbigenschwärmerei"*) was counterproductive to Nazi political ends. However, only a year or two later, the Nazi teachers' association (NS-Lehrerbund), the NS-Jugendschriftenwarte (literally, "National Socialist Guardian Agency for Books for Youth"), and the Nazi association for writers (NS-Schriftstellerverband) agreed to use Indian books to propagate Nazi ideals such as *Führerkult* (cult of the Führer), *Rassenlehre* (race theory), and *Wehrertüchtigung* (preparing for military prowess). And they did!

7 In his memoirs, Karl Speer, another Nazi politician and a prominent architect and sculptor, recalled that Hitler had said that "Karl May would be a proof that it is not necessary to travel in order to get to know the world. The character of Winnetou, for example, as created by Karl May, had always impressed [Hitler] deeply by his flexibility and foresight as a tactitian. In Winnetou he saw embodied almost the ideal qualities of a '*Kompanieführer.*' Even today, when faced with seemingly hopeless situations, in his nightly reading hours, he would turn to these narratives, which would uplift him internally as other people might be uplifted by philosophical texts or older people by the Bible; besides, Winnetou had always incorporated the ideal of a truly noble person. It was necessary, of course, through a hero figure to teach youth the proper ideas about nobility; youth needed heroes like daily bread. In this lay the great importance of Karl May. But instead those idiots of teachers were hammering the works of Goethe or Schiller into the heads of their pitiable pupils" (qtd. in Lutz, *"Indianer"* 361; author's translation).

8 Often, Native people touring Europe as representatives of their nations use humour to combat stereotyping. The Anishnabe activist, actor, and author Dennis Banks, cofounder of the American Indian Movement, knows one sentence in German, which he tries on the German people he encounters: "Ich bin ein stolzer Indianer!" ("I am a proud Indian").

9 Still, in postunification Germany, Germans seem prone to identifying politically with Indians. In December 1991, a colleague of mine, Dr. Annette

Brauer of the University of Greifswald (in the former GDR), gave a paper in which East Germans were compared to Indians as victims. She said that East Germans, like First Nations people in North America, are being turned into a minority in their own territory by the colonial power of an alien bureaucracy, the German federal trust agency, *Treuhand*, which holds in possession and sells what had formerly been held communally, just as the Bureau of Indian Affairs in the United States and the Department of Indian Affairs and Northern Development in Canada held Native land in trust and then sold its assets on the private market. And there are further parallels.

[10] This is my own eye- and ear-witness rendering of his words. I am confident that this is what Bellecourt said.

[11] The most profound and fascinating study of the relatedness of land and ethnic identity as reflected in Native American literature is Robert M. Nelson's *Place and Vision: The Function of Landscape in Native American Fiction*.

[12] See Rudolf and Michaela Kaiser, *Diese Erde ist uns heilig*.

[13] There is a great variety of ironic terms used for individual Natives or impostors who cater, for money, to the spiritual needs of (dis-)enchanted non-Native followers. The term "instant medicine men" was used by the late spiritual counsellor of the American Indian Movement, Philip Deere (Muskogee-Creek), in the presence of Archie Fire Lame Deer and Rolling Thunder at a Native American health conference in San Francisco in November 1979. The term "plastic shamans" is in wide use among First Nations people in Canada today (see Greg Young-Ing), and "Indian ersatz gurus" is my own coinage.

[14] The geographical givens of the continent do indeed shape the cultural regions that characterize North America today. This is obvious when the cultural geography as established by the map in Joel Garreau's popular regionalist cultural geography *The Nine Nations of North America* (204f.) is compared to a map of Native American ethnocultural regions as established by ethnographers for the First Nations — for example, in Lindig and Münzel's *Die Indianer* (16). Many cultural regions are congruous, although there is little awareness of this fact (see Lutz, "Regional Cultures").

[15] Despite all intentions to the contrary, a similar danger is inherent in discourses about multiculturalism and the mosaic in literature, because they tend to see all literatures as equally important and potentially powerful, regardless of the very real inequalities in power and impact between the various ethnic groups.

[16] See Brydon and Tiffin, *Decolonising Fictions*; Williamson, *Sounding Differences*; Kamboureli, *Making a Difference* — the latter really "makes a difference" in that it presents, for the first time in an anthology, the multiple ethnic voices of Canada, including First Nations, "visible minorities," and even European.

[17] There are several monographs and small magazines reflecting this process. The most established academic journal, which is published in Austria and Hungary, *European Review of Native American Studies* (ERNAS), has brought out two issues a year since 1987 and is edited by Christian F. Feest.

[18] Here are just a few of the doctoral theses that have appeared in Germany: Janine Bohlinger, "Zeitgenössische Autobiographien kanadischer Ureinwohnerinnen"; Brigitte Georgi-Findlay, "Tradition und Moderne in der zeitgenössischen indianischen Literatur der USA"; Wolfgang Hochbruck, " 'I Have Spoken': Die Darstellung und ideologische Funktion indianischer Mündlichkeit in der nordamerikanischen Literatur"; Audrey Huntley, "Widerstand schreiben! Entkolonialisierungsprozesse im Schreiben indigener kanadischer Frauen"; Holger Möllenberg, "Die Rhetorik indianischer Literatur: Gedankliche Voraussetzungen moderner Literatur der Indianer Nordamerikas und ihre rhetorische Verwendung zur Beeinflussung einer differenzierten Leserschaft"; Frauke Zwillus, " 'Today Talks in Yesterday's Voice': Zentrale Themen und ihre erzählerische Gestaltung im indianischen Roman der Gegenwart."

[19] So far, we have published sixteen regular issues, two of which present the works of First Nations authors from Canada: Peter Blue Cloud, *I Am Turtle/Ich bin Schildkröte* 5 (1991); and a number of Indian and Métis authors, *Four Feathers/Vier Federn* 10 (1992). Other authors included in OBEMA are Joe Bruchac, Melba Boyd, Bobbi Sykes, Cathie Dunsford, Rolando Hinojosa, Carmen Tafolla, Lance Henson, Meiling Jin, Audre Lorde, Gerald Vizenor, Lorenzo Thomas, Claire Harris, and Carol Lee Sanchez. As well, one issue of OBEMA has taken the form of a collection of Maori writing and another anthology of Australian Aborigine literature. While I served as founding editor from 1989 until 1993, the series is now edited by my Osnabrück colleague, comrade, and friend Sigrid Markmann.

WORKS CITED

Anzaldúa, Gloria. "Haciendo caras, una entrada." Anzaldúa, ed. xv–xxviii.
——, ed. *Making Face, Making Soul: Haciendo Caras*. San Francisco: aunt lute, 1990.
Armstrong, Jeannette. "Rocks." *Breath Tracks*. Penticton, BC: Theytus, 1991. 21–24.
——. *Slash*. Übersetzt von Audrey Huntley, Nachwort von Hartmut Lutz und Marlowe Sam. Münster: Unrast, 1997.
——, et al. *Telling It: Women and Language across Cultures*. Vancouver: Press Gang, 1990.
——, ed. *Looking at the Words of Our People: First Nations Analysis of Literature*. Penticton, BC: Theytus, 1993.

Ashcroft, Bill, Gareth Griffiths, and Helen Tiffin. *The Empire Writes Back: Theory and Practice in Post-Colonial Literatures*. London: Routledge, 1989.

Bannerji, Himani, ed. *Returning the Gaze: Essays on Racism, Feminism and Politics*. Toronto: Sister Vision, 1993.

Berkhofer, Robert F. *The White Man's Indian*. New York: Random House, 1979.

Bohlinger, Janine. *Zeitgenössische Autobiographien kanadischer Ureinwohnerinnen*. Diss. Mainz: Johannes Gutenberg-Universität, 1995.

Bosanquet, Mary. *Ein Mädchen reitet durch Kanada*. Braunschweig: Westermann, 1950.

Bruchac, Joseph, ed. *Returning the Gift: Poetry and Prose from the First North American Native Writers' Festival*. Tucson: U of Arizona P, 1994.

Brydon, Diana, and Helen Tiffin, eds. *Decolonising Fictions*. Sydney: Dangaroo, 1993.

Buffalo Child Long Lance. *Long Lance*. New York: Cosmopolitan, 1928.

Campbell, Maria, et al. *Give Back: First Nations Perspectives on Cultural Practice*. North Vancouver: Gallerie, 1992.

Christian, Barbara. "The Race for Theory" Anzaldúa, ed. 335–45.

Chrystos. *Wilder Reis*. Übersetzt von Audrey Huntley. Berlin: Orlanda, 1997.

Culleton, Beatrice. *Halbblut! Die Geschichte der April Raintree*. Aus dem Englischen von Annette Kohl-Beyer, Nachwort von Hartmut Lutz. Wuppertal: Peter Hammer, 1994.

Dempsey, Hugh A. "Sylvester Long, Buffalo Child Long Lance, Catawba Cherokee and Adopted Blackfoot, 1891–1932." *American Indian Intellectuals*. Ed. Margot Liberty. St. Paul: West, 1978. 196–203.

Dickason, Lovat. *Wilderness Man: The Strange Story of Grey Owl*. Toronto: Macmillan, 1973.

Egoff, Sheila E. "Children's Literature" *Literary History of Canada: Canadian Literature in English*. 2nd ed. Ed. Carl F. Klinck. Vol. 3. Toronto: U of Toronto P, 1976. 134–42. 3 vols. 1976.

Emberley, Julia V. *Thresholds of Difference: Feminist Critique, Native Women's Writings, Postcolonial Theory*. Toronto: U of Toronto P, 1993.

Francis, Daniel. *The Imaginary Indian: The Image of the Indian in Canadian Culture*. Vancouver: Arsenal, 1992.

Garreau, Joel. *The Nine Nations of North America*. New York: Hearst, 1982.

Georgi-Findlay, Brigitte. *Tradition und Moderne in der zeitgenössischen indianischen Literatur der USA*. Diss. Köln: Pahl-Rugenstein, 1986.

Grant, Agnes, ed. *Our Bit of Truth: An Anthology of Canadian Native Literature*. Winnipeg: Pemmican, 1990.

Haible, Barbara. *Indianer im Dienste der NS-Ideologie: Untersuchungen zur Funktion von Jugendbüchern über nordamerikanische Indianer im Nationalsozialismus*. Hamburg: Kovač, 1998.

Herms, Dieter. "La Chicana: Dreifache Diskriminierung als Drittweltfrau." *Gulliver 10: "Frauenstudien."* Berlin: Argument, 1981. 79–93.

Hochbruck, Wolfgang. *"I Have Spoken": Die Darstellung und ideologische Funktion indianischer Mündlichkeit in der nordamerikanischen Literatur.* Diss. Tübingen: Gunter Narr Verlag, 1991.

Hodgson, Heather, ed. *Seventh Generation: Contemporary Native Writing.* Penticton, BC: Theytus, 1989.

Huntley, Audrey. *Widerstand schreiben! Entkolonialisierungsprozesse im Schreiben indigener kanadischer Frauen.* Diss. Münster: Unrast, 1996.

Hutcheon, Linda, and Marion Richmond, eds. *Other Solitudes: Canadian Multicultural Fictions.* Toronto: Oxford UP, 1990.

Jaine, Linda, and Drew Hayden Taylor, eds. *Voices: Being Native in Canada.* Saskatoon: U of Saskatchewan, Extensions Division, 1992.

Kaiser, Rudolf, and Michaela Kaiser. *Diese Erde ist uns heilig: Die Rede des Indianerhäuptlings Seattle, Original und Nachdichtung.* Münster: Iris Blaschzok, 1984.

Kamboureli, Smaro, ed. *Making a Difference: Canadian Multicultural Literature.* Toronto: Oxford UP, 1996.

King, Thomas, ed. *All My Relations: An Anthology of Contemporary Canadian Native Fiction.* Toronto: McClelland, 1990.

Klooss, Wolfgang. *Geschichte und Mythos in der Literatur Kanadas: Die englischsprachige Métis- und Riel-Rezeption.* Heidelberg: Carl Winter, 1989.

Knowles, Richard Paul. "Voices (off): Deconstructing the Modern English-Canadian Dramatic Canon." *Canadian Canons: Essays in Literary Value.* Ed. Robert Lecker. Toronto: U of Toronto P, 1991. 91–111.

Krupat, Arnold. *The Voice in the Margin: Native American Literature and the Canon.* Berkeley: U of California P, 1989.

LaRocque, Emma. "Preface: Or, Here Are Our Voices — Who Will Hear?" *Writing the Circle: Native Women of Western Canada.* Ed. Jeanne Perreault and Sylvia Vance. Edmonton: NeWest, 1990. xv–xxx.

——. "Tides, Towns, and Trains." *Living the Changes.* Ed. Joan Turner. Winnipeg: U of Manitoba P, 1990. 76–90.

Larsen, Fred. *Männer im roten Rock: Abenteuer eines kanadischen Nordwest-Polizisten.* Gütersloh: C. Bertelsmann, 1958.

Lindig, Wolfgang, and Mark Münzel. *Die Indianer.* München: Deutscher Taschenbuch, 1985.

Lutz, Hartmut. "Anglocanadian Women Writers and Canadian Female Identity." *Anglistentag 1986: Kiel.* Ed. R. Böhm and H. Wode. Giessen: Hoffmann, 1987. 520–35.

——. "Canadian Native Literature and the Sixties: A Historical and Bibliographical Survey." *Canadian Literature* 152–53 (1997): 167–91.

——. "Confronting Cultural Imperialism: First Nations People Are Combatting Continued Cultural Theft." *Multiculturalism in North America and Europe: Social Practices/Literary Visions*. Ed. Hans Braun and Wolfgang Klooss. Trier: Wissenschaftlicher, 1995.

——. *Contemporary Challenges: Conversations with Canadian Native Authors*. Saskatoon: Fifth House, 1991.

——. "Contemporary Native Literature in Canada and 'The Voice of the Mother.'" *O Canada: Essays on Canadian Literature and Culture*. Ed. Jörn Carlsen. Aarhus: Aarhus UP, 1995. 79–96.

——. "Cultural Appropriation as a Process of Displacing Peoples and History." *Canadian Journal of Native Studies* 10.2 (1990): 167–82.

——. "First Nations Literature in Canada and the Voice of Survival." *London Journal of Canadian Studies* 11 (1995): 60–76.

——. *"Indianer" und "Native Americans": Zur sozial-und literarhistorischen Vermittlung eines Streotyps*. Hildesheim: Georg Olms, 1985.

——. "'Is the Canon Colorblind?': On the Status of Authors of Color in Canadian Literature in English." *ZAA: Zeitschrift für Anglistik und Amerikanistik: A Quarterly of Language, Literature and Culture* 44.1 (1996): 51–81.

——. "'O Canada!' The National State and International Ecology in Contemporary Native Literature in Canada." *Literary Responses to Arctic Canada*. Ed Jörn Carlsen. Lund: Nordic Association for Canadian Studies, 1993. 105–13.

——. "Regional Cultures, Ethnicity and the Displacement of Indian Heritage in the United States Academia." *Englisch Amerikanische Studien* 8 (1985): 684–95.

——. "Von den Ladies im Busch zu den Heldinnen der Prärie: Anglokanadische Erzählerinnen und das Land." *Gulliver 19: "Kanada: Geschichte, Politik, Kultur."* Eds. W. Klooss and H. Lutz. Berlin: Argument, 1986. 58–74.

Maracle, Lee. *Bobbi Lee, Indian Rebel: Struggles of a Native Canadian Woman*. Toronto: Women's, 1990.

——. *Bobbi Lee, Indian Rebel: Das Leben einer Stadtindianerin aus Kanada*. Übersetzt von Werner Waldhoff, nachwort von Claus Biegert. München: Trikont, 1977.

Möllenberg, Holger. *Die Rhetorik indianischer Literatur: Gedankliche Voraussetzungen moderner Literatur der Indianer Nordamerikas und ihre rhetorische Verwendung zur Beeinflussung einer differenzierten Leserschaft*. Diss. Frankfurt am Main: Fischer, 1982.

Moses, Daniel David, and Terry Goldie. "Preface: Two Voices." *An Anthology of Canadian Native Literature in English*. Ed. Moses and Goldie. Toronto: Oxford UP, 1992. xii–xxii.

Nelson, Robert M. *Place and Vision: The Function of Landscape in Native American Fiction*. New York: Peter Lang, 1993.

Petrone, Penny. "Indian Legends and Tales." *The Oxford Companion to Canadian Literature*. Ed. William Toye. Toronto: Oxford UP, 1983. 387.

Rieder, Hans Rudolf. Introduction. *Häuptling Büffelkind Langspeer erzählt sein Leben*. Ed. and trans. Rieder. München: Paul List, 1958. 7–9.

Ruffo, Armand Garnet. *Grey Owl: The Mystery of Archie Belaney*. Regina: Coteau, 1996.

———. *Opening in the Sky*. Penticton, BC: Theytus, 1994.

Smith, Donald B. *From the Land of Shadows: The Making of Grey Owl*. Saskatoon: Western Producer Prairie, 1990.

———. *Long Lance: The True Story of an Impostor*. Lincoln: U of Nebraska P, 1982.

Sollors, Werner. "Introduction: The Invention of Ethnicity." *The Invention of Ethnicity*. Ed. Sollors. Oxford: Oxford UP, 1989. ix–xx.

Wäscha-Kwonnesin [Grey Owl]. *Das einsame Blockhaus*. Stuttgart: Franckh'sche, 1938.

Williamson, Janice, ed. *Sounding Differences: Conversations with Seventeen Canadian Women Writers*. Toronto: U of Toronto P, 1993.

Young-Ing, Greg. "The Estrangement and Marginalization of Aboriginal Writers in Canada." *Paragraph* 15.3 (1993–94): 23–27.

Zwillus, Frauke. *"Today Talks in Yesterday's Voice": Zentrale Themen und ihre erzählerische Gestaltung im indianischen Roman der Gegenwart*. Diss. Frankfurt am Main: Peter Lang, 1989.

Why Native Literature?

ARMAND GARNET RUFFO

If we consider the titles of Jeannette Armstrong's essay "The Disempowerment of First North American Native Peoples and Empowerment through Their Writing," Emma LaRocque's "Here Are Our Voices — Who Will Hear?" or even Jordan Wheeler's "Voice," we come to some understanding of the position in which many Native writers see themselves in relation to their work, their people, and Canadian society at large. In fact, it would not be hyperbole to say that the kind of writing to which these writers refer faces with an unblinking eye the realities of what it means to be a people under siege. For Native people, this is the history of the Americas and the legacy of colonialism. We only have to think back to the 1990 Oka Crisis, or the confrontation at Ipperwash and the death of Dudley George (who was shot by an Ontario Provincial Police officer), to consider the appalling social conditions in which most Native people are forced to live. Indeed, the situation at the end of the twentieth century for Native people is critical. For many, it is a matter of life and death. In a 1994 interim report, the Royal Commission on Aboriginal Peoples documented that the suicide rate among young Native people is five to six times higher than it is among their non-Native peers — and rising. In a country that boasts one of the highest standards of living, obviously something has gone terribly wrong.

This intolerable situation, as Wheeler sees it, is only exacerbated by having the Native voice stymied by the dominant society, where "a novel written by a non-aboriginal writer [about Native people] sell[s] millions of copies when it is riddled with stereotypes, racial attitudes, shallow, one-dimensional characters and cultural inaccuracies. Tell a people that they are poor and hopeless enough times and they will begin to believe it" (40). Clearly, the only alternative to this kind of colonizing imposition is for Native people to claim their own voice and thereby give insight into their own values, traditions, concerns, and needs. It is a reality that for the most part is still unheard and unheeded in a country whose first inhabitants are but a mere afterthought, an anachronism to be dealt with at best, "material" for constructing a sense of Canadian national identity in a multicultural state. Any wonder that Elleke Boehmer, in her *Colonial and Postcolonial Literature*, observes that "Indigenous writers rightly remain wary of . . . (the) implications of the postcolonial. For they see themselves as still colonized, always-invaded, never free of a history of white occupation" (229).

As an expression of voice, or, more correctly, a community of voices, Native writers are attempting to find expression in a society that does not share their values and concerns. The form of these voices, like content itself, varies according to individual author, but as community, theirs is a collective voice that addresses the relationship between colonizer and colonized, the impact of colonialism, and, moreover, functions on a practical level by striving to bring about positive change. Thus, my claim is that Native literature, while grounded in a traditional, spiritually based worldview, is no less a call for liberation, survival, and beyond to affirmation. As the tradition of Native spirituality is inherent in the literature, beginning with European contact, so, too, is the tradition of addressing historical, secular concerns. To proceed with this position, I will foreground a number of prominent theoretical and functional perspectives in the context of the relationship between language and power to point out that Native people were subjected to ideologies that have had very real and dire consequences. In doing so, I will confirm that while Native culture may be appropriated due to the imbalance of power between colonizer and colonized, it is ironically this very imbalance that makes it impossible for the dominant culture to position itself within the Native worldview. Finally, I will consider some prominent characteristics and motifs of Native literature in order to arrive at a methodology for understanding and approaching it.

Back in the mid-seventies, prior to the popularizing of such terminology as *postcolonial* and *postmodern*, Canadian literary critic and theorist Northrop Frye, in an essay entitled "Haunted by Lack of Ghosts: Some Patterns in the Imagery of Canadian Poetry," stumbled upon the difference between Native and non-Native perception. He writes:

> I said in an article on Canadian literature that the Canadian problem of identity seemed to me primarily connected with

locale, less a matter of "Who am I?" than of "Where is here?" Another friend, commenting on this, told me of a story about a doctor from the south (that is, from one of the Canadian cities) travelling on the arctic tundra with an [Inuit] guide. A blizzard blew up, and they had to camp for the night. What with the cold, the storm, and the loneliness, the doctor panicked and began shouting "We are lost!" The [Inuit] looked at him thoughtfully and said, "We are not lost. We are here." (27)

It is through this simple anecdote that Frye goes on to observe that "a vast gulf between an indigenous and an immigrant mentality opened at that point" (27). In his text *The Bush Garden*, Frye presents a thematic analysis of Canadian literature, referring to what he calls the "garrison mentality," which he says has had the tendency to manifest itself as a "tone of deep terror in regard to nature" (225). This theme supposedly persists throughout Canadian literature and, in fact, has developed as the literature itself developed, moving from the physical to the psychological, a position that Margaret Atwood further developed into her thematic guide to literature, *Survival*. Thus, Frye moves us along a trajectory in which nature becomes the embodiment of the unanswerable denial of human and moral values, equated with all that is uncivilized.

It goes without saying that where Native people figure in Frye's Canadian landscape they are inevitably connected to the land, and, as the land is considered terrifying, the embodiment of a denial of Western cultural values, so too do Native people symbolize this perception (*Bush Garden* 140). (Although Frye does not provide a detailed analysis of this observation, one only has to consider his reference to E. J. Pratt's martyrdom of Brébeuf. In a contemporary context, one might consider the portrayal of the Mohawks on the front page of *Maclean's* during the Oka Crisis.) Accordingly, as it has been illustrated by Daniel Francis in *The Imaginary Indian: The Image of the Indian in Canadian Culture* and Leslie Monkman in *A Native Heritage: Images of the Indian in English-Canadian Literature*, these imaginings run a gamut of variations from the noble savage embodying spirituality to the savage lacking spirituality with a myriad of versions of the degraded and doomed. In the American context, Robert Berkhofer picks up a similar theme. He writes that "Only civilization had history and dynamics in this view, so therefore Indianness must be conceived of as ahistorical and static" (27).

With the rapidly depleting natural environment, however, and the

New Age, posthippy search for spiritual enlightenment in a wasteland of mass consumerism, contemporary Western writers have come to realize that their own humanity is indelibly linked to nature. Accordingly, this notion of Native as anachronism, of being static and locked into the past, has of late been viewed in a positive light and has gained new prominence. It is this latest incarnation that has recently become the most problematic, namely, "We as Native," which is essentially a reworking of the noble savage motif tempered by the contemporary agenda of self-fulfilment and preservation. In this context, the writer dons the persona (or shall I say headdress) of the Native, as indicated in Doug Fetherling's poem "Explorers as Seen by the Natives" (463). As with older variations, again, the dominant merely perpetuates stereotypes and continues the legacy of objectifying Native people.

Francis succinctly sums up these transitory imaginings. He concludes that "Our thinking about Indians relates to our thinking about ourselves as North Americans" (222). Likewise, Berkhofer writes that "American authors increasingly looked to the experiences of other peoples to criticize their own society" (107). Without getting into the whole appropriation issue, I will merely say that this is most controversial in that it raises issues of exploitation, power relationships, and domination, all of which are put into sharp relief against questions of freedom of expression, artistic licence, and censorship. (Interestingly, one of the finest works written about Native people, Rudy Wiebe's Governor General's Award-winning novel *The Temptations of Big Bear* [1973], ultimately presents Big Bear not merely as a Christian but even as Christlike. That Wiebe's title is reminiscent of Nikos Kazantzakis's *The Last Temptation of Christ* [1951] seems hardly a coincidence. For some, such a portrayal may not be necessarily negative; nevertheless, for others, it is certainly a cause for concern. Gail Anderson-Dargatz's bestselling novel *The Cure for Death by Lightning* provides a recent example of a controversial representation of Native culture by the dominant. This, however, is a topic of discussion in itself.)

The important thing to consider among these numerous variations of the "Imaginary or Whiteman's Indian" is that historically each of these imaginings has been projected and readily imposed upon Native people for the purpose of subjugation, whether it be physical, psychological, or spiritual. What makes this all the more insidious is that these projections have taken on a life of their own. According to Albert Memmi, "racism appears . . . not as an incidental detail, but as a consubstantial part of colonialism" (74). Janice Acoose explains the impact of such imagery in the portrayal of Native women in Canadian literature: "They were generally represented in Canadian literature somewhere between the polemical stereotypical images of Indian princess . . . and the easy squaw. Such representations create very powerful images that perpetuate stereotypes and perhaps more importantly, foster dangerous cultural attitudes that affect human relationships and inform institutional ideology" (39). To be sure, this imagery and the language associated with it are far from neutral. We only have to consider the term *Indian*, which as an imperial construct serves to wipe out any trace of a unique culture and history among individual First Nations. Consider also the social policy that was implemented in response to the stereotypical and racist perception of Native people as being "uncivilized," particularly as it pertains to the residential school system. I need not dwell on the catastrophic results.

Reconsidering Frye's anecdote as it relates to perception of place and, accordingly, identity, in light of the kinds of stereotyping that has been imposed upon Native people over the centuries, we can begin to see how the imposition of language has not only compounded the problem of meaningful communication between Native and non-Native peoples but has resulted in those catastrophes for Native people in the real world. This legacy leads us to consider the theories of Edward Said, particularly that of the relationship between discourse and power and its impact on what we may term "historical truth." From this perspective, "the power to narrate, or to block other narratives from forming and emerging, is very important to culture and imperialism, and constitutes one of the main connections between them" (Said xiii). Hence, the unabated misrepresentation and appropriation of Native voice. Yet, despite it all, the colonizer, no matter how hard he tries to get out of his skin, must always remain the colonizer because, simply put, he is the one wielding power.

According to George Steiner, "One need not subscribe to romantic 'personalism' in order to know that it is mere artifice to seek to immunize the meanings of a work of literature from the life and milieu of the writer" (8). Considering the cataclysmic postcontact experience of Native people on this continent, we can conclude that Native literature represents a response to an experience that literally turned life and milieu upside down. Moreover, this expression is of an experience of such magnitude that it has moved beyond an individual response and into the realm of the collective psyche of a people. Where new experiences come into play, the individual translates these into the context of this communal experience, which has never been forgotten but passed from one generation to the next (Gunn Allen 8). In other words, Native writers, while writing from their individual perspectives, are in a sense adjuncts of the collective experience, of what we may call "community." This is no doubt a very different frame of reference from that of non-Native writers, who traditionally place great emphasis on individuality and hence personal isolation.

Considering these observations, then, in regard to what I have termed the imposition of language, its codification signifying a relationship to real power, the question "Why Native literature?" becomes at least partially answered. It arises because it must if authentic Native voices are to be heard and addressed within a country that to date has been satiated by projections of what Native people are supposed to be, projections that have been used to keep "The Native Under Control" (Said 162). What this leads us to, however, are even more questions, such as, "What is this Native voice?" And, ultimately, "What is Native literature?" In the words of Thomas King, "perhaps our simple definition that Native literature is literature produced by Natives will suffice for the while" (xi). At this point, I will say only that the literature itself tells us what it is; theories of criticism, ways of approaching the literature, will necessarily come from the literature and not be foisted upon it.

What we see in turning to the writing itself is a body of work that differs remarkably from that of non-Native people. Beginning with the oral tradition, nowhere does the land appear, in Frye's words, "immoral and terrorizing" (*Bush Garden* 225); on the contrary, it is considered a living entity, a mother who must be respected and honoured even at the harshest of times. As such, one only has to consider the relationship to the land and environment, relationships to people and other life forces, to material possessions, and, certainly, to the Creator. It is these inherent traditions and values, then, emphasizing what we may call a holistic, connected, or integrated approach to life, that one finds throughout the work. However, for those who may think that Native literature is solely about spiritual matters (which much literature *about* Native people tries to be), I must reiterate that the contemporary Native worldview is post-contact and therefore also inherently secular/political.

At this point, I will shift the discourse to a more personal level and present a poem of mine entitled "Sahquakegick." The reason for choosing the poem is twofold: first, because it provides an effective and immediate way to illustrate my position; and second, because it was recently reprinted in a McGraw-Hill Ryerson Senior Issues school anthology (the significance of this second point will become clear by the conclusion of this essay). To proceed, I will use the poem as a starting point to illustrate my central thesis, that of liberation, survival, and beyond, while examining some of the common motifs that one finds throughout Native literature.

                    Sahquakegick
        Although I never knew him
        I am told when my great-great-grandfather
        signed away miles of home and bush
                        campfires hugged Lake
                        Biscotasing like moons
        in treaty, with the government of Canada
                        official men in offical
                        black suits
        It is a special day he pronounced
        looking stern and proud
                        in this photograph
                        shot in front of the Hudson Bay Company
                        store
        while faces in the background
        looking bewildered looked on

        And he knew also the momentous day
        meant change
                        change, yes, like the seasons
                        he knew that
        and standing like the trunk of a tree
        dressed in leather and balancing
        his rifle, I am told he said slowly
        in grave concern
        looking beyond the heads of all
        to me now, squarely,
        some will learn
        and speak. (24)

The central theme is clearly the land, particularly its passing from Native control to Canadian control during the treaty process. As well, there is the idea of passing the torch, so to speak, from one generation to the next, the writer using his knowledge of the English language to address the ramifications of the treaty process and loss of land. The significance of this cannot be overstated. From the earliest prayers and songs, the land and all the forms of life upon it have always been regarded as sacred by the people. That is a constant, a given. An example of this may be found in a traditional Midewiwin (Anishnabe Medicine Society) death song, which, translated, reads:

You are a spirit,
I am making you a spirit.
In the place where I sit,
I am making you a spirit.

The speaker centres himself on the land, which becomes an integral part of the process of communication with the spirit world. When we speak of the land, it is not any land but a specific piece of Mother Earth that is as much spiritual as physical. For me, in "Sahquakegick," it is the land of northern Ontario, Biscotasing, Anishnabe country. As for the Midewiwin singer, it is literally the land beneath his feet.

Another theme evident in the poem, one that is considered among the most predominant in Native literature, is that of community and a sense of family. What we notice is a return to the community rather than a going away. In "Sahquakegick," the return is metaphorical as well as spiritual; the poet finds his great-great-grandfather speaking to him through an old photograph. In numerous other Native works, the movement is in fact physical with spiritual overtones. For example, one only has to think of Richard Wagamese's *Keeper 'n Me*, in which a Native protagonist finds strength and well-being by returning to his community after a life in the non-Native world. Community is necessarily linked to identity, the return to community signifying the protagonist's recognition of himself as a Native person who has survived the colonizing and assimilating forces of the dominant society.

Garnet Raven, the young Anishnabe protagonist in Wagamese's novel, returns to White Dog Reserve after twenty years of trying to be everything from Mexican to African. Through it all, he comes to learn that his identity and well-being are inseparable from the traditions of his own Anishnabe community. "What I'm tryin' to say is tradition gives strength to the culture," he later concludes. After remaining on the reserve for two years, he comes to further under-stand that "the land is a feeling" (155). In other words, he discovers that it is just as much inside his people as it is under their feet. While his return to the community signals a movement towards spiritual enlightenment, particularly the knowledge of who he is and what it means to be Anishnabe, it also finally gives him a role and identity within the community, that of storyteller; the book we are reading is his contribution to community life.

In "Sahquakegick," the theme of identity and voice is implied in the writer's identification with his relations who appear in the background of the photograph "looking bewildered." The task of learning and speaking has been passed on to him, and he, through writing the poem, has taken up the call to speak for those who cannot. This, of course, is a theme that has pervaded much contemporary Native literature. In this regard, we can consider Maria Campbell's *Halfbreed* and Beatrice Culleton's *In Search of April Raintree*. In both, the author employs a first-person, autobiographical perspective. Certainly, these authors go a long way towards breaking the silence and showing "what it was like . . . what it still is like," to be a Native person in Canada (Campbell 9). Theirs are moving testimonies that are not unique to a few Native people in this country but relate the racism and oppression that is the norm for so many. In Campbell's case, her narrator's poverty and destitution lead her to a life of prostitution, drugs, and alcohol. Through it all, she manages to move away from her despair and begin a process of healing, eventually returning to her community where she once again finds "happiness and beauty" (2). Campbell refers to herself as "a community healer and teacher" (Griffiths and Campbell 69), and it is in the writing of *Halfbreed* that she most forcefully expresses the healing process. April Raintree, the protagonist of Culleton's work, likewise goes through a personal hell of family suicide and sexual abuse. In the end, she, too, comes full circle, "accepts who she is" as a Native woman (Culleton 228), and learns the value of speaking out for herself and her people.

I would like to take this idea of voice a step further and note that the historical branch of Native literature can be traced directly through such poems as "Sahquakegick" to a central concern: the pressure put on Native people to sign away their land for immigrant settlement, when they had little knowledge of the significance of their signature and little or no command of the English language. This branch, then, begins with the genre of petitions and protest letters, which were a direct response to the rapid influx of settlers and the deteriorating living conditions of Native people. From the letters of

Joseph Brant, writing to the colonial government in 1798 to demand control of his lands along the Grand River, and Catherine So-nee-goh Sutton, writing in 1860 to the editor of the Owen Sound *Leader* to protest against speculators buying up Native land, this spirit of indignation can be traced to the poetry and fiction of contemporary writers. One only has to consider the work of renowned Mohawk poet Pauline Johnson, whose poem "The Cattle Thief" is essentially a woman's protest against the racist treatment of her husband and family. In her essay "Here Are Our Voices — Who Will Hear?" Emma LaRocque remarks that "much of Native writing, whether blunt or subtle, is protest literature in that it speaks of the processes of our colonization, dispossession, objectification, marginalization, and that constant struggle for cultural survival expressed in the movement for structural and psychological self-determination" (xviii). In fact, it is said that one cannot be a Native writer and not be political; it comes with the territory.

The other branch of Native writing to which I would like briefly to allude is that of the spiritually based mythological. Although "Sahquakegick" does not use mythology per se, it does refer to sacred elements: *gisiss*, the moon; and *ishkote*, fire. The "campfires hugged Lake / Biscotasing like moons" — the metaphor here draws the reader into the relationship between community and time. Prior to the arrival of white settlers, Native literature in its oral form was spiritually centred in that it was, and is, informed by an Indigenous worldview that sees humans not at the top of an evolutionary pyramid but rather as a link in a circle of creation in which every entity is endowed with spirit. Essentially, this body of literature revealed through culturally specific myth(s) the values, customs, attitudes, and religious and philosophic beliefs of a particular nation.

As a consequence of contact, however, these myths and sacred songs of the oral tradition, which had flourished as part of daily life prior to the arrival of the Europeans, were forced to go underground in order to survive the onslaught of zealous Christian missionaries. Some also found their way into the hands of professional and amateur ethnologists. The point is that many of these myths and songs managed to survive and remain intact, and it is this wealth of material that has provided an alternative to the influence of the so-called historical/secular writing that Native people found themselves by necessity forced into doing. Moreover, it is this branch, originating in the earliest stories of the Manitous, such as Trickster, in all his/her guises from Coyote to Weesaykayjac to Nanabush to Raven, as well as in the prayers and chants of the earliest poems and songs, that is having a profound influence on contemporary Native writers. In light of the work of Tomson Highway, whose plays *The Rez Sisters* and *Dry Lips Oughta Move to Kapuskasing* are constructed around the transformative qualities of the mythological Nanabush, or Thomas King, whose short stories in addition to his novel *Green Grass, Running Water* feature a sly and mischievous Coyote as a central character, this branch appears, ironically, to offer new possibilities for literary creation.

In contemporary Native literature, these two influences (or branches, as I have called them) — the mythic/sacred and the historical/secular — are not exclusive. For while Highway and King both draw on mythological sources, their work is still profoundly historical/political in that it challenges the dominant power structures, be it the church and its impact on Native people (as in Highway's *Dry Lips Oughta Move to Kapuskasing*) or the state and its officially sanctioned history (as in King's "The One about Coyote Going West"). This, of course, is not to say that the force of the political message does not vary depending on the individual author. According to Gerald Vizenor, "comic signs and tragic modes are cultural variations . . . they are not structural opposition" (introduction 9). Writers such as Highway and King are not bound to what Vizenor refers to as the tragic language of the social sciences. Rather, in using mythic trickster figures, they move towards a "comic narrative" ("Trickster Discourse" 195), which, of course, does not mean that the work shouldn't be taken seriously. On the contrary, the use of humour as an important survival tool is evident in the work of numerous serious writers.

Finally, I draw attention to the words of the late Anishnabe Elder Art Solomon, who, in his last collection of poems and essays, *Eating Bitterness*, appears to set out the task, or perhaps the challenge, for the contemporary Native writer: "When enough Native people feel good about themselves, about their beliefs, spirituality and culture, then we have hope for the future simply because we may express ourselves according to the way we are" (58). The message here is clear: the need for healing, the need for expression, go hand in hand with each other. To bring hope to young Native people so they too can express themselves and heal is a communal task. With new writers continually emerging in the communities, where once there were a handful of Native people expressing themselves creatively there is now no less than a flowering, what has been termed an "Aboriginal renaissance." In the recent community-based publication *Steal My Rage*, Joel Maki, the editor, says that "we had envisioned producing a thin volume featuring perhaps a dozen authors. This changed with the response to our advertisement: only a week after sending out a call for unpublished Native writers, the submissions began to flow in until we had received almost four hundred works" (1).

Why Native Literature? For an answer we can turn to the work of these young authors. What they write about — in poems such as "Prayer for Oka," "The Survivors," "Healing Begins with Me," and "Guardian Spirit Winds," which begins with the line "steal my rage" — is none other than liberation, survival, and beyond . . . to affirmation. This is not to say that the work of these writers is not at times dark and despondent, but, nevertheless, it is in the very act of expressing themselves, of ironically putting down words in the language of the colonizer, that these authors reveal their determination to liberate themselves and to choose life over death. To address Native people themselves so that they can empower and heal themselves through their own cultural affirmation, as well as to address those in power and give them the real story: this too is the answer. And if collections such as *Steal My Rage* are any indication of things to come, then it is evident that there is no lack of creativity and self-expression among Native people. The last word, however, goes to Art Solomon, who succinctly grounds us in reality: "We can only make ourselves understood if others are willing to listen" (58).

WORKS CITED

Acoose, Janice. *Iskwewak — Kah' Ki Yaw Ni Wahkomakanak: Neither Indian Princesses nor Easy Squaws*. Toronto: Women's, 1995.

Berkhofer, Robert F. *The Whiteman's Indian: Images of the American Indian from Columbus to Present*. New York: Vintage, 1979.

Boehmer, Elleke. *Colonial and Postcolonial Literature*. Oxford: Oxford UP, 1995.

Campbell, Marcia. *Halfbreed*. Toronto: McClelland, 1973.

Culleton, Beatrice. *In Search of April Raintree*. Winnipeg: Pemmican, 1983.

Fetherling, Doug. "Explorers as Seen by the Natives." *The New Oxford Book of Canadian Verse in English*. Ed. Margaret Atwood. Toronto: Oxford UP, 1982.

Francis, Daniel. *The Imaginary Indian: The Image of the Indian in Canadian Culture*. Vancouver: Arsenal, 1992.

Frye, Northrop. *The Bush Garden: Essays on the Canadian Imagination*. Toronto: Anansi, 1971.

——. "Haunted by Lack of Ghosts: Some Patterns in the Imagery of Canadian Poetry." *The Canadian Imagination.* Ed. David Staines. Cambridge: Harvard UP, 1977.

Griffiths, Linda, and Maria Campbell. *The Book of Jessica.* Toronto: Coach House, 1989.

Gunn Allen, Paula. Introduction. *Spider Woman's Granddaughters: Traditional Tales and Contemporary Writing by Native American Women.* Ed. Gunn Allen. New York: Ballantine, 1990.

King, Thomas. Introduction. *All My Relations: An Anthology of Contemporary Canadian Native Literature.* Ed. King. Toronto: McClelland, 1990.

LaRoque, Emma. "Preface: Or, Here Are Our Voices Who Will Hear?" *Writing the Circle.* Ed. Jeanne Perreault and Sylvia Vance. Edmonton: NeWest, 1990.

Maki, Joel T. Introduction. *Steal My Rage: New Native Voices.* Ed. Maki. Toronto: Douglas, 1995.

Memmi, Albert. *The Colonizer and the Colonized.* Boston: Beacon, 1965.

Monkman, Leslie. *A Native Heritage: Images of the Indian in English-Canadian Literature.* Toronto: U of Toronto P, 1981.

Ruffo, Armand Garnet. "Sahquakegick." *Opening in the Sky.* Penticton, BC: Theytus, 1994.

Said, Edward W. *Culture and Imperialism.* New York: Vintage, 1994.

Solomon, Arthur. *Eating Bitterness: A Vision beyond the Prison Walls.* Toronto: NC, 1994.

Steiner, George. *George Steiner: A Reader.* New York: Oxford UP, 1984.

Vizenor, Gerald. Introduction. Vizenor, ed.

——. "Trickster Discourse: Comic Holotropes and Language Games." Vizenor, ed.

——, ed. *Narrative Chance: Postmodern Discourse on Native American Indian Literatures.* Norman: U of Oklahoma P, 1992.

Wagamese, Richard. *Keeper 'n Me.* Toronto: Doubleday, 1994.

Wheeler, Jordan. "Voice." *Aboriginal Voices: Amerindian, Inuit, and Sami Theatre.* Ed. Per Brask and William Morgan. Baltimore: Johns Hopkins UP, 1992.

"Great Stories Are Told":
Canadian Native Novelists

AGNES GRANT

Much has been said about Aboriginals in Canadian literature; much more remains to be said. In *A Native Heritage: Images of the Indian in English-Canadian Literature*, Leslie Monkman traces the treatment of Indians in Canadian literature from the earliest times to 1981. He predicts a changing role for Aboriginal writers when he says, in a footnote: "the emergence of writers such as George Clutesi, Maria Campbell, and Marty Dunn, and the development of new translation techniques through the study of ethnopoetics ensure that the red man's perspective will be expressed" (184). He does not, however, include literature written *by* Natives in his discussion. Native literature has been forced to develop as an independent genre, parallel to other "Canadian literature."

Early Canadian literature portrayed Indians as barbaric, uncivilized, frightening, evil, degraded, and unworthy of inclusion in the human race, let alone Canadian society. Government policy was assimilationist; Indians were an obstacle to the orderly progress of white settlement. Imperialism, colonialism, racism, and Christian proselytizing were values generally subscribed to by all Canadians. Deputy Superintendent General of Indian Affairs Duncan Campbell Scott stated in 1920, "Our object is to continue until there is not a single Indian in Canada that has not been absorbed into the body politic and there is no Indian question . . ." (qtd. in Haig-Brown 27). The public generally accepted the government's policy direction.

Scott's tenure at Indian Affairs spanned over fifty years, much of it spent in senior administrative positions. He is better known for his poetry than for his bureaucratic career. It was during his time in office that the most repressive legislation regarding Indians was passed by the Canadian government. It could be argued that Scott was only a bureaucrat and that the responsibility for Indians rested with the minister of the interior, who also was the superintendent general of

Indian Affairs. In practice, the minister delegated responsibility for Indians to the deputy superintendent, and parliament rarely concerned itself with issues regarding Indians except when making budget allocations. This practice led to a system of bureaucratic capriciousness, lack of accountability, unfettered abuse (as in the residential schools), and petty tyranny. Much of the Indian Affairs staff feared Duncan Campbell Scott.

As Indian parents and children were separated, their languages were destroyed, leading to a breakdown of the transmission of oral narratives, which was an integral component of Native identity. This was no accidental by-product of other government policies; it was a deliberate method of destroying a culture. Scott was instrumental in introducing legislation that made attendance of residential schools mandatory and in banning the sundances of the plains and the potlatch ceremonies of the West Coast — both central to the spiritualism of Native societies. Much of the West Coast dance paraphernalia was forfeited in lieu of prison terms. Most was placed in museums, but some artefacts found their way into Scott's private collection.

In 1898, Scott began to write poetry about Indian life. He had made a number of wilderness canoe trips, and these experiences were reflected in his poetry. English literature strongly influenced what Canadians believed about Indians, and Scott's poetry was no exception. When he writes, in "The Onondaga Madonna," that the woman comes from "a weird and waning race" (14), his words were accepted; few understood that Scott was making a major contribution to government policies intended to ensure that Indians would, indeed, wane.

Ethnocentrism and European attitudes of superiority surface repeatedly in Scott's poetry. "Night Hymns on Lake Nipigon," considered by many to be one of his best poems, speaks of the melding of languages: the Latin is "sonorous" and "noble"; Ojibway is "Uncouth" and "mournful" (34). The stereotyped brutality of Indians of the past and the helplessness of contemporary Indians was always present in Scott's poetry, greatly adding to its popularity.

Once the threat that Indians posed to European expansionist plans diminished, so did most of the denigrating literature. Subjugation of Aboriginal societies all over the world led to the establishment of the Aborigines Protection Association in the late 1800s, and literature began to adopt a "noble savage" portrayal of Indians. The novels of James Fenimore Cooper are still popular, but Indians gradually lapsed into relative obscurity for half a century.

By the mid-twentieth century, another phenomenon had arisen: a plethora of literature using Natives as a vehicle for defining Canadian identity or as a symbol for a wide variety of constructs. Better-known novels in this category include Rudy Wiebe's *Peace Shall Destroy Many* (1966), Leonard Cohen's *Beautiful Losers* (1966), W. O. Mitchell's *Vanishing Point* (1973), Robert Kroetsch's *Gone Indian* (1963) and *The Studhorse Man* (1969), and Margaret Atwood's *Surfacing* (1973). Though Monkman's use of the generic "he" in this passage and his depersonalizing of Indians detracts from his work today, he accurately pointed out that "we must acknowledge that throughout our literary history, the Indian and his culture are vehicles for the definition of the white man's national, social, or personal identity. Only a few dozen works focus directly on the red man and his culture, and even these works are governed by the white man's perspective" (163).

Even in historical fiction, Native cultures were presented within a non-Native paradigm. The danger of misrepresentation was great. Maria Campbell expresses frustration with this kind of writing: ". . . I don't need you to tell the story of our people to other white people. How can somebody interpret or tell? How can a white person tell you, another white person, about my community and my people, when he's only coming from half a place? He has to believe the other half, too" (Lutz 58). Campbell was especially concerned about the lack of respect for Indian culture. She pointed out:

> I don't think that you have any right to come into my community and tell my stories for me. I can speak for myself. I share them with you, and you can read them. And if you come into my circle, and I tell you the stories, then you should respect that you've been invited into the circle. . . . Either you are a friend of the people, or you're not. And if you are a friend of the people, you don't steal. . . . You don't go walking into somebody's personal places and pick through their stuff and decide what you're going to walk off with! It doesn't matter what culture you come from, it's bad manners to do that! (Lutz 57)

This, however, has continually happened to Native cultures and dates back to colonial policies. Policies and practices denied human equality to Indians and established the assumption that Indians were automatically excluded from the circle of respect generally accorded other Canadians, a mind-set that continues to plague Canadian society to this day. Any challenge to these attitudes is a relatively recent phenomenon.

A further phenomenon of the 1960s was the fact that Aboriginal people were beginning to attend universities in significant numbers. The literature confused, angered, and sometimes insulted their very humanity as they shared classrooms with members of mainstream society. Students were being taught to view Aboriginal Canadians as little more than symbols. Bitter resentment flared as educated young Natives saw themselves reduced to symbolic entities while their real history and culture were ignored or misrepresented. This resentment deepened as their attempts to explain their feelings were drowned out by those who argued for the freedom to write what and how they chose. Educational institutions and the literary community became polarized around the issues, arguing that any objections to their appropriation of Native materials was tantamount to censorship.

Aboriginal writers were poorly equipped to enter this controversy and the realms of academe on an equal basis. Deliberate government policies had kept them undereducated for over a hundred years. Appropriation was challenged, however, and the most notable spokesperson was Lenore Keeshig-Tobias. Her exasperation, impatience, and despair were evident when she said, "They have our land, and now they want our stories, too." She went on to explain:

> . . . I don't think that non-Natives should be telling Native stories. And, of course, the immediate reaction is: "You are censoring my imagination!"
>
> Which makes me wonder why God has given the white man such a broad, all-encompassing imagination? If it's so broad why can't white men just make up their own fictional cultural society? Why draw on Native society? They show us nothing new. They make no new discoveries. They simply embellish and prop up old stereotypes. (Lutz 79)

To understand how emotional the issue of appropriation is, we must examine it from a Native perspective. Hartmut Lutz, after speaking with many Canadian Native writers, arrived at the conclusion that in a book such as Atwood's *Surfacing* the central character seeks "Indian roots" that are not hers:

> Two, three hundred years of colonization and dispossession just disappear in this one person's quest to find a meaningful

way of worshipping at sacred places. . . . [I]t leaves out and displaces the whole historical process, and just acts as if *any* culture that there is, is for the having, and can be tapped into by whoever feels a need for that culture's spirituality, regardless of history and the politics of oppression. (81)

Appropriation has been particularly damaging in the area of Native spirituality. The Trickster has historically been portrayed as male, and, in keeping with Christian guilt and patriarchal preoccupation with sexuality, has been portrayed in sexual terms, usually licentious. The Trickster *is* a sexual being, but he/she is much, much more than that. This kind of writing is, indeed, coming from "half a place."

No English literary work has made any attempt to portray the Trickster in anything but a male, patriarchal manner. The extent of the misconceptions under which Europeans laboured is only beginning to be understood today as Aboriginal writers themselves attempt to explain their belief system to non-Aboriginals utilizing a language inadequate to the task. Often concepts cannot be adequately explained because the vocabulary simply does not exist in English. Playwright Tomson Highway attempts to explain the difference:

> The most explicit distinguishing feature between the North American Indian languages and the European languages is that in Indian . . . there is no gender. In Cree, Ojibway . . . the male-female-neuter hierarchy is entirely absent. So that by this system of thought, the central hero figure from our mythology — theology, if you will — is theoretically neither exclusively male nor exclusively female, or is both simultaneously. (*Dry Lips* 12)

Because of the gender-specific nature of the English language, even Highway resorts to the generic "he" to explain the importance of the Trickster: the Trickster is "as pivotal and important a figure in our world as Christ is in the realm of Christian mythology . . . he can assume any guise he chooses . . . his role is to teach us about the nature and meaning of existence on the planet Earth; he straddles the consciousness of man and that of God, the Great Spirit" (*Dry Lips* 12).

Highway told a Brandon University audience in 1992:

> Essentially, when Mr. Columbus came in 1492 there was this system where there was this matriarchy, this very female

earth-based system with this highly sophisticated theology system. . . .

So along comes the patriarchal God and the male hero figure meets the female/male from this side. Mostly because this hero figure was part female, the male just knocked him/her down and this little Trickster figure . . . was so shocked by this initial contact, this initial insult, that he/she has been passed out under some bar table for some five hundred years!

Aboriginal languages reflect the gender-free worldview of Aboriginal societies. It is virtually impossible to capture this in European languages. In Aboriginal societies, there is an understanding of male/female relationships that does not pit gender against gender or place genders in hierarchical relationships to each other. To portray the Trickster as either "he" or "she" is inadequate, since even when the Trickster assumes a specific role the opposite role is equally influential. The gender-neutral "it" renders the Trickster inanimate. This neutrality is a misrepresentation of the vitality of the Trickster, since inanimate objects in European/Christian terminology occupy a lower position in the hierarchy than animate objects do.

Daniel David Moses expresses his frustration with non-Natives who misrepresent Native spirituality: "It's when people from the opposite culture try and tell those stories, they don't know what's going on. They are just going to screw them up. . . . [T]hat's what's getting us upset. You say you want freedom to tell our stories, and then you just screw it up. Freedom of the imagination shouldn't be freedom to destroy" (Lutz 166).

Nowhere has this frustration been expressed more strongly than in feminist interpretations of Native cultures. Keeshig-Tobias has expressed concern about Native stories being used "to give credence to . . . white feminist politics" (Lutz 80), and Jeannette Armstrong has pointed out that the holistic thinking found in Aboriginal culture is "not dependent on sex, men or women." Armstrong objects to her writing being described by critics as "feminist thought" because, she explains, "it's fundamental to our thought as humans, and the real humanity in us" (Lutz 18).

By far the most notorious appropriator in this area is Lynn Andrews. Winnipeggers can dismiss her ignorance of Canadian geography with amusement when she places Winnipeg on the tundra (21); however, when she presents Agnes Whistling Elk as an authentic Canadian elder, and Canadian academics accept her as one, it is cause for deep concern (Godard 10). Keeshig-Tobias expresses her concern over the misrepresentations that are widely accepted while the human beings living within the cultures are ignored: "If you want to hear the stories then you come to me. And you go to my grandmother or my grandfather. If you want to hear stories, don't go over there to W. P. Kinsella, or Lynn Andrews, or even M. T. Kelly for that matter, or Rudy Wiebe" (Lutz 84).

A further example of a feminist critique is Angelika Maeser-Lemieux's examination of Margaret Laurence's writing. She advances the theory that Laurence needed the mediation of Métis characters to enable her women protagonists to make contact with the archetypal Feminine. Maeser-Lemieux believes that the Métis "serve as a metaphor for the alienated and repressed parts of the individual and collective psyche in patriarchal culture." She also argues that Laurence uses the symbolism of colour and race because the darker Native coloration is associated with the "feared primitive, unconscious instinctual forces, repressed psychic powers." She ends her essay on an optimistic note: "we may expect changes in the types of roles assigned to Native peoples. Instead of dying out, vanishing, or destroying themselves, they may, in the future, be presented as energetically alive and thriving" (King et al. 121, 116, 129).

How could I accept such critical thinking, surrounded as I was by "energetically alive and thriving" Ojibway university students while the paper was being read? Their hurt and bewilderment was evident, and the best I could do was reassure them later that this analysis was only one person's opinion. I pointed out that Laurence did not write *about* the Métis, she wrote about white society's ambivalence towards Native people. She was ahead of her time when she agonized over the huge gulf separating Native and non-Native Canadians. Even at the end of *The Diviners*, as Jules Tonnerre is dying, Morag Gunn tells herself: "Perhaps he, too, had found that although you needed to do battle, you didn't always need to, every minute. Or was she interpreting him, as usual, only through her own eyes?" (363). Perhaps his acceptance comes from the fact that the killer in his throat can no longer be denied, or that the continual battle will at last be over for him, too, as it is for the rest of his family.

In *Heart of a Stranger*, Laurence states: "The spirits of Dumont and Riel, of Big Bear and Poundmaker, after the long silence, are speaking once again through their people, their descendants. Will we ever reach a point when it is no longer necessary to say Them and Us? I believe we must reach that point or perish" (211). It is no accident that

Margaret Laurence and Maria Campbell, a descendant of Big Bear, were friends. Laurence came to understand intercultural dynamics better, perhaps, than any other Canadian writer: "There are many ways in which those of us who are not Indian or Métis have not yet earned the right to call Gabriel Dumont ancestor. But I do so, all the same. His life, his legend, and his times are a part of our past which we desperately need to understand and pay heed to" (Laurence, *Heart* 212). It could be argued that Laurence earned this right with *The Diviners* when Morag, who had insisted all along on the uniqueness of Pique's journey to adulthood because of her mixed heritage, came to realize that, "although at this point it might feel to be unique, [it] was not unique" (360).

It has been a long, uphill battle for Native writers. Discriminated against in every conceivable way, only a few have had the opportunity to express their ideas in writing. The difficulty of getting published has presented another obstacle: usually only the small publishing houses consider manuscripts from Native writers. Maria Campbell's *Halfbreed* was an anomaly in the 1970s as publishers concentrated on literature about Natives by established non-Native writers. The lucrative textbook business remains largely closed to Native writers.

Beatrice Culleton's *In Search of April Raintree* was for many years the lonely forerunner of the Native novel, but today Culleton is joined by such Canadian novelists as Thomas King, Lee Maracle, Jeannette Armstrong, Jordan Wheeler, Ruby Slipperjack, and Richard Wagamese. Critical articles are beginning to appear in journals, a few written by Native critics, and several books of critical writing exist, among them *Looking at the Words of Our People: First Nations Analysis of Literature*, edited by Jeannette Armstrong.

Though Maria Campbell's latest book, *Stories of the Road Allowance People*, is not a novel, it is unique and merits particular attention. In it, Campbell collects stories from the old men of her culture — men who speak a mixture of Cree and English. Campbell accurately portrays the vernacular, leaving a rare record of a group of people who once played a prominent role in the history of western Canada; these voices will soon be nothing but a memory. The story "Dah Teef" begins:

You know
me I talk about dah whitemans like dere dah only
ones dat steal.

But dats not true you know
cause some of our own peoples dey steal too.

Oh yeah dats true.
We gots some damn good teefs among us
an dah worse ting about dem
is dey steal from us dere very own peoples. (126)

The unorthodox spelling is soon forgotten as readers chuckle over the stories or wince with the understated pain of Canada's largely forgotten people. Campbell's book is a refreshing contrast to the writing of W. P. Kinsella, who continues to churn out stories of contemporary Indian men who are forever doomed to speak in stereotyped pidgin English as they express their preoccupation with ways to beat the system.

Thomas King has received critical acclaim, public recognition, and movie contracts. Jordan Wheeler's work has also been adapted for television. Two other writers, Ruby Slipperjack and Richard Wagamese, are making less-well-known, but valuable, contributions to the literary scene.

Ruby Slipperjack's *Honour the Sun* is a novel, but it reads more like autobiography. The story is told through the perceptions of a young girl, the Owl, from 1962 to 1968. She records events that are exciting, frightening, joyful, horrifying, and simply mundane with painstaking detail and great authenticity. Readers familiar with boreal forests experience waves of nostalgia as they see, feel, smell, and hear along with Owl. The maturation of Owl and her changing perceptions provide the threads from which the book is woven. Slipperjack creates an intimate portrait of a single-parent family in an isolated Ojibway community in northern Ontario.

Slipperjack is a superb storyteller. With a great economy of words, she manages to convey a picture of a small cabin, full to bursting with permanent occupants as well as relatives who come and go. Keeping track of characters could be a bewildering task were it not for the fact that readers soon realize that actual numbers are unimportant; the relationships are what make life joyful.

But not all is joy and love. Violence lurks under the surface of the community. Men become the enemy when they drink — they smash doors, rape women, terrorize children, and kill animals wantonly. The women and children can only protect themselves with well-rehearsed escape procedures. But the violence is transmitted to the children, and the older and stronger bully and terrorize the younger and weaker, deliberately inflicting pain. The younger ones can only cope with the abuse stoically. Damaged, psychopathic children grow up in this community, and alcoholism is rampant. It is only the strong who survive unscathed.

This is a moving book. Slipperjack writes "from the heart," as the Ojibway say, and captures the joys and sorrows of what it is to be an Indian in this century. She does not sentimentalize, nor does she excuse or blame. She records Owl's perceptions and interpretations. Slipperjack has said of her book: "The only thing I can do is to remind you of the person you once were, to wake you up and make you remember what it felt like to be that small. . . . The child has memory of creation, because the child has not yet lost that connection. That is one thing that we all have in common, and I think that is one way we can all communicate" (Lutz 209).

Owl is a cherished child — cherished by her mother, her extended family, and her community. So Owl grows up to be a strong young woman capable of determining the direction her future will take. On the surface, the book appears to be simple; however, the simple style is deceptive. Slipperjack probes and explores, gently uncovering universal truths and leaving readers with haunting and unforgettable images.

Keeper 'n Me by Richard Wagamese is also set on an isolated Ojibway reserve in northern Ontario. It tells the story of Garnet Raven, who is victimized by the baby-snatching practices of social-service agencies in the 1960s. Garnet grows up in various foster homes with no sense of personal identity. The book is about his quest for identity. *Keeper 'n Me* is basically a "happy ever after" book, but it is also much more than that. It demonstrates how family and elders wait to teach and heal those who have been robbed of their roots. A significant character is Keeper, a one-time protégé of Garnet's grandfather. Keeper, too, is seeking healing, since he did not avail himself of the opportunities to learn that were offered to him in his younger years. He is given a second chance when he helps his mentor's grandson.

The book is a significant contribution to Canadian literature and Canadian society in general. Wagamese fictionalizes an experience that has been only too common in Native society, and an era mainstream society today prefers to forget. He presents Ojibway culture from the point of view of one who is attempting to regain his rightful place within it.

Wagamese is a colourful and expert writer who uses colloquial language and regional mannerisms to great advantage. The story is told with great integrity and humour. As is to be expected, Garnet Raven laughs at himself and his own foibles. When he first goes "home," he is unsure that this is where he wants to be, and he sets out to impress the country yokels with his "city smarts." And, indeed, they are "gawking like crazy" as he arrives. Small wonder. Influenced by the black buddy whose family has adopted him as one of its own, Garnet is wearing mirrored shades, an afro "all picked out to about three feet around my head" (31), a balloon-sleeved yellow silk shirt, lime green baggy pants with little cuffs, hippy platform shoes with silver spangles, three gold chains around his neck, and a lot of perfume. One relative wonders if he had been adopted by Liberace, another comments that he smells so strongly he could attract fruit flies, and a third warns against the dangers of playing with electricity. Keeper muses: "Guess if he could survive walkin' around lookin' and smellin' like that, learnin' to live and learn off the land was gonna be simple" (39).

Customs and practices of reserve life are woven into the story artfully. The most significant teachings come from Keeper. The duality of the Trickster is demonstrated by a theme of the book, a theme of gender balance, both within the culture and within each human being. Keeper elaborates on the philosophy of *Soo-wanee-quay*, which means "power of the woman":

> See, when we get sent out into the world we come here carryin' two sets of gifts. The gifts of the father an' the gifts of the mother. . . . We come here carryin' those two sets of gifts, each one equal to the other. . . . Lotta us kinda start ignorin' the gifts of our mother. Go through life just usin' gifts of the father. Bein' tough, makin' our own plans, livin' in the head. But if you do that you can't be whole on accounta you gotta use both of them equal setsa gifts to live right, to fill out the circle of your own life. Be complete. Gotta use the mother's gifts, too. . . . Them that's tryin' to chase the female outta themselves an' their world are chasin' out half of who they are. Busy bein' incomplete. That's not our way. (115)

Keeper 'n Me carries a strong message about the importance of regaining cultural balance after the holocaust that Native societies have endured. Wagamese continues this theme with an ironic twist in *A Quality of Light*. In this novel, the Aboriginal protagonist helps his neglected non-Aboriginal friend, who is searching for meaning in his life by adopting an Aboriginal identity.

The disharmony and imbalance created by racist, patriarchal, proselytizing societies will be slow to heal; artists such as Wagamese will do much to facilitate the healing process. Tomson Highway believes it is the responsibility of artists to breathe new life into the Trickster so "he/she can stand up, back on his own two feet — so we can laugh and dance again!" ("Tomson Highway at Brandon University"). Wagamese acknowledges his role when his alter ego, Garnet Raven, states: "You gather [at the seventh fire] with all the travelers who made the journey too and you are alone no more. There's feasting and celebration. Great stories are told and you learn that you gotta keep the fire going on accounta there's more to come. There's always more to come" (*Keeper 'n Me* 213).

A common theme throughout all Native writing is the need for Natives to reclaim and tell their own stories. Maria Campbell regrets that "dah teef" did not leave a legacy of *good* stories for his children:

> An dah stories you know
> dats dah bes treasure of all to leave your family.
> Everyting else on dis eart
> he gets los or wore out.
> But dah stories
> day las forever.
> Too bad about dah man hees kids.
> Jus too bad. (142)

Slipperjack, Wagamese, and other novelists are revealing a richness that has long been dormant in Canada. Great stories are, indeed, being told. They make valuable contributions to a greater understanding of the Canadian mosaic.

WORKS CITED

Andrews, Lynn V. *Medicine Woman*. Toronto: Fitzhenry, 1981.
Campbell, Maria. *Stories of the Road Allowance People*. Penticton, BC: Theytus, 1995.
Godard, Barbara. *Talking about Ourselves: The Literary Productions of the Native Women of Canada*. Ottawa: CRIAW, 1985.
Haig-Brown, Celia. *Resistance and Renewal: Surviving the Indian Residential School*. Vancouver: Tillicum, 1988.

Highway, Tomson. *Dry Lips Oughta Move to Kapuskasing.* Saskatoon: Fifth House, 1989.

———. "Tomson Highway at Brandon University." Brandon Access TV, c. 1992.

King, Thomas, Cheryl Calver, and Helen Hoy, eds. *The Native in Literature.* Toronto: ECW, 1987.

Laurence, Margaret. *The Diviners.* Toronto: McClelland, 1974.

———. *Heart of a Stranger.* Toronto: Bantam-Seal, 1976.

Lutz, Hartmut. *Contemporary Challenges: Conversations with Canadian Native Authors.* Saskatoon: Fifth House, 1991.

Monkman, Leslie. *A Native Heritage: Images of the Indian in English-Canadian Literature.* Toronto: U of Toronto P, 1981.

Scott, Duncan Campbell. *Duncan Campbell Scott: Selected Poetry.* Ed. Glenn Clever. Ottawa: Tecumseh, 1974.

Slipperjack, Ruby. *Honour the Sun.* Winnipeg: Pemmican, 1987.

Wagamese, Richard. *Keeper 'n Me.* Toronto: Doubleday, 1994.

———. *A Quality of Light.* Toronto: Doubleday, 1997.

Aboriginal Writing in Canada and the Anthology as Commodity

MARGERY FEE

This essay began with my attempt to review the first edition of Daniel David Moses and Terry Goldie's *An Anthology of Canadian Native Literature in English* (1992) — a chronologically arranged "national" survey anthology published by a university press primarily for classroom use. It was a task I never completed for two good reasons (and doubtless several not so good ones). First, I found myself balking at writing a review of an anthology put out by a multinational publishing house if length restrictions meant I could not also list the many anthologies put out by several small presses, two of them Aboriginal-run. (Thus, the list appended to this essay of as many anthologies and literary magazines as I could find that include material by Aboriginal writers working in Canada.) Second, the review got out of control and turned into a paper on the ideological effects of the anthology, particularly the national historical anthology, using Moses and Goldie as its main example. Since it is this essay that you are now reading rather than a review of Moses and Goldie as such, I must add that I do use this anthology (a second edition of which was published in 1998) in my courses and think highly of it for providing a useful overview of important literature with a good bio-bibliographical apparatus and thoughtful introduction. However, I plan here to discuss the implications the use of such an anthology carries with it for First Nations literature.[1]

Insufficient academic attention has been paid to the "book genre": the encyclopedia, the dictionary, the textbook, the coffee table book, the cookbook, the travel guide, the children's picture book, the anthology. These are commodities that flow into and out of bookstores, and readers almost take their conventions for granted. Yet what we take for granted, what seems most "natural," conveys powerful ideological messages. Therefore, the structures and purposes of particular book types and their target markets — connoisseurs, students, children, middle-class travellers — deserve far more scrutiny than they usually get. As Homi Bhabha points out in "Signs Taken for Wonders," the "idea of the English book is presented as universally adequate" (105), although clearly it is not. To examine books as commodities, rather than as proofs of national achievement, say, or as maps of social reality, is to highlight their connections to a variety of ideological discourses.

Nationalism affected literary discourse differently in various places, but despite this the historical survey anthology became a standard book form in many parts of the world. With the rise of nationalism, this sort of anthology of the best and most representative literary work became crucial in establishing a particular literature as worthy of regard, and there is a long history of such anthologies of Canadian literature, beginning with E. H. Dewart's *Selections from Canadian Poets with Occasional Critical and Biographical Notes and an Introductory Essay on Canadian Poetry*, published in Montreal by John Lovell in 1864. Dewart's introduction reflects beliefs that still operate with great force: "A national literature is an essential element in the formation of national character. It is not merely the record of a country's mental progress: it is the expression of its intellectual life, the bond of national unity, and the guide of national energy. It may be fairly questioned, whether the whole range of history presents the spectacle of a people firmly united politically, without the subtle but powerful cement of a patriotic literature" (ix).

These beliefs about literature were developed during the Romantic period by critics and philosophers, beginning in Germany and spreading with nationalism across the world.[2] A nation without a literature grounded in a long history was not really a nation, this ideology held, and its power explains the collection of German folk-tales by the brothers Grimm, the Celtic revival in Ireland, Thomas Chatterton's brilliant and disastrous construction of Ossian, and many other intellectual enterprises, such as the writing of literary histories, the development of nationalist curricula, and the founding of associations, journals, and other institutions devoted to particular national literatures.

A particular kind of anthology, the historical survey that attempts to select the best of a whole literature, including poetry, fiction, drama, and sometimes prose, is exemplified nowadays in North America by the various Norton anthologies, particularly the *Norton Anthology of English Literature* (first edition, 1962), which, as the cliché has it, goes from Beowulf to Virginia Woolf. This sort of anthology is explicitly designed for survey courses in North American English departments. And this sort of anthology does more than demonstrate that a national literature exists: it consolidates a canon. It is arranged by period and by national origin, just like the standard English curriculum — not surprisingly, since it arises from the same historical forces (see Young on Matthew Arnold, whose ideas supported the founding of English as a discipline in Great Britain, the United States, and Canada). Its commodity nature is marked by the ease with which professors can get desk copies and by how quickly it goes into a new edition, which, of course, means secondhand copies of the old edition are no longer saleable. There is no Norton anthology of Canadian literature, but Oxford has a large share of the Canadian teaching-anthology market. The exemplary Canadian survey anthology is the two-volume *Anthology of Canadian Literature in English*, edited by Donna Bennett and Russell Brown (1983). Another similar anthology, Douglas Daymond and Leslie Monkman's *Literature in Canada* (1978), gambled that those teaching Canadian literature in English Canada would want to have French literature in translation included — and lost. Just as nations are supposed to be linguistically homogeneous, so are anthologies. (Further, disciplinary boundaries indirectly enforce ethnic lines; I suspect French departments feared losing students to English, and English-speaking professors felt uneasy about teaching works that were not in the original.) Anthologies, particularly what are sometimes called "teaching anthologies," have attracted some critical attention in the last few years, mainly in the context of the canon debate.[3] As Lucia Re points out in "(De)Constructing the Canon," "precisely through its status as an institution, the anthology partakes of the dynamic of the 'instituting process' by breaking with a pre-existing order and contributing to the foundation of a new one. In particular, the anthology is one of the fundamental means of forming and transforming the canon: an anthology can in fact reflect, expand, or modify (in more or less radical ways) the existing canon" (585–86). Anthologies, in other words, are connected to the cultural practices of reading and are designed to fit into the conceptual categories used by publishers, booksellers, reviewers, book buyers, and (at least for some anthologies) teachers.

The Moses and Goldie anthology closely resembles the similarly titled *An Anthology of Canadian Literature in English* (1990), edited by Russell Brown, Donna Bennett, and Nathalie Cooke, a one-volume revision of the anthology mentioned earlier (this version presumably designed for the ever-increasing number of half-courses in the English curriculum). This resemblance triggered my first insight: that these literatures are packaged as parallel commodities by the publisher, Oxford, just as a course I teach at the University of British Columbia, Studies in First Nations Writing, comes right after Studies in Canadian Literature in the calendar. Just as some have seen the "add-on" model of the curriculum as problematic, in that it leaves the old, established courses untouched by new forces such as feminism, postcolonialism, or theory, so this parallel anthology model leaves aside the question of whether literature by First Nations writers is part of Canadian literature or not. It is parallel, implicitly "equal" in the liberal model, but also separate, so we don't have to tackle difficult questions about quality such as "Is Thomas King as good a writer as Timothy Findley?" or, "Does Daniel David Moses write poetry as compelling as Erin Mouré's?"

Barbara Herrnstein Smith has said that "One of the major effects of prohibiting or inhibiting explicit evaluation is to forestall the exhibition and obviate the possible acknowledgement of divergent systems of value and thus to ratify, by default, established evaluative authority" (11). Goldie says in the introduction to his anthology that he "would feel personally a bit of a failure if people thought that [the anthology] therefore establishes what is the best in Native writing, or even establishes what is the best in Native writing in 1992" (xx), but his intentions cannot overturn conventional assumptions about anthologies. That these works have been selected for this anthology implies that they were seen as better than others that were not selected, whatever the editors may say. Quality should be discussed, particularly in courses on Aboriginal literature, where often students assume that this body of writing is inferior because it does not match what they are trained to expect in their other literature courses. As Goldie points out in his article "Fresh Canons: The Native Canadian Example," it is "difficult to see any canon as much more than a series of power relationships" (374), and this issue also needs exploration in any class that uses this anthology. The ways in which the dominant culture establishes its aesthetic assumptions as universal can be explored in many ways — indeed, this essay is an exploration of how the reception of First Nations writing is made problematic by presenting it in the structure of the national historical anthology, a form designed to support alien cultural practices and assumptions.

"Parallel" ethnic anthologies not only separate the "ethnic" from the supposedly "nonethnic" Anglo-Celtic mainstream but also separate writers who are profoundly interconnected in their writing life.

Thus they forestall the discussion of, for example, the influence of Leon Rooke on Thomas King or of Michel Tremblay on Tomson Highway. It is as if Native and non-Native writers live in different worlds, thus supporting the model of us and them, self and other, which racial/ethnic difference is constructed to maintain. Although the publication of new anthologies of minority writing, such as *Making a Difference: Canadian Multicultural Literature* (published by Oxford and edited by Smaro Kamboureli), appears to signal inclusion, ethnicity remains in what Kamboureli has called a "quarantined position" ("Canadian Ethnic Anthologies" 13). Nonetheless, as Alan C. Golding notes, their very existence can destabilize the authority of "the canonical teaching text" and prevent it from achieving the hegemony of earlier anthologies whose influence sometimes lasted for decades (303). Anyone putting together a new survey anthology of Canadian literature will certainly begin by looking at anthologies like the one edited by Moses and Goldie.

Constructing Aboriginal writing in Canada as a "national" literature and collecting works only by those who have some Native ancestry does support the claim of Aboriginal peoples to be dealt with as nations with important cultures, rather than as a small population of federal wards whose cultures must necessarily vanish if they are to flourish in a modern world. Despite increasing globalization, the force of the term *First Nations* shows the currency of nationalist beliefs. The essentialism implicit in such terms is also implicit in the selection process of national anthologies although, of course, ethnicity and race have repeatedly been shown to be rather dubious constructs of the same ideology that drives Dewart's message. Anthologies are part of a system — a set of interconnected institutional practices — that construct ethnic and racial identity. Thomas King tackles this complex issue in the introduction to *All My Relations: An Anthology of Contemporary Canadian Native Fiction*:

> [The] definition — on the basis of race — however, makes a rather large assumption. . . . It assumes that the matter of race imparts to the Native writer a tribal understanding of the universe, access to a distinct culture, and a literary perspective that is unattainable by non-Natives. In our discussions of Native literature, we try to imagine that there is a racial denominator which full-bloods raised in cities, half-bloods raised on farms, quarter-bloods raised on reservations, Indians adopted and raised by white families, Indians who speak their

139

tribal language, Indians who speak only English, traditionally educated Indians, university-trained Indians, Indians with little education, and the like all share. We know, of course, that there is not. We know that this is a romantic, mystical, and in many instances, a self-serving notion that the sheer number of cultural groups in North America, the variety of Native languages, and the varied conditions of the various tribes should immediately belie. (x–xi)

After noting that some non-Native writers may be "more perceptive" about Native culture than Native ones, King goes on to say that his "simple definition that Native literature is literature produced by Natives" will work "providing we resist the temptation to define a Native" (xi).[4] Elsewhere, he describes the "demand for authenticity" as a "whip that we get beaten with" and notes that "some people don't see me as an Indian at all," concluding that his identity comes finally from "what I know and feel about myself" and from "the community in which we exist" (interview 2). King points out the problems of anthologies (and identities) based on ancestry without giving up his project to introduce a range of new writers dealing with a particular cultural and sociopolitical experience in Canada.

Some non-Native people have shared this experience, at least to some extent, which might support the inclusion of a writer without Native ancestry in such an anthology. Grey Owl, for example, has claims on being a Native writer, since he lived as a Native, published as a Native, and died as a Native. Of course it was, for him, a lifetime project, and few non-Natives have the persistence for that. However, even Lenore Keeshig-Tobias, one of the strongest critics of what has been called "appropriation of voice," takes such experience into account. In "Stop Stealing Native Stories," she quotes Maria Campbell: "If you want to write our stories then be prepared to live with us." Then Keeshig-Tobias adds her own comment: "And not just for a few months." The piece concludes, "If you want these stories, fight for them. I dare you" (73). Although Goldie and Moses "both agreed" that they didn't want to include non-Native writers, neither goes into much detail as to why. Goldie does raise the issue of Rudy Wiebe's *The Temptations of Big Bear* as a "Native" text because many "Native undergraduate students . . . believed it to be an empowering book for them" (xxvii). However, given that it is only recently that Native people in Canada have begun to find publishing outlets for their work, the decision to exclude non-Native writers is hardly surprising. As King says, "most Canadians have only seen Natives through the eyes of non-Native writers" (introduction xi), and thus, King and Moses and Goldie obviously felt it was time mainstream readers were given a different perspective. This matches Arnold Krupat's comment in *The Turn to the Native*: "Thus, for all my insistence that Indian 'experience' is not monolithic, not always and everywhere the same, there is no doubt that Native people have a variety of experiences that differ from (many of) those of non-Native people and that make them more likely to be sensitive, aware, in touch with the experiential dimension of a variety of Native texts in a way that non-Natives (like myself) simply can't be" (10).

Recent shifts in the names used for Native people have rendered the title of this anthology problematic (it was doubtless chosen by the publisher to be parallel to that of the Brown, Bennett, and Cooke anthology), simply because some Aboriginal peoples living in Canada, most notably many of the Mohawk, do not consider themselves Canadian; still others, however willing they are to describe themselves as Canadian, would put it in a way that emphasizes that they are Native first, Canadian second.[5] And, of course, the border is problematic for many First Nations peoples — those whose traditional territory straddles the border, or who were forced from territory in the United States, often as the result of military alliances with the British during the American Revolution or the War of 1812, or those of Native ancestry who are Canadian citizens, but whose Indigenous ancestors lived in territory outside the borders of Canada. It is precisely these sorts of problems with terminology that reveal the provisional and shifting nature of the relation of Indigenous peoples in Canada to the state and the dominant culture. For example, the rubric "Aboriginal" in Canada subsumes many different groups. Indeed, it only became current here after the Constitution Act of 1982 used the expression, stating explicitly that "'aboriginal peoples of Canada' includes the Indian, Inuit and Métis peoples of Canada" ("Constitution Act, 1982"). Here the Métis, a group of part-European descent that had long been excluded from even the limited rights and privileges granted to the Inuit and the Indians, are brought into a multiethnic grouping that is produced as equivalent to a nation. That Canada itself is such a multiethnic nation makes the idea of a pan-Aboriginal "national" culture easier to convey.

Indeed, some feel it is almost too easy to convey, and thus anyone teaching from the anthology has to ensure that students understand the cultural variety that underlies it. The main danger of the pan-Aboriginality inevitably conveyed in the title is that it is easily assimilated into the stereotype of the Indian, a traditional person whose culture is depicted as a mishmash of icons belonging to different groups, such as the totem poles of the West Coast cultures and the tepees and feather headdresses of the Plains cultures. Aboriginal writers often want to preserve the distinctive practices of their cultures and to pass them on to the next generation, and thus are concerned that the differences between Cree and Nuu-chah-nulth and Mohawk be preserved, even if all these groups share a similar relation to the state and the dominant culture. But one cannot pretend that contemporary Aboriginal artists and writers work in isolation from each other or from the dominant culture, nor should one see earlier groups as totally isolated from each other, either. As Helen Carr notes, "a segmented view of the different groups of Indians has helped to perpetuate a sense that their culture consists of limited, simple units, and has obscured the existence of traditions and forms of knowledge shared in much the same way as, for example, cultural traditions in Europe and Western Asia" (qtd. in Haig-Brown 98). Attention to these complexities reminds us how seriously flawed the nationalist paradigm has always been, even in Britain, where because *English* is both the name of an ethnic group and of a language, it is possible to teach W. B. Yeats and T. S. Eliot as the greatest modern English poets (as in a Yeats-Eliot graduate course I once took) without ever discussing what that might mean.

And here the issue of a literary tradition surfaces: Who belongs, and why? The Brown, Bennett, and Cooke anthology begins with an excerpt from Frances Brooke's *History of Emily Montague* (1769), often described as the first Canadian novel (even though Brooke rather gratefully shook the snow of Canada off her feet after only five years in the country). Moses and Goldie begin, however, with a section entitled "Traditional Songs: Inuit" and another entitled "Traditional Orature: Southern First Nations," both taken from anthologies edited by John Robert Colombo, *Poems of the Inuit* (1981) and *Songs of the Indian* (1983). In the note on these pieces, Moses and Goldie are careful to point out that these works were collected after contact (indeed, the Inuit material was all collected in the early twentieth century, mostly by Knud Rasmussen), and that their authenticity cannot be taken for granted since they are "samples of a recording process which comments on both cultures involved" (493). Nonetheless, these pieces come first in the collection, before written material from the nineteenth century, and these "early versions" are included "to suggest the cultural and aesthetic *roots* of this collection" (492; emphasis added).

That it seems natural for oral material produced in the twentieth century to precede written material produced earlier in what is otherwise a chronologically ordered collection, implies a great deal about our general assumptions concerning oral poetry. First, these songs and speeches are rendered atemporal, implying that the oral tradition must be static. No matter when they are told, or by whom, they are automatically "early" — if not authentically precontact, at least close. However, the oral tradition does assimilate new material, as the discovery that a myth collected by Diamond Jenness in 1924 and ascribed to the Tsimshian was in fact a retelling of "a French fabliau brought into the Canadian West by early *coureurs de bois*" (Maud 95n1). Harry Robinson tells "White man stories," including "Cat with the Boots On" (*Write It* 282). Further, the speakers of this material are not named, although it is widely agreed that oral storytellers vary in skill (see Kimball for an analysis of the "same" stories by different storytellers). Thus, contemporary oral and literate poets are separated, the former living anonymously in a kind of pre-history, the latter as individuals in the modern world, because of conceptions about the differences between oral and written poetry.[6] In fact, Joel Scherzer and Anthony C. Woodbury, editors of *Native American Discourse*, state that "there is no simple dichotomy between oral and written discourse, between literate and nonliterate societies" (10; see also Fee, "Writing Orality").

That it seems logical to put oral poetry before written also derives from a progressive model of literacy that supports the assumption that so-called literate societies are at a later, more developed stage of communication and, therefore, superior to those labelled "oral." Jacques Derrida's discussion of Claude Lévi-Strauss in *Of Grammatology* is devoted to disputing these assumptions:

> If writing is no longer understood in the narrow sense of linear and phonetic notation, it should be possible to say that all societies capable of producing, that is to say of obliterating, their proper names, and of bringing classificatory difference into play, practice writing in general. No reality or concept would therefore correspond to the expression "society without writing." This expression is dependent on ethnocentric oneirism, upon the vulgar, that is to say, ethnocentric, misconception of writing. (109)

The tendency to put oral poetry at the beginning of anthologies also comes from the Romantic nationalist belief that great national literatures require an oral origin, by analogy with the Homeric tradition, which was appropriated as the (constructed) origin of Western civilization by European nations. Indeed, one of the defects of Canadian literature, according to critics, was its lack of this origin. Northrop Frye writes that the emphasis on the conceptual in Canadian literature results from the fact that "the Canadian literary mind, beginning as it did so late in the cultural history of the West, was established on a basis, not of myth, but of history" (347). J. D. Robins (who became head of English at Victoria College, Toronto, in 1938) shares the assumption that the mythic is the best ground for literature in his essay "The Backgrounds of Future Canadian Poetry," published in 1915. He sums up a commonplace belief that myths are "the spontaneous expression of the thought and soul of the individual race," goes on to argue that myths "are more myths of the soil than of the race, " and concludes: "If this be so, it only serves as an excellent precedent for embodying in this background the weird and fascinating legends of the soil that are to be found in Canada among our Indians, and whose spirit breathes so strongly and beautifully through the work of Pauline Johnson. Of these we are the sole heirs, and the necessity of preserving them is urgent" (316). There is a lot to analyse in this passage ("our" Indians, for example), and the chilling but commonplace assumption (based on the incredibly high mortality rate among Native peoples around the turn of the century) that Native people would die out, leaving their culture for the salvage anthropologists and the poets.

However, I would like to focus on the assumption that Native oral tales can form, as the notes in Moses and Goldie imply, the roots for later Native written literature or, as Robins implies, the background for Canadian literature more generally. First, this is not just a Canadian literary idea. Herbert Piper comments, in "The Background of Romantic Thought," that nineteenth-century Australian writers believed that "the culture of the inhabitants of Australia who had been longest in contact with the natural surroundings . . . that is the Aborigines, had more relevance for Australians than their European cultural inheritance, and that the Aboriginal's understanding of nature, expressed in his myths, provided a suitable mythology . . . for poets and readers of wholly European descent" (68). Indeed, this belief explains the Jindyworobak group of Australian poets who, in the 1930s and 1940s, published poetry using

144

Aboriginal motifs. As Lawrence Bourke points out, many early anthologies of Australian and New Zealand literature begin with Aboriginal or Maori pieces. And Mary Austin argues that "American poetry must inevitably take, at some period of its history, the mold of Amerind verse, which is the mold of the American experience shaped by the American environment" (qtd. in Krupat, "Native" 318; see also Carr on Austin). Louis Untermeyer's widely used *American Poetry: From the Beginning to Whitman* (1931) contains a section of American Indian poetry. And this belief affected English literature anthologies too, although clearly their Indigenous peoples were the Anglo-Saxons (and not the Celts!). The Romantic nationalist belief in the need for oral literary origins meant that *Beowulf*, previously the domain of German scholars, was swung into place at the beginning of anthologies of English literature beginning in the 1920s.[7] Yet *Beowulf* can scarcely be said to be written in English, despite the relation of Anglo-Saxon to modern English. First-year students can't read *Beowulf* in the original, but they can struggle through Chaucer, previously the first author in most general English literature anthologies. What the desire for oral origins occluded was the Norman Conquest. In a similar way, to place Aboriginal oral transcriptions at the beginning of anthologies, whether of Native literature or Canadian literature, occludes the conquest that changed the main means of literary production in North America from spoken to written, sung to published.

Canadian anthologists shared the view that Aboriginal writing was important to the Canadian literary tradition. John Reade suggested producing an anthology of Native Canadian poetry to the Royal Society of Canada in 1884 (Clements 184), and Lorne Pierce planned to include an anthology of Native material in his Makers of Canadian Literature series, edited by Marius Barbeau, but neither appeared (Fee, "Lorne Pierce" 62). However, several early and important anthologies open with transcribed, translated Native oral material, including Ralph Gustafson's *Anthology of Canadian Poetry (English)* (1942), which begins with two songs from the Haida; A. J. M. Smith's *The Book of Canadian Poetry: A Critical and Historical Anthology* (1943), which begins with a section titled "Indian Poetry and French Canadian Folk Songs," including Haida and Abenaki material;[8] and Desmond Pacey's *A Book of Canadian Stories* (1947), which includes four "Indian Tales."[9] The point is that national historical anthologies construct a tradition retroactively, implying that the writers at the end have a comprehensive and organic knowledge of the whole range of work, when, in fact, scarcely any of the writers in the *Norton Anthology of English Literature* ever read *Beowulf*, and the writers in Moses and Goldie probably had their first contact with the oral works in it when they got their authors' copies. Dell Hymes says that "the underlying patterns revealed by ethnopoetics are not available in consciousness, even to those with an uninterrupted heritage" ("Anthologies" 42). The tradition of oral storytelling rarely connects seamlessly with the contemporary written tradition except in anthologies.

As Hymes points out, "Conquest, disruption, conversion, schooling, decimation eliminated most [oral] learning" (*"In Vain"* 6), and so although there are important connections between oral tales and contemporary writers, these are not usually the traditional ones of having a story passed from one teller to the next within a culture. Instead, someone like Thomas King, a part-Cherokee, part-Greek, American-born Canadian, *reads* the transcribed oral stories of Harry Robinson, a Shuswap storyteller, and is inspired (see King, "Godzilla" 14). But what King discovers in oral stories is not content so much as "technical aspects of writing," such as "repetition and the kind of cadences . . . normally only . . . associated with poetry" (interview 5). Moses comments that the mainstream image of "traditional Native storytelling places Native people in the museum with all the other extinct species. We're living now, in this world, and like everyone else we have to deal with mass media, everything from video to paperback books. Of course our ways of expressing ourselves are no longer only oral storytelling" (xx). Again, for Moses as for King, the influence of oral stories has been formal: "the example of traditional Native storytelling, its orality or whatever you would call it, has been for me a freeing thing. The pieces I write look like plays or poems or short stories, but I'm interested in how they sound and how they work when they're spoken" (xx). King and Moses are wary of being too closely identified with the stereotype of the oral, inarticulate, grunting Indian. However, their use of the formal markers of orality is striking. This is particularly so in King's stories, and the move is a recuperative one: King is claiming his right to use this tradition in a new way (see Fee, "Writing Orality").

Further, the singers of the songs and the orators at the beginning of this anthology were speaking in Indigenous languages. Thus, the first pieces are not only transcriptions, but also translations.[10] The difficulties inherent in our assumptions about translation, assumptions that include the idea that words contain a transparent meaning that can be faithfully rendered in another language without any consideration of power relations or cultural context, have been examined by Tejaswini Niranjana in *Siting Translation*. She notes that "Translation as a practice shapes, and takes shape within, the asymmetrical relations of power that operate under colonialism. What is at stake here is the representation of the colonized, who need to be produced in such a manner as to justify colonial domination, and to beg for the English book by themselves" (2). Moreover, to write oral tales — even when they are, like those of Harry Robinson, told in English — is inevitably to strip them of their performative aspect: gesture, facial expression, audience interaction, and so on.

The point is not that I think that oral material should be excluded from anthologies, but that the difficulties of including it should be recognized and made clear to readers. As William M. Clements points out, there has been a long-standing tendency for collections of "Native American verbal art" (as he calls it) to decontextualize the works as if they could be read by anyone for their "universal" qualities, when, like every work of art, they are tied firmly to a particular culture and its aesthetic. He draws an analogy with the way in which Native material art is displayed in museums and galleries, a mode of presentation that implies that "Westerners don't need to reorient themselves culturally to appreciate the texts" (183). Yet even contemporary oral tales, songs, and speeches are produced outside the art institutions of the West. And a great deal of Native oral and written art differs from mainstream productions of a similar sort because it is often aimed at different audiences and intended to perform different sociopolitical functions. Lenore Keeshig-Tobias edited *Into the Moon* (1996) as a healing project as much as a literary one since it gives the women in it a place to speak of the abuse and prejudice that has shaped their lives. Ron Hamilton (Ki-ke-in) notes that "the Western literary traditions will have to adopt some new forms of writing . . . in order to speed up the approaching understanding so much looked forward to by natives and non-natives alike. I don't want to have to launder my thoughts and bleach my words 'white' in order to have them published" (91).

Without knowledge of cultural differences, the reader will simply read his or her own cultural traditions over the work, obliterating its difference. A similar point is made by Brian Swann and Arnold Krupat in their introduction to *Recovering the Word: Essays on Native American Literature*. They warn of the "dangers in welcoming Native literatures into classroom discussion or journal debate as though they were 'just like any other,' just like what 'we' English teachers were familiar with" (1–2). Reading these literatures properly, they argue, involves the interdisciplinary knowledge of language, poetics, and culture produced by linguists, literary critics, and ethnologists working together. Several recent collections have begun to overcome the problem, for example: *Coming to Light: Contemporary Translations of the Native Literatures of North America*, edited by Brian Swann (1994); Julie Cruikshank's *Life Lived like a Story: Life Stories of Three Yukon Native Elders* (1990); Harry Robinson's *Write It on Your Heart* (1989); and *Nature Power* (1992), collected, transcribed, and edited by Wendy Wickwire; the works of Nora Marks Dauenhauer and Richard Dauenhauer on Tlingit verbal art, *Haa Shuká, Our Ancestors: Tlingit Oral Narratives* (1987), *Haa Tuwunáagu Yís, For Healing our Spirit: Tlingit Oratory* (1990), *Haa Kusteeyí, Our Culture: Tlingit Life Stories* (1994); and the "Performances and Texts" section of *New Voices in Native American Literary Criticism*, edited by Arnold Krupat (1993). The example of such works will make it easier to introduce oral texts into anthologies and the English classroom without simultaneously subjecting them to reductive ethnocentric interpretations.

After the oral pieces, Moses and Goldie include a few letters and speeches written by Joseph Brant (1742–1807), George Copway (1818–69), Catherine Soneegoh Sutton (1822–65), and John Brant-Sero (1867–1914). These are not oral works nor are they literature, strictly speaking, but they do draw attention to the long tradition of prose writing in English by Aboriginal peoples, also foregrounded in Penny Petrone's two anthologies (see anthologies list). Helen Jaskoski, in *Early Native American Writing* (1996), notes that it is commonplace to ignore Native writers who "wrote in European languages, and . . . directed their words to an audience of non-Native people" (xi), and yet this tradition helps to dissolve the ideological binary constructed between illiterate, traditional Native person and literate, contemporary Native person. This is the binary that King attacks in *Green Grass, Running Water*; when Eli Stand Alone is accused of not being a real Indian because he is a university professor of English, he replies that he not only speaks English better than his interlocutor, but "Blackfoot too" (141). It is not an either/or proposition.

This essay's running commentary has been facilitated by a renaissance in oral storytelling and writing by Aboriginal people in North America, as well as a renewed scholarly interest in the whole range of Native cultural production. So it is not only the advent of new writers that will force a third edition of Moses and Goldie but also the advent of new approaches and attitudes to the material, particularly the oral and early written material. This anthology has forced me to think about a host of issues — just those issues that courses on First Nations writing must raise with students: authenticity, quality, the canon, appropriation, cultural contextualization, translation, transcription, orality, literacy, history. Anthologies, then, make the teaching task both simpler, by providing us with texts and information, and more complex, because their implicit messages must be made explicit and discussed. Lucia Re notes that

> The anthology is intended to map out the literary canon of a given period in its entirety, giving the illusion of essential thoroughness and totality and occluding any transgression of its self-established borders. The reading of the anthology replaces the direct exploration of a literary field whose contours are uncomfortably shifting and unstable, thus apparently economizing the reader's energies and simplifying his or her hermeneutic efforts. (587)

Students must be moved from the security of "essential thoroughness" to the sense of the ways a literary field is "uncomfortably shifting and unstable" in order to understand the ways in which culture is constantly broken down and reconstructed.

Perhaps one way to raise these issues in a classroom would be to ask students to find samples of transcribed oral work, of "non-literary writing" (such as a letter or deposition), and of contemporary literary writing to present to the class, commenting on the difficulties of properly contextualizing and understanding them. The entire collection could then become a class resource and a supplement to the "official" anthology.[11] But this is only one way that students can learn to be critically self-conscious of the institution that they are trained in, its pedagogical practices (including the use of anthologies), its curriculum, and its often unquestioned assumptions about the world.

NOTES

[1] I thank my colleagues Sneja Gunew and Siân Echard for their help.

[2] See Young, chapters 1 through 3, for a useful overview of this history.

[3] See Bourke; Golding; Hymes, "Anthologies"; Johnson; Kamboureli; Lecker; Re.

⁴ The whole process of definition requires an essence, and I would argue that this relation between definition and essence is the product of another book type: the standard dictionary. Of necessity, given the size of the English lexicon and the size of a book that can be sold for under thirty dollars, the desk dictionary must isolate the word from its sociopolical context and create the impression that words contain their meaning, rather than being sites of struggle.

⁵ A "recommendation notice" from the Terminology and Language Standardization Board, Public Works, Canada, comments: "because of Indigenous people's interest in self-government, do not use the terms Aboriginal Canadian(s), Native Canadian(s), or Indigenous Canadian(s)." It suggests that "Aboriginal people(s) in Canada" is preferable (Public Works 3).

⁶ Moses and Goldie do include dated transcriptions of oral stories by Mary Augusta Tappage and Harry Robinson, which certainly helps to counter the idea that oral poetry cannot be contemporary.

⁷ See, for example, McClelland and Baugh, eds.; Watt and Munn, eds.

⁸ The linking of the Native and the French Canadian here is interesting; both have "folk" cultures, which can be appropriated by Anglo-Celtic immigrants, who presumably have lost the connection to their own folk past through the process of becoming modern, civilized individuals.

⁹ Pacey includes a two-page note on these tales, which relies heavily on the ideas of Marius Barbeau and points out that the tales were transcribed from an oral performance and translated. He also warns against "free" adaptations, as they are inauthentic, and gives sources for other such tales.

¹⁰ For an overview of the difficulties of both, see Maud, and Hymes, "In Vain."

¹¹ See Warren for this idea in terms of American literature anthologies.

WORKS CITED

Bhabha, Homi K. "Signs Taken for Wonders: Questions of Ambivalence and Authority under a Tree Outside Delhi, May 1817." *The Location of Culture*. London: Routledge, 1994. 102–22.

Bourke, Lawrence. "Maori and Aboriginal Literature in Australian and New Zealand Poetry Anthologies: Some Problems and Perspectives." *New Literatures Review* 25 (1993): 23–38.

Carr, Helen. *Inventing the American Primitive: Politics, Gender and the Representation of Native American Literary Traditions, 1789–1936.* Cork, Ire.: Cork UP, 1996.

Clements, William M. "The Anthology as Museum of Verbal Art." *Native American Verbal Art: Texts and Contexts*. Tucson: U of Arizona P, 1996. 179–98.

Derrida, Jacques. *Of Grammatology*. Trans. Gayatri Chakravorty Spivak. Baltimore: Johns Hopkins UP, 1974.

Dewart, E. H. "Introductory Essay." *Selections from Canadian Poets with Occasional Critical and Biographical Notes and an Introductory Essay on Canadian Poetry*. Ed. Dewart. Montreal: Lovell, 1864. ix–xix.

Fee, Margery. "Lorne Pierce, Ryerson Press, and the Makers of Canadian Literature Series." *Papers of the Bibliographical Society of Canada* 24 (1985): 51–69.

——. "Writing Orality: Interpreting Literature in English by Aboriginal Writers in North America, Australia and New Zealand." *Journal of Intercultural Studies* 18.1 (1997): 23–39.

Frye, Northrop. Conclusion. *Literary History of Canada: Canadian Literature in English*. Gen. ed. Carl F. Klinck. 2nd ed. Vol. 2. Toronto: U of Toronto P, 1976. 333–61. 4 vols.

Goldie, Terry. "Fresh Canons: The Native Canadian Example." *English Studies in Canada* 27.4 (1991): 373–84.

Golding, Alan C. "A History of American Poetry Anthologies." Von Hallberg 279–307.

Haig-Brown, Celia. *Taking Control: Power and Contradiction in First Nations Adult Education*. Vancouver: UBC, 1995.

Hamilton, Ron (Ki-ke-in). "I Invite Honest Criticism: An Introduction." *In Celebration of Our Survival: The First Nations of British Columbia*. Ed. Doreen Jensen and Cheryl Brooks. Spec. issue of BC *Studies* 89 (1991): 89–91.

Herrnstein Smith, Barbara. "Contingencies of Value." Von Hallberg 5–39.

Hymes, Dell. "Anthologies and Narrators." Swann and Krupat, eds. 41–84.

——. *"In Vain I Tried to Tell You": Essays in Native American Ethnopoetics*. Philadelphia: U of Pennsylvania P, 1981.

Jaskoski, Helen. *Early Native American Writing: New Critical Essays*. Cambridge: Cambridge UP, 1996.

Johnson, Glen M. "The Teaching Anthology and the Canon of American Literature: Some Notes on Theory in Practice." *The Hospitable Canon: Essays on Literary Play, Scholarly Choice, and Popular Pressures*. Ed. Virgil Nemoianu and Robert Royal. Philadelphia: Benjamins, 1991. 111–35.

Kamboureli, Smaro. "Canadian Ethnic Anthologies: Representations of Ethnicity." *Ariel* 25.4 (1994): 11–52.

——, ed. *Making a Difference: Canadian Multicultural Literature*. Toronto: Oxford UP, 1996.

Keeshig-Tobias, Lenore. "Stop Stealing Native Stories." *Borrowed Power: Essays on Cultural Appropriation*. Ed. Bruce Ziff and Pratima V. Rao. New Brunswick: Rutgers UP, 1997. 71–73.

Kimball, Geoffrey. "Koasati Narrator and Narrative." Krupat, ed. 3–36.

King, Thomas. "Godzilla vs. Post-Colonial." *World Literature Written in English* 30.2 (1990): 10–16.

—. *Green Grass, Running Water*. Toronto: Harper-Perennial, 1993.

—. Interview. With Jeffrey Canton. *Paragraph* 15.1 (1994): 2–6.

—. Introduction. *All My Relations: An Anthology of Contemporary Canadian Native Fiction*. Toronto: McClelland, 1990. ix–xvi.

Krupat, Arnold. "Native American Literature and the Canon." Von Hallberg, ed. 309–35.

—. *The Turn to the Native: Studies in Criticism and Culture*. Lincoln: U of Nebraska P, 1996.

—, ed. *New Voices in Native American Literary Criticism*. Washington: Smithsonian Institution, 1993.

Lecker, Robert. "Anthologizing English-Canadian Fiction: Some Canonical Trends." *Making It Real: The Canonization of English-Canadian Literature*. Concord, ON: Anansi, 1995. 113–51.

Maud, Ralph. "Ethnographic Notes on Howard O'Hagan's *Tay John*." *Silence Made Visible: Howard O'Hagan and Tay John*. Ed. Margery Fee. Toronto: ECW, 1992. 92–96.

McClelland, George Wm., and Albert C. Baugh, eds. *Century Types of English Literature*. New York: Century, 1925.

Moses, Daniel David, and Terry Goldie. "Preface to the First Edition: Two Voices." *An Anthology of Canadian Native Literature in English*. Ed. Moses and Goldie. 2nd ed. Toronto: Oxford UP, 1998. xix–xxix.

Niranjana, Tejaswini. *Siting Translation: History, Post-Structuralism, and the Colonial Context*. Berkeley: U of California P, 1992.

Piper, Herbert. "The Background of Romantic Thought." *Twentieth Century Australian Literary Criticism*. Ed. Clement Semmler. Melbourne: Oxford UP, 1967. 67–74.

Public Works and Government Services Canada. Terminology and Language Standardization Board. "Recommendation Notice: Aboriginal Peoples in Canada." No. 2. Jan. 1994.

Re, Lucia. "(De)Constructing the Canon: The Agon of the Anthologies on the Scene of Modern Italian Poetry." *Modern Language Review* 87.3 (1992): 585–93.

Robins, J.D. "The Backgrounds of Future Canadian Poetry." *Acta Victoriana* 36.6 (1915): 300–17.

Robinson, Harry. *Nature Power: In the Spirit of an Okanagan Storyteller*. Ed. Wendy Wickwire. Vancouver: Douglas, 1992.

—. *Write It on Your Heart: The Epic World of an Okanagan Storyteller*. Ed. Wendy Wickwire. Vancouver: Talonbooks-Theytus, 1989.

Scherzer, Joel, and Anthony C. Woodbury, eds. *Native American Discourse: Poetics and Rhetoric*. Cambridge Studies in Oral and Literate Culture. Cambridge: Cambridge UP, 1987.

Swann, Brian, and Arnold Krupat. Introduction. Swann and Krupat, eds. 1–9.

———, eds. *Recovering the Word: Essays on Native American Literature.* Berkeley, U of California P, 1987.

Untermeyer, Louis, ed. *American Poetry: From the Beginnings to Whitman.* 1931.

Von Hallberg, Robert, ed. *Canons.* Chicago: U of Chicago P, 1983.

Warren, Kenneth. "The Problem of Anthologies: Or, Making the Dead Wince." *American Literature* 65.2 (1993): 338–42.

Watt, Homer A., and James B. Munn, eds. *Ideas and Forms in English and American Literature.* Chicago: Foresman, 1925.

Young, Robert J. C. *Colonial Desire: Hybridity in Theory, Culture and Race.* London: Routledge, 1995.

ANTHOLOGIES

(multiauthor collections including works written in English by Aboriginal writers working in Canada, with the exception of Pauline Johnson, who is routinely included in most early and many later general anthologies)

Alford, Edna, and Claire Harris, eds. *Kitchen Talk: Contemporary Women's Prose and Poetry.* Red Deer, AB: Red Deer College P, 1992.

Brant, Beth, ed. *A Gathering of Spirit: A Collection by North American Indian Women.* Ithaca, NY: Firebrand, 1988.

Bruchac, Joseph, ed. *Returning the Gift: Poetry and Prose from the First North American Native Writer's Festival.* Tucson: U of Arizona P, 1994.

Camper, Carol, ed. *Miscegenation Blues: Voices of Mixed Race Women.* Toronto: Sister Vision, 1994.

Columbo, John Robert, ed. *Songs of the Great Land.* Ottawa: Oberon, 1989.

———. *Poems of the Inuit.* Ottawa: Oberon, 1981.

———. *Songs of the Indians.* 2 vols. Ottawa: Oberon, 1983.

Day, David, and Marilyn Bowering, eds. *Many Voices: An Anthology of Contemporary Canadian Indian Poetry.* Vancouver: Douglas, 1977.

Fife, Connie, ed. *The Colour of Resistance: A Contemporary Collection of Writing by Aboriginal Women.* Toronto: Sister Vision, 1993.

Fireweed: A Feminist Quarterly 22 (1986).

Gatherings: The En'owkin Journal of First North American Peoples 1.1 (1990–).

Gedalof, Robin [now Robin McGrath], ed. *Paper Stays Put: A Collection of Inuit Writing.* Drawings by Alootook Ipellie. Edmonton, AB: Hurtig [1981]. With a separate Teacher's Handbook. Dept. of Education, Northwest Territories. 1981.

Gooderham, Kent, ed. *I Am an Indian.* Toronto: Dent, 1969.

Grant, Agnes, ed. *Our Bit of Truth: An Anthology of Canadian Native Literature.* Winnipeg: Pemmican, 1990.

Grauer, Lally, and Jeannette Armstrong, eds. *Anthology of Native Poetry in Canada.* Peterborough, ON: Broadview, 1998.

Harjo, Joy, and Gloria Bird, eds. *Reinventing the Enemy's Language: Contemporary Native Women's Writings of North America.* New York: Norton, 1997.

Hodgson, Heather, ed. *Seventh Generation: Contemporary Native Writing.* Penticton, BC: Theytus, 1989.

Jaine, Linda, and Drew Taylor, eds. *Voices: Being Native in Canada.* Saskatoon: U of Saskatchewan Extension Division, 1991.

Keeshig-Tobias, Lenore, ed. *Into the Moon: Heart, Mind, Body, Soul. The Native Women's Writing Circle.* Toronto: Sister Vision, 1996.

Keon, Wayne, Orville Keon, and Ronald Keon, eds. *Sweetgrass: An Anthology of Indian Poetry.* Comp. Wayne Keon. Elliott Lake, ON: Algoma, 1972.

King, Thomas, ed. *All My Relations: An Anthology of Contemporary Canadian Native Fiction.* Toronto: McClelland, 1990.

———. *An Anthology of Canadian Native Fiction.* Spec. issue of *Canadian Fiction Magazine* 60 (1987).

Kivioq: Inuit Fiction Magazine (1987–).

Lesley, Craig, ed. *Talking Leaves: Contemporary Native American Short Stories.* New York: Dell-Laurel, 1991.

Lutz, Hartmut, ed. *Four Feathers: Poems and Stories by Canadian Native Authors/Vier Federn: Gedichte und Geschichten Kanadischer Indianer/innen und Metis.* Osnabrucker Bilinguale Editionen von Minoritäten Auto(inn)en. No. 7. Osnabruck: Verlagscooperative, 1992.

Maki, Joel T., ed. *Let the Drums Be Your Heart: New Native Voices.* Vancouver: Douglas, 1996.

———. *Steal My Rage: New Native Poems.* Vancouver: Douglas, 1996.

Moses, Daniel David, and Terry Goldie, eds. *An Anthology of Canadian Native Literature in English.* 2nd ed. Toronto: Oxford UP, 1998.

Mowat, William, and Christine Mowat. *Native Peoples in Canadian Literature.* Themes in Canadian Literature. Gen. ed. David Arnason. Toronto: Macmillan, 1975.

Nolan, Yvette, Betty Quan, and George Bwanika, eds. *Beyond the Pale: Dramatic Writing from First Nations Writers and Writers of Colour.* Toronto: Playwrights Canada, 1996.

Perreault, Jeanne, and Sylvia Vance, eds. *Writing the Circle: Native Women of Western Canada.* Edmonton: NeWest, 1990.

Petrone, Penny, ed. *First People, First Voices.* Toronto: U of Toronto P, 1983.

———. *Northern Voices: Inuit Writing in English.* Toronto: U of Toronto P, 1988.

Sullivan, Rosemary. *Poetry by Canadian Women*. Toronto: Oxford UP, 1989.

Trans 2. Ed. Geoffrey Hancock. Spec. issue of *Canadian Fiction Magazine*. 36/36 (1980).

Whetstone (1971–). Spec. issues spring 1985; spring 1987; fall 1988.

Witalec, Janet, ed. *Smoke Rising: The Native North American Literary Companion*. Detroit: Visible Ink, 1995.

"There Is Nothing but White between the Lines": Parallel Colonial Experiences of the Irish and Aboriginal Canadians

RON MARKEN

Now talk is around of a loosening in republics,
retrievals of subtle water: all the peoples
who call themselves The People,
all the unnoticed cultures,
remnants defined by a tilt in their speech

. . . .
— all these are being canvassed.
The time has come round for republics of the cultures
and for rituals, with sound: the painful washings-clean
of smallpox blankets.
                                    — Les A. Murray ("The Action" 95)

In this essay, I will explore parallels between the experiences of the Irish in the eighteenth and nineteenth centuries and those of Canada's Aboriginal peoples since the Indian Act of 1876, and I will also interrogate the roles of literature in twentieth-century re-creations of their respective cultures.[1] My approach will be historical and literary, comparing the separate but similar experiences of two ruthlessly colonized peoples. My tone of voice will be subjective, since much of what I have to present has grown and developed from personal experience, primarily in the classroom. Patricia Monture Angus, in *Thunder in My Soul: A Mohawk Woman Speaks*, sets her tone, and mine: "We can only experience the world through the prism of self. This is one of the differences between the two cultures, First Nations and Canadians, that I have experienced. In academic writing, the rule is that the authors do not identify their voices. They speak from a pedestal of knowledge. . . . The knowledge is outside the self" (45). Monture Angus goes on to describe the comparative subjectivity of Native writing, examining the light of awareness as it refracts through that "prism of self." Coming out of the detached academic tradition,

I will try to get down from my pedestal, to speak what I have experienced through my own prism, my own experience and education. Little of what I encountered in books through thirty-five years as an academic prepared me adequately for the voices and life experiences that Native students and colleagues have taught me. I am having to learn new ways of learning and to speak with my own voice, not the disembodied "one" of traditional academic discourse. My approach will be narrative and heavily subjective.

* * *

I grew up in central Alberta, acquiring my public school education there and pursuing my undergraduate studies in Minnesota. By the time I graduated with my BA, I had travelled through most of Europe, forty-two of the fifty American states, and seven of Canada's ten provinces and two territories. Since early childhood, I have been an insatiable reader: literature, criticism, mystery, history, mythology, religion, science, photography, news — anything made of words. I have an honours BA, an MA, and a PhD in English; I have two-thirds of a Bachelor of Divinity degree; I can read five languages (including Greek, Hebrew, and Old Norse). But when I started my university teaching career as a "fully qualified" English professor in 1966, I had read none of the few Native writers, nor did I have enough curiosity to determine if, indeed, there were any in print. I could have named only two: Buffy Saint-Marie and Chief Dan George. Others came to prominence in the last fifteen years, precipitated by the publication in 1973 of Maria Campbell's *Halfbreed*, but I did not know of their existence until the mid-1980s. I read *Halfbreed* two years ago, twenty years after its publication.

In 1981, I taught an introductory English class to a group of fifteen Cree students in La Ronge, a northern extension branch of the University of Saskatchewan, six hundred kilometres north of Saskatoon. The students' first language was Cree; they were not strong in English, but they wanted to become teachers. Many had decided to master English and to return to their home settlements to teach. My syllabus included no Native literature for two simple reasons: I had read none and, even though it was only fifteen years ago, there was very little available in Canada. Since then, of course, there has been an outpouring of writing by First Nations people.[2] On the reading list for my La Ronge class I placed *King Lear* (it became their favourite!), John Donne, Gerard Manley Hopkins, Andrew Marvell,

157

Robert Frost, Margaret Laurence, Sheila Watson, as well as *Translations* by Irish playwright Brian Friel.

Set in County Donegal, Ireland, in the 1830s, *Translations* dramatizes two or three days in the life of a tiny peasant village, Baile Baeg. The British army and its surveyors are systematically changing all the country's place names from Irish into English, making Ireland "coherent," less "barbarous" (87). Irish responses to these transformations are varied. Some decide, pragmatically, that learning English is their best hope for a successful future. At the other extreme, inhabitants such as the Donnelly twins see the translation of their maps as an invasion. They appear to be responsible for the disappearance of several English soldiers. One turncoat Irishman, Owen, who works as a translator for the British, even calls the transformation a "baptism" in "a kind of Eden" (94). In the end, of course, the British forces succeed by sheer force of arms, threatening to lay waste the countryside and to burn the houses and barns if the resistance does not stop.

The play opens with a mute girl, Sarah Johnny Sally, learning to speak her own name. By the end of act 1, she can speak her name and a few words. Before the play is over, however, as the ruthless English sweep the Irish names from the landscape, Sarah, traumatized, loses her tongue again. She, like Ireland, is symbolically doomed to a life of silence. Irish poet Seamus Heaney contends that Sarah's struggle to pronounce her own name "constitutes a powerful therapy, a set of imaginative exercises that give her [and Ireland] a chance to know and say herself properly to herself again" (1199). I find his connected metaphors of healing, self-knowledge, and speech profoundly convincing.

I have made *Translations* sound far simpler than it is. The text, for instance, is written entirely in English, but the audience has to understand that the Irish characters are speaking Gaelic and the English soldiers are speaking English. It is difficult in other ways too. Audiences of *Translations* will benefit immensely from familiarity with nineteenth-century Irish peasant life, marginalized agrarian economics, and cultural critic George Steiner's philosophy of language as articulated in *After Babel*, a text from which Friel has borrowed considerably. My La Ronge students had none of those prerequisites. Only one had ever seen a play. Reading Friel on the cold page puzzled them. When I asked simple plot or character questions, they looked at me quizzically.

So, in one of those moments of frustration that can lead to

inspiration, I set up ten chairs at the front of the room, arbitrarily assigned roles, aimed ten students at the chairs, and asked them to start reading their parts. Naturally, there was a good deal of initial confusion, giggling, and self-consciousness, but before long they began to enjoy themselves, noting differences in character, sensing motivations, discovering Friel's humour — and their own. They began to laugh. As they found their way into their roles, the Irish names came out sounding soft and rich, like their own Cree language (Seamus became "Seeamoos"; Maire, "Mah-eer-ah"; Hugh, "Hoogh"). During the "love duet" between Gaelic-speaking Maire and British soldier Yolland, the room was very quiet. I learned that some of the young women in the class had also, from time to time, tried to communicate across language barriers with similarly charming and dangerous English-speaking men. When that unrehearsed reading was over, I remember the tall grandson of a chief announcing:

"This is the first book I've respected that's been written by a white man."
"Why?"
"Because, that Irish guy, he understands what happens when you steal peoples' places, their language."
"Do you have a personal example?" I asked.
"Yes," another student replied. "Last summer I worked for a survey crew too. Just like Owen in the play. And we camped every night at Nelson's Crossing. . . . In the fall, when I came back home, my grandfather asked me where I was working. He'd never heard of Nelson's Crossing. Just after New Year's, my grandfather died and then I found out that he was born at Nelson's Crossing, only it wasn't called that. It had a Cree name, but the white men — and surveyors like me — rubbed out that name. Part of my grandfather and me disappeared when that happened."[3]

Likewise, in Friel's masterpiece, "translation" happens on many levels. Places are erased only to return under new designations. Near the end of the play, one of Friel's older characters says that he can no longer find his way home; he is lost and astray in his own countryside: "Lis na Muc . . . has become Swinefort. And to get to Swinefort you pass through Greencastle and Fair Head and Strandhill and Gort and Whiteplains. And the new school isn't at Poll na gCaorach — it's at Sheepsrock. Will you be able to find your way?" (350). Every single road sign, hill, spring, forest, and village has been retitled. "My job," says an interpreter, "is to translate the quaint, archaic tongue you people persist in speaking into the King's good English" (338). The Irish natives are told that national schools — some of them residential — have been established where their children will learn English under a compulsory system of universal education.[4] The "old language," with its cargo of signs, emblems, myths, memory, and tradition, is arbitrarily devalued, humiliated, rendered powerless. Hugh, the community's venerable schoolmaster — a poet, scholar, storyteller, and master of at least four languages (Irish, Latin, Greek, and English) — is seen as a mere drunken buffoon by a military force that is unthinkingly monolingual. The young student in La Ronge saw that the surveyors had come between himself and his own family, his personal oral history, just as surely as the British Army ordnance surveyors had come between the people of Baile Baeg and their oral histories. Each of us in that northern Saskatchewan classroom realized that a work of literature by a living Irishman had helped us to understand ourselves, realize our histories. Could literature also be instrumental, as Seamus Heaney hints, in healing wounds and scars, forging positive and creative visions for all our futures, giving ourselves a chance to know and "say [ourselves] properly"?

At that moment, the likelihood of other parallels between the experiences of the Irish and Canadian Native people occurred to me. Fourteen years later, in the fall of 1995, I was invited to address the daily assembly of the Saskatchewan Indian Federated College. In the forty or so minutes allotted to me, I hastily summarized the often grim history of Catholic Ireland from 1790 to 1890. Afterwards, a Cree man in his sixties came up to me and shook my hand: "Thank you for telling us this story. All my life, I thought we were the only ones." Two winters ago, Celtic scholar Angela Bourke visited our campus from University College, Dublin. She and Métis writer Maria Campbell held an unrehearsed public conversation about the oral traditions of women in their respective cultures. What emerged, to their delight, was another confirmation that the First Nations of Canada and the Irish have many historical issues in common. Sharing that commonality was restorative for both women. And so, in my roundabout way, I come to the major issues of this essay. I have been nurturing these separate episodes and others like them for many years, sensing that some good might come, first, by rehearsing a series of coincident events in the histories of Ireland and the Natives of colonized Canada; and second — and this is the main thrust of my theme — by arguing the favourable effects of artistic expression as one of the most dependable roads to recovery and healing from the wounds of postcolonial trauma. "Therapy," is Seamus Heaney's powerful noun. I will look simultaneously at Irish peasants and at Canada's Aboriginal people.

To set these observations in a deeper historical and literary-critical context, I can add a voice from 1596, Edmund Spenser: "But if that country . . . whence you lately came be so goodly and commodious a soil as you report, I wonder that no course is taken for the turning thereof to good uses, and reducing that savage nation to better government and civility" ("View" 171). Spenser wrote those words in "A View of the Present State of Ireland." Not only was he a distinguished English poet, but he was also colonial administrator for the imperial government of Queen Elizabeth I, whose armies were in the process of thoroughly subduing Ireland, its culture, and its people. When Spenser says "good," of course, he implies that the people of Ireland's use of their land and soil is *not* good, and that reducing their so-called savagery will partially elevate them to an English civility.

He is as pointedly clear in his celebrated poem *The Faerie Queene*:

They held this land and with their filthinesse
Polluted this same gentle soyl long time:
That their own mother loathed their beastlinesse,
And gan abhorre her broods vnkindly crime,
All were they borne of her owne natiue slime. (II.x.9)

Contemporary Irish poet and scholar Eiléan Ní Chuilleanáin responds to Spenser's indictment: "Rhetoric provides the tautological insistence on 'filthinesse' as well as 'polluted,' and the personification which embellishes the conquest of the [Irish] aborigines by Arthur's ancestors and nullifies their rights as indigenous people by a poetic license; the land itself, rather *herself*, rejected them" (238).

Spenser's views are startlingly similar to those of Canadian poet and Indian administrator Duncan Campbell Scott, who was determined to assimilate Canada's Indigenous peoples — with their "senseless drumming and dancing" — totally. Scott, says Stan Dragland, "has become the most visible representative of a government whose Indian policy was based on the definition of an Indian as a ward of the state — as little more than a child. . . . The First Nations have almost literally been seen and not heard" since the Indian Act of 1876 (6–7). An extraordinary novel of mystery and detection by Danish writer Peter Hoeg, *Smilla's Sense of Snow* (1992), helps restore the perspective. Smilla, who has a Greenland Inuit mother and a Danish father, says:

> Any race . . . that allows itself to be graded on any scale designed by European science will appear to be a culture of higher primates. Any grading system is meaningless. Every attempt to compare cultures with the intention of determining which is the more developed will be [only] . . . one more bullshit projection of Western culture's hatred of its own shadows. (89)

Wise in a dozen ways, this statement especially invites subjugated people to refuse to measure themselves by any but their *own* standards of excellence, to recover (in both senses of that word) their voices. "If a people is inferior," said Grand Chief Ovide Mercredi in a speech entitled "The Proposed Amendments to the Indian Act," "they are not capable of ownership. This is a myth that has shaped constitutional law in New Zealand, the USA, and Canada since contact."

Even when I recall the stories of my gentle grandparents, Norwegian homesteaders in southern Alberta and Saskatchewan, their vocation appears to have been to represent a government and civility that could reduce that "savage nation" and put the land to "good uses," although they would never have killed to do so. My great-uncle Erik, in fact, was a private in the United States Cavalry under General Custer. He deserted rather than follow the orders of a man he described laconically as "crazy." Erik eventually settled in Swift Current, Saskatchewan. However, Boyce Richardson vividly documents that as a group arriving to settle Canada, our European and American forbears had to invent a language, like Edmund Spenser's, that would justify their actions against the land and its First Peoples. The Aboriginal inhabitants had to be de-humanized, characterized as childlike, shiftless, violent, dirty, and drunken. Such stereotypes have been perpetuated in the popular culture of North America for several generations. And we can examine the consequences of such thinking over the course of several hundred years of *Irish* history: consider Elizabeth I, the penal laws, Oliver Cromwell, the Year of the French, the Great Hunger, and the Shankhill Road. Whatever tactics the British learned about dealing with the "savages" in Ireland came with them to British North America, where they were deployed against the Natives.

There are several such parallels. The first is found in the attitudes or inclinations of generations of colonial governments. According to the editors of *The Field Day Anthology of Irish Writing*, Spenser "was the first of his nation to advance a coherent movement for the systematic colonization of Ireland by the English people. In taking this stance, he became the prime apologist for the destruction of the Gaelic and Hiberno-Norman civilizations of Ireland" (Deane et al., eds. 16).[5] Olive Dickason demonstrates that three ideas concerning Native North Americans dominated the imperial civil administration for British North America in 1830: that as a people they were disappearing; that those who remained should either be removed and confined to reserves, communities isolated from whites; or that they should be assimilated (225). "Our object is to continue until there is not a single Indian in Canada that has not been absorbed into the body politic," states Scott, speaking to the House of Commons in 1920, "and there is no Indian question and no Indian department" (qtd. in Richardson 131). The government perceived that its duty was to "civilize" Natives by assimilating them, then giving their land to Europeans, people who, in Spenser's words, could put it to "goodly" use.

Spenser also regarded the Irish people as less worthwhile than the soil they lived on. His views, transmitted to his betters in London and to subsequent generations of settlers, became dangerously influential, his attitudes infecting the outlook of English conquerors, Scots planters, and other Anglo-Irish settlers of the country. Spenser's dialogues, Platonic conversations between imaginary philosophers, are written in a deliberate and balanced manner. The style is civilized in its urbanity, in its assumption of its own superiority and, therefore, of Irish barbarism. "Barbarians," literally, are people who do not speak Greek. Like the ancient Greeks, in his English supremacist view, Spenser could assume he was civilized because he spoke his own language; the Irish were barbaric because they did not. They spoke gibberish. Spenser's tempered and temperate style, according to the editors of *The Field Day Anthology*, coupled with his serene and supremacist theme of Civilization, influenced his "readers into feelings of self-righteousness which, when pushed to excess, could justify all manner of atrocities. . . . His work had a lasting influence on successive generations of Irish Protestant writers and politicians: he provided them with a ready-made sense of purpose and well-being" (Deane et al., eds. 174). "Much of the vocabulary favoured in [Spenser's 'A View of the Present State of Ireland']," writes Sheila

Cavanagh, "provides insight into the most unsettling of the perceived threats against order and virtue in the two worlds [England and Ireland] considered here. The repetition, for example, of terms such as 'lewd,' 'licentious,' and 'barbarous,' as well as the emphasis upon wide-ranging models of incivility express a multitude of fears into a few short syllables" (270). According to the *Oxford English Dictionary*, *barbarous* "had probably a primary reference to speech. . . . The sense-development in ancient times was (with the Greeks) 'foreign, non-Hellenic,' later 'outlandish, rude, brutal,' . . . and later 'savage, rude, savagely cruel, inhuman.' " The word appears to have onomatopoeic origins; in *bar bar*, the Greeks might be mimicking the grunting, incomprehensible noises made by foreigners when they spoke their own languages. As did English speakers in Ireland, English speakers in Canada routinely assumed the Indigenous languages to be barbaric, their sounds and syllables being foreign and outlandish to their ears.

A second parallel is found in acts and statutes adopted to bring the "barbarous savages" under control. The infamous penal laws of eighteenth-century Ireland, statutes based on race, language, and religion, were designed to subjugate and humiliate an entire people under an odious form of apartheid. The Irish were forbidden appropriate education; denied the vote; barred from public office; prohibited from owning land, weapons, or even a horse worth five pounds. Their priests and bishops were placed under universal interdict.

A century and a half later, in Canada, Her Majesty's Government of British North America enacted its own "penal laws," the father of which was the Indian Act of 1876, which found "its principal inspiration in the assumptions of nineteenth-century evangelical religion, cultural imperialism, and laissez-faire economics" (Tilley 201). Denying Natives the right to vote, the government, under the act, took charge of Native lands, systems of community government, education, health, inheritance, ceremonies, rituals, and amusements. Indian women were even more thoroughly restricted; they could not even vote in Indian Act elections. Assembly and free speech were restricted and confined, as were all means of gainful production (Richardson 97–106). In fact, if a Native were to qualify as a professional of any kind or to earn a university degree, that person was deemed by the act to have ceased to be Native. The act calls this dubious process "enfranchisement." Native people were prohibited by the act from retaining lawyers to fight for any cause, and the act attempted to annihilate Native culture, banning potlatches, thirst dances, and sun dances, "substitut[ing]," in the patronizing words of Scott, "reasonable amusements for this senseless drumming and dancing" (qtd. in Tilley 177). The act proscribed all appearances in "Indian costume," unless countenanced by white society at displays such as parades, rodeos, and fairs, where costumed Natives could be seen as curiosities, outlandish attractions for white tourists to gawp at and photograph. Failure to comply resulted in confiscations and burnings, fits of righteousness enacted by missionaries and Indian agents (Richardson 102). "Power was taken to secure compulsory attendance of all Indian children at school, but with the added provision for 'the arrest and conveyance to school and detention there' of any children who might be prevented . . . by their parents" (Richardson 101).

Once in school, Native children were punished ferociously if they spoke their own language. Irish scholars and their grandparents will remember the infamous tally sticks — *bata scior* — Irish children were forced to wear after the Education Act of 1831 made English the official language of Ireland. Gaelic-speaking children wore sticks around their necks. When they did not speak in English, the teacher notched the stick, once for every word of Irish uttered. When the child's stick was full of notches, he or she was beaten with it. Unable to keep similar horrors from being visited on their children, Native parents suffered devastating sadness and guilt at their helplessness. Irish scholars agree that the Irish language came to be associated with shame and poverty too. At least two generations of Canadian Natives were treated this way, creating a schism between the culture of the past and the shame-filled emptiness of the present. Linda Jaine, a Saskatchewan Cree and a survivor of a residential school, writes, "the last one hundred years of our history is full of black holes made by the theft of our language . . . and traditions. Especially sad are the decades of torment our nations' children had to endure in the church-run, government-sponsored residential schools" (viii). Cree poet Skydancer (Louise Halfe) is a survivor of the residential school system:

> In the late fall
> ice waited
> outside our cabin.
> . . . .
> Two white-skins
> talked in tongues.

Father's long face
stretched further
to the floor.
Mother's crimson cheeks
turned like swirling ashes
in the stove-pipe.

Behind
Mother's draping dress
a six-year-old sister.
Her small fist
white against
brown skin.
. . . .
My stomach couldn't hold
the fresh cinnamon roll.

The air was
wrapped in
raven darkness.
Namoya maskoc.
It's a mistake.
Father's voice
shook.
Mother swayed.

The white-skins
left.
The cold seeped in the
cracks of the door,
its fingers wrapped
in silence.

The world
was silent.

The family gone.
The family not ever more. (63–64)

"The Indian Act . . . created a nation-wide framework that is still fundamentally in place today" (Dickason 283). Briefing Canada's diplomatic heads as recently as 1992, Ted Moses said: "As Indians we live in a dictatorship every bit as real, every bit as offensive as the dictatorships that were overthrown in Eastern Europe. Many Native Canadians watched that situation with intensity, sympathy, and understanding. They hope that they too will some day be liberated" (qtd. in Richardson 350). The act's major goal was assimilation; among its major effects has been cruel repression. According to Ovide Mercredi, "The Indian Act is not a bill of rights; it's an instrument of oppression. . . . It dehumanized our people. It made the white man superior." The residential schools established under these laws were among the most arbitrary and indefensible institutions ever created in my country, all the more vicious because their gross cruelties were visited upon children, and usually by the churches.

I offer a third parallel example. In the 1820s, Britain under Sir Robert Peel created the Royal Irish Constabulary, a different kind of force from the usual decentralized British law enforcement agencies (Dickason 281). For one thing, the RIC (the "Peelers") were armed, while the ordinary British metropolitan police ("Bobbies") were not. The RIC was organized along military lines. When Louis Riel began the Métis resistance in Manitoba and Saskatchewan in the 1870s and 1880s, Sir John A. MacDonald's government in Ottawa sent the North West Mounted Police to deal with him. The NWMP was, of course, an all-white constabulary, and it was modelled after the Royal Irish Constabulary: armed and trained like soldiers (Dickason 281). It was deemed acceptable after all to open fire on, in the words of an old missionary hymn, "lesser breeds without the law" but not on civilized white people.[6]

Another parallel is the popular humiliation of the ethnic stereotype. The Irish people grew weary long ago of the fanciful leprechaun land to which other nations were wont to transport them. Much of Irish literature of the last hundred years has been an attempt to correct stereotypes, some of them vicious, like the simian "Paddy" of Victorian *Punch* magazine cartoons. Heinz Kosok is one of several scholars who have carefully documented the popular but humiliating images of the Irishman; he does so in his essay "John Bull's Other Ego: Reactions to the Stage Irishman in Anglo-Irish Drama."

The "Stage Irishman" is probably the most long-lived of all the ethnic stereotypes of the international theatre; in the twentieth-century international cinema, the "Hollywood Indian" has endured too. From movies and television, the world has learned to antici-pate a score of familiar images and patterns. Westerns have shaped racial perceptions of Natives, foregrounding and glamourizing the poisonous ethnic stereotypes of Eurocentric, nineteenth-century popular melodrama. The redskins are evil; the palefaces are good. Occasionally, the stereotype flips to the other extreme of romantic sentimentalism. The hawkeyed warrior chieftain rides along the ridge of foothills, scanning the horizon; his glamorous, doeskin-clad consort prepares his meals, rears his children, and whines vapid song lyrics about the colour of the wind: he is the Noble Savage. The Stage Irishman was usually confined to one or more of five discernible characteristics: his garrulousness, his vaingloriousness, his laziness and unreliability, his unquenchable thirst, and his equally untamable desire for quarrels and duels. Any student of North American culture will recognize that these same racial traits are applicable to Hollywood Indians too. The buffoon names — O'Blunder, MacBrogue, Big Chief Rain-in-the-face, Sittum-on-Possum — indicate the extent to which these figures became stereotyped. When they spoke, they said "B'gosh and begorrah" or "How. Ugh."

The fifth parallel example is less dramatic but no less urgent. In our late-twentieth-century setting, Native writers and intellectuals have warned that they are being marginalized by the blind presuppositions of criticism and theory. In Ireland, alien standards are repeatedly imposed on Irish imaginative creations, marginalizing them from the start. Yeats's early "Ballad of Father O'Hart," for instance, was praised by Daniel Hoffman (in *Barbarous Knowledge*) as a competent example of the literary ballad, but marred by "daubing" of "local colour" — by which he meant the inclusion of certain Irish place names that had escaped Anglicization (such as Glen Car, Innisfree, Ben Bulben, Kilvarnet). The question, of course, is, "What was Yeats supposed to call these places?" These are not touches of "local colour" but names of real places. Nineteenth-century scholars and writers who first dismissed the early, orally transmitted Irish stories and songs as primitive then translated them into domesticated and more sophisticated literary forms, snatching them from the voices and minds of their creators. Angela Bourke's research into the oral songs of eighteenth-century Irish women has shown just how much nineteenth-century publishers and romantic Hibernophiles laundered, modified, distorted, then silenced the voices. Trying to place Native literature in the canon, trying to *define* the adjective "Native," Canadian scholars have found themselves engaged in a bewildering debate. Some manifest a polite racism, treating Native literature as some kind of rare and exotic growth to be handled delicately and kept apart from other literatures. Others find it interesting purely from a sociological or anthropological point of view, just as the initial Eurocentric opinions about Inuit sculpture were that these majestic, powerful pieces were created by a race of idiots savants. What impresses such people "is not that the bear dances poorly or well," complains a Métis friend, "but that he dances at all." Maria Campbell, translating oral narratives of her Métis people for *Stories of the Road Allowance People* (1995), spoke of the stifling effects of "imperial English" on the voices of the originals, forcing her to translate back into "village English." The process went something like this: Métchif rendered in standard English was then transcribed back into village English to capture some of the flavour, rhythm, and intent of the prototype in the published version. Louis Owens, in *Other Destinies*, says that "The task before [the Native writer] was not simply to learn the lost language of his tribe but rather to appropriate, to tear free of its restricting authority, another language — English — and to make it accessible to Indian discourse" (13).

In this pair of words, "tear free," one can hear a cultural imperative, a shift into the concluding section of this essay. Applied to literature, the words "tear free" advise Natives first to reclaim and then to develop their own voices. A powerful precedent can be found, beginning in the Irish literary renaissance of the 1890s. Whatever I have read in recent Native literature, one theme comes through repeatedly, summarized in this single rhythmic assertion by Kateri Damm, an Ontario Chippewyan author: "[Writing] is a means of affirming the cultures, of clarifying lies, of speaking truth, of resisting oppression, of asserting identity, of self-empowerment, of survival, of moving beyond survival. . . . In words, the healing continues" (113).

There has been a great loss and a discontinuity between the lives once lived and the lives lived now. One loses history; one loses memory. The greatest loss is the loss of language. Images of the world sustained by language are often deauthenticated in the now unfamiliar old setting; the words and ways of seeing the old world scarcely work any more. This new world is haunted by absence. I am reminded of Nelson's Crossing and what was erased so that Nelson, whoever he was, could be honoured somewhere in northern Saskatchewan. Chief Bighetty of the Cree has said recently that he was often terrified: "The people could go back to the sorrowful years of the seventies. At that time, you know, we almost lost our language. My wife, who now teaches Cree, didn't know how to speak it. . . . The nuns always told us to speak English. We were taught to be ashamed of our culture.

. . . Now everybody is proud to be Missinippi Cree." (qtd. in Richardson 222)

A narrow escape from silence. Olive Dickason, in her invaluable study, *Canada's First Nations: A History of Found Peoples from Earliest Times*, says that seventeenth-century Jesuits "noted the power of the word and song among the peoples of the St. Lawrence Valley. . . . The Amassalik Inuit of East Greenland use the same word for 'to breathe' and 'to make poetry'; its stem means 'life force'" (66–67). The same gist of meaning — breath, life, poetry — applies in Cree. Monture Angus has told me in conversation that "Indian languages have no nouns, no things. All the words in Indian describe the connection (verb) between things. For example, in Mikmaq the trees were named by the sounds they made."

Canada's Natives are beginning to speak and write in languages that come from their own hearts and minds and that do not mimic the bureaucratic gobbledygook of the Faceless Ones in the Federal Department of Indian Affairs (imagine those people being named by the sounds they make!). The best Native literature is showing them how to re-create their world. Although it is an uphill climb, these strays — transitional generations — are using lodges of the imagination as sites of refuge and healing, places of vantage, to inspire themselves, from which to re-search themselves. It happened in nineteenth-century Ireland, and in this century it is happening in Canada.

The final parallel, then, is the hope-filled one. When Irish parliamentarian Charles Stewart Parnell died, hope for Irish home rule virtually died with him; Irish historians speak of the great political vacuum that occurred in Irish republican life. The Great Hunger preceded a Great Silence, both of which drained the Irish people. As O'Connell, the Fenians, Parnell disappeared into the earth, the vital energies they had imparted to their people were sapped. But out of that void there came a rebirth: the Irish literary renaissance, a determination to rescue Irish culture, songs, stories, and myths. Thirty years later, Eire was born (in blood and civil war, yes, but as an independent republic). A hundred years later, we in Canada have witnessed and read an outpouring of fine work by Native artists. There is an ancient prophecy among the Iroquois, a simple and astounding belief: "One day, our people will speak to the world." Most Native writers I know believe that such a day has come. "Each day," Monture Angus has said to me, "repeats itself so it will continue to come and come. Wait 'til my kids get hold of this place!" Art is one way to attain self-discovery, pride, and spiritual independence. "The Great Mystery," writes Skydancer,

> entered my dreams, and I heard its voice through its creation. Squirrels shared their chatter, and the wind blew its soul into my ears, and the water spoke its very ancient tongue. . . . The stories inside me demanded face. . . . My bare feet had felt the drum of the earth and the heartbeat of my palms . . . I became a wolf, sniffing and searching, pawing, muzzling, examining every visible track I made or saw. . . . I will no longer be a binding sinew of stifling rules, but rather a sinew of wolf songs, clear as morning air. (126–27)

Says Campbell more bluntly: "I can't believe you're saying culture isn't political" (Campbell and Daniels 15).

Trying to write my way towards conclusion, I complained to a colleague that instead of coming to a point my paper was sprawling like the Fraser Delta. "Then *that's* your point," he retorted. Another wise colleague challenged us both: "You need to think of this as a circle, not a straight line. Circles have no points!" The subject has seized me, making me feel more excited and more ignorant with every book I read. Skydancer proclaims: "The land, the Spirit doesn't betray you. I was learning to cry with the Spirit. I was safe to tear, to lick, to strip the stories from my bones and to offer them to the universe" (126). These images are sacred, painful, and powerfully creative. And Skydancer's words are far from isolated. On a recent album, *Coincidence (and Likely Stories)*, Buffy Saint-Marie sings with defiant assurance: "We're only getting started."

NOTES

[1] The phrase I use for my main title is taken from "Paper" by Daniel David Moses: "It's too bad if anyone imagines / words have ever bled when the clean blackness / of letters on this paper should imply / that it's easy to live. . . . there is nothing but white between the lines" (295).

[2] A bibliography compiled by Janice Acoose, acting head of the English Department, Saskatchewan Indian Federated College, runs to over a thousand items.

[3] "What could be more intimate," asks Stan Dragland while commenting on one of Duncan Campbell Scott's expeditions, "than a route that needs no names? . . . [I]t's a far cry from the obsession that generated place names

along the CPR in advance of any settlement or even experience of the locales"
(25).

4 The English established compulsory schooling in Ireland before they
did so in their own country, using the Irish situation as an educational laboratory.

5 In what was actually the first of the Crusades, the Normans, who had
originated in France of Viking stock a hundred years earlier, conquered
Ireland during the twelfth century, setting themselves up as Ireland's rulers,
building castles, taking lands. Five hundred years later, those "Hiberno-
Normans" or "Irish Normans" had integrated themselves into the fabric of
the country, sometimes intermarrying and always calling themselves "Irish."
After several humiliating defeats, the Gaelic and Anglo-Norman chieftains
fled the country, leaving the Gaelic-speaking poor and the peasants behind.
This sad event is called the Flight of the Wild Geese in Irish history and
legend. With their departure, the old Irish civilization was, for all intents
and purposes, annihilated.

6 More recently, the NWMP has become the RCMP. Only within the last
ten years have Natives been allowed to join the force, even though the RCMP
is still the sole protector of law and order in every nonurban settlement in
western Canada, and even though the majority of residents of those settlements are Native (seventy-five to eighty-five percent).

WORKS CITED

"Barbarous." *Oxford English Dictionary*. 1989 ed.

Bourke, Angela. "Eighteenth-Century Irish Women's Work Songs." Departments of English and Native Studies. University of Saskatchewan, Sept.
1994.

Campbell, Maria. *Halfbreed*. Toronto: McClelland, 1973.

——. *Stories of the Road Allowance People*. Penticton, BC: Theytus, 1995.

——, and Harry W. Daniels. *One More Time*. Dir. Tom Bentley-Fisher.
Twenty-Fifth Street Theatre, Saskatoon. 20 Apr.–7 May 1995.

Cavanagh, Sheila. " 'Licentious Barbarism': Spenser's View of the Irish and
The Faeries Queene." *Irish University Review* 26.2 (1996): 268–89.

Damm, Kateri. "Dispelling and Telling: Speaking Native Realities in Maria
Campbell's *Halfbreed* and Bernice Culleton's *In Search of April Raintree*." *Looking at the Words of Our People: First Nations Analysis of
Literature*. Ed. Jeannette Armstrong. Penticton, BC: Theytus, 1993.
93–114.

Dickason, Olive Patricia. *Canada's First Nations: A History of Founding
Peoples from Earliest Times*. Toronto: McClelland, 1992.

Dragland, Stan. *Floating Voice: Duncan Campbell Scott and the Literature
of Treaty 9*. Toronto: Anansi, 1994.

Deane, Seamus, Andrew Carpenter, and Jonathan Williams. "The Early Planters: Spenser and His Contemporaries." Deane, Carpenter, and Williams, eds. vol. 1. 171–74.

——, eds. *Field Day Anthology of Irish Writing*. 3 vols. Derry, N. Ire.: Field Day, 1991.

Friel, Brian. *Translations. Modern Irish Drama*. Ed. John P. Harrington. New York: Norton, 1991.

Heaney, Seamus. Rev. of *Translations*, by Brian Friel. *Times Literary Supplement* Oct. 1980: 1199.

Hoeg, Peter. *Smilla's Sense of Snow*. New York: Farrar, 1992.

Hoffman, Daniel. *Barbarous Knowledge: Myth in the Poetry of Yeats, Graves, and Muir*. New York: Oxford UP, 1967.

Jaine, Linda, ed. *Residential Schools: The Stolen Years*. Saskatoon: University Extension, 1993.

Kosok, Heinz. "John Bull's Other Ego: Reactions to the Stage Irishman in Anglo-Irish Drama." Eighteenth Annual Conference of the Canadian Association for Irish Studies, University of Alberta. Edmonton, 14 Feb. 1985.

Mercredi, Ovide. "The Proposed Amendments to the Indian Act." Department of Native Studies, University of Saskatchewan. Saskatoon, 27 Feb. 1997.

Monture Angus, Patricia. *Thunder in My Soul: A Mohawk Woman Speaks*. Halifax: Fernwood, 1995.

Moses, Daniel David. "Paper." *An Anthology of Canadian Native Literature in English*. Eds. Daniel David Moses and Terry Goldie. Toronto: Oxford UP, 1992. 295.

Murray, Les A. "The Action." *The Vernacular Republic: Poems, 1961–1983*. North Ryde, Austral.: Angus, 1988. 95.

Ní Chuilleanaán, Eiléan. "'Forged and Fabulous Chronicles': Reading Spenser as an Irish Writer." *Irish University Review*. 26.2 (1996): 337–51.

Owens, Louis. *Other Destinies: Understanding the American Indian Novel*. Norman: U of Oklahoma P, 1992.

Richardson, Boyce. *People of Terra Nullius: Betrayal and Rebirth in Aboriginal Canada*. Vancouver: Douglas, 1993.

Saint-Marie, Buffy. *Coincidences (and Likely Stories)*. Chrysalis, 1992.

Skydancer (Louise Bernice Halfe). *Bear Bones and Feathers*. Regina: Coteau, 1994.

Spenser, Edmund. *The Faerie Queene*. Ed. Lilian Winstanley. Vol. 2. Cambridge: Cambridge UP, 1955. 2 vols. 1952–55.

——. "A View of the Present State of Ireland." Deane, Carpenter, and Williams, eds.

Tilley, E. Brian. *A Narrow Vision: Duncan Campbell Scott and the Administration of Indian Affairs in Canada*. Vancouver: UBC, 1986.

"That Murderin' Half-Breed": The Abjectification of the Mixedblood in Mark Twain's Adventures of Tom Sawyer

Patricia Riley

In *The Half-Blood: A Cultural Symbol in Nineteenth-Century American Fiction*, William Scheik observes that "American writers of the nineteenth century, more than those of any other period, probed into the nature of the half-blood's identity, of his place in the scheme of things (universal and American), and of his future in relation to the New World" (x–xi). Published seven years after General Phil Sheridan's infamous assertion that "the only good Indian [he] ever saw was dead" (qtd. in Brandon 366), and "only six months after Custer made his last stand" (Backus 263), Mark Twain's *Adventures of Tom Sawyer* (1876) represents one of the more prominent links in a literary chain whose portrayals of Mixedblood characters often serve to illustrate and reinforce a nineteenth-century Euro-American desire to keep racial borders intact, to protect oneself from, and in some cases, rid oneself of, that which one considers to be abject.

According to Julia Kristeva in *The Powers of Horror: An Essay in Abjection*, the notion of the abject is linked to that which "disturbs identity, system, order. What does not respect borders, positions, rules. The in-between, the ambiguous, the composite . . ." (4). As Cynthia Nakashima notes in "An Invisible Monster: The Creation and Denial of Mixed-Race People in America," those of mixed race "have always upset . . . the understanding of race, ethnicity, culture, and community in the United States" (163). Indeed, Nakashima further notes that "People who do not fit into a clearly defined race category threaten the psychological and sociological foundations of the [American] 'we' and 'they' mentality that determines so much of an individual's social, economic, and political experience in the United States" (164).

Twain's unsavoury characterization of his Mixedblood antagonist as abjection personified exemplifies how the presence of the Mixedblood in nineteenth-century American society represented a salient threat to the Euro-American desire for a racially pure citizenry. As Nakashima also observes, the fact that "antimiscegenation laws were [primarily] aimed at marriages between Whites and non-Whites . . . is indicative of the ultimate concern with keeping the White race apart from all others" (166). Furthermore, according to Ramon Saldivar in "Narrative, Ideology, and the Reconstruction of American Literary History," an "ideology of exclusion remained central to the American creed throughout the nineteenth century. And we see its effects in other historical and literary movements" (14). We certainly see its "effects" in Twain's *Adventures of Tom Sawyer.*

The perceived threat to white racial purity, no doubt a reaction to the increasing presence of Mixedbloods in various communities throughout North America, precipitated a scapegoating impulse with sacrificial overtones that is based on a biologically deterministic belief that the wages of the so-called sin of miscegenation can be found in the biracial offspring who are subsequently portrayed in literature as doomed, defective, dangerous, and double-crossed by virtue of the genetic contribution of the Indian parent. Consequently, the character of Injun Joe functions within the text not only as demonic arch villain, but as a hieroglyph for Euro-America's fear of miscegenation as well.

In "Discovery of River and Town," Henry Nash Smith asserts that while "the novel celebrates conformity and bourgeois respectability" (8), the demonization of Injun Joe is little more than a literary device used by Twain to "sustain the story" (8) and solve a plot problem: "It is the absence of a basic conflict between Tom [Sawyer] and the society of the village that obliges Mark Twain to look elsewhere for the conflict he considered essential to the plot of the novel. He solves his problem by introducing evil in the form of Injun Joe, whose mixed blood labels him as an outsider . . ." (85).

In spite of the fact that Smith briefly acknowledges that it is Joe's racial makeup that determines his "outsider" status in the novel, he fails to probe the darker reasons behind this. In the depiction of the consequences of race mixing as embodied by Injun Joe, Twain delineates his character in a way that echoes the skewed viewpoint held by J. C. Nott, a nineteenth-century southern physician who, in his study of animal hybrids, concluded that "the Mulatto or Hybrid is a *degenerate, unnatural* offspring, *doomed by nature* to work out its own destruction" (qtd. in Beider 24; emphasis added). In light of this line of thinking, Joe's negative depiction, his rejection as one who is unfit to exist even on a textual level, tells us far more about the psychotic shadows that lurk within the nineteenth-century Euro-American imagination than it does about the Mixedblood subject, for, as Kristeva, citing a Freudian concept, points out, "*rejection . . .* [is] a means of situating psychosis" (7).

Twain's "consistently savage attack on the Indian" in "Fenimore Cooper's Literary Offenses" (Backus 262), and the "bitter racism against 'Digger' Indians in . . . *Roughing It*" (Owens 32), is fairly well known. Unfortunately, however, Twain gives the impression that his opinion that Indians "are mean, vengeful, deceitful, dirty, stupid and in all ways depraved" is based on his having "met them face to face on the western frontier" (Backus 263). Unfortunate, too, is the fact that readers often fail to question that opinion and tend to "take Twain's word . . . as final" when "in fact he saw American Indians only briefly and from a distance; Indians [who were] dispossessed and demoralized" (Backus 263). Therefore, it seems that Twain, imbued as he was with a host of nineteenth-century stereotypes about America's Indigenous people, "had a personal axe to grind" (Backus 263). From his vicious and degrading characterization of the Mixedblood Injun Joe, it would seem that Twain's particular axe was sharpened on his fear of miscegenation.

Nakashima observes that oftentimes "The mixed-race person is seen as the product of an immoral union between immoral people, and is thus expected to be immoral him or herself" (168). This belief is consistent with the notion of one who is considered to be abject. Abjection, as Kristeva further describes it, "is immoral, sinister, scheming, and shady: a terror that dissembles, a hatred that smiles . . . a friend who stabs you . . ." (4). Interestingly, Kristeva's description of the abject closely resembles Twain's portrayal of Injun Joe.

The reader first encounters the character of Injun Joe in chapter 9. Tom and Huck are in the midst of a boyish, late-night adventure involving a dead cat and a trip to the local graveyard. After arriving at the cemetery, the two boys hear voices and see three men approaching on a grave-robbing expedition. The men are identified by the boys as Injun Joe, "that murderin' half-breed" (68); his partner in crime, Muff Potter, a known drunk; and young Dr. Robinson, a man of science. Twain immediately characterizes Joe as worse than demonic through Huck's reaction when Tom recognizes the Mixedblood's voice: "I'd druther they was devil's a dern sight" (68). Twain also brands Joe as lawless and unnatural through his mercenary participation in an act that is illegal as well as immoral and macabre.

According to Kristeva, "decay. . . and corpse[s] . . . stand for the danger to identity that comes from without . . . society threatened by its outside" (71). Therefore, by bringing Joe into intimate contact with a decaying corpse, Twain also immediately associates his character with the threat of decomposition and pollution that the Mixedblood, as an outsider in white society, represents to nineteenth-century Euro-America.

Twain's characterization of Potter and Dr. Robinson, Joe's partners in crime, allows the reader to construct points of redemption for them in spite of the fact that they have participated in a grotesque criminal action. Potter is a poor man and an alcoholic who, while intoxicated, clearly lacks good judgement; he probably would not have helped to commit the grave robbery if he had been sober. The reader learns later that Potter "hain't ever done anything to hurt anybody" (146), and that he has been good to the children in the community, "mend[ing] all the boys' kites and things, and show[ing] 'em where the good fishin' places was" (147). Justifications for Dr. Robinson's role as instigator of the crime can also be found. He is a man of science and humanity. A greater illumination of the workings of the human body would increase his ability to serve his community as a medical professional. While his act is illegal, his motive is scholarly, altruistic, and ultimately humanitarian. In contrast, Joe's participation in the crime remains unmitigated and unredeemed. His motivation is rooted in a desire to revenge himself for a slight perpetrated against him by the good doctor and his father in the past.

Once the chosen body is disinterred, Potter threatens to abandon the night's work unless the doctor pays his two cohorts an additional five dollars. When Robinson reminds them that they have already been paid in advance, Joe erupts in a violently bitter tirade against the doctor. True to the stereotypical attitudes of the nineteenth century, Twain casts Joe as a shiftless, vindictive halfbreed with a dangerously patient memory, one of those Mixedbloods who, according to "George Flower, an Englishman travelling to the Illinois country in 1817," resemble "lank curs" who "lurk with thief-like look about the door" (qtd. in Petersen 25). Therefore, in order to underscore the representation of Mixedbloods as a dangerous, chaotic threat to an otherwise orderly and racially pure society, Twain draws upon the nineteenth-century notion "of blood as the agent of the transmission of [ethnocentrically perceived] racial characteristics" (Spickard 15), making it clear that it is precisely Joe's "Indian blood" that induces him to remember the slight, allows him to nurse a grudge for years, and urges him on to act out his revenge when the opportunity finally presents itself: "Five years ago you drove me away from your father's kitchen one night, when I come to ask for something to eat, and you said I warn't there for any good; and when I swore I'd get even with you if it took a hundred years, your father had me jailed for a vagrant. Did you think I'd forget? The Injun blood ain't in me for nothing. And now I've *got* you, and you got to *settle*, you know!" (68–69). Additionally, Twain's focus on Joe's "Indian blood" labels the Mixedblood as a kind of vector who carries the dreaded dis-ease of miscegenation, an enormously dangerous "Indian" plague, within his very platelets, and threatens to unleash it on the world around him in the form of vengeance, murder, and mayhem.

When the doctor lashes out and knocks Joe down, Potter, in a gesture that carries the redemptive quality of loyalty to one's associates at least in the context of honour among thieves, attempts to defend his partner. A scuffle ensues in which Potter's knife falls to the ground and is taken up again by Joe. Twain's construction of his Mixedblood antagonist as a natural man, in the most pejorative sense, becomes clear in a way that marks Joe as irrational and unreasonable. His eyes are aflame "with passion" (69). His movements are likened to those of an animal circling its prey — sinuous, calculated, and opportunistic. Twain writes that Joe "snatched up Potter's knife, and went creeping, catlike and stooping, round and round about the combatants, seeking an opportunity" (69). When the doctor knocks Potter unconscious with a headboard, Joe moves in for the kill and stabs the doctor in the heart. Twain continues to play on the notion that Mixedbloods are treacherous by situating Joe as both Judas figure and bad thief in a passion play between the races. After robbing the doctor's body and taking his metaphorical thirty pieces of silver, Joe betrays the man who had attempted to defend him. By placing the murder weapon in Potter's hand, Joe leads Potter to believe that he, himself, has committed the murder. When Potter regains consciousness and jumps to that conclusion, Joe assures the frightened man that he will never tell anyone about the night's events. Grateful for this gesture of friendship, Potter says, "Oh, Joe, you're an angel. I'll bless you for this the longest day I live" (70). However, the reader, being privy to Joe's deception and betrayal, is acutely aware that if Joe is an angel, he is of the Luciferian variety. Twain tightens this association by invoking the supposedly demonic nature of the Mixedblood, whose unnatural proclivity and capacity for revenge extends even to children. Tom and Huck, the sole witnesses to the night's treacherous events, fear the Mixedblood's revenge and are forced into a compromising silence: "Tom, we *got* to keep mum. *You* know that. That Injun devil wouldn't make any more of drownding us than a couple of cats, if we was to squeak 'bout this and they didn't hang him. Now, look-a-here, Tom, less take and swear to one another — that's what we got to do — swear to keep mum" (72).

As if Injun Joe's initial private betrayal of Muff Potter is not enough to paint the Mixedblood as cunning, crafty, and untrustworthy, Twain continues to push the point even further, deepening and reinforcing it through a second, public, betrayal. Prior even to the arrival of the townsfolk on the murder scene, rumours circulate around town linking Potter to the murder. Although Joe's name is not immediately put forward as an informant, an anonymous "somebody" recognizes the murder weapon as "belonging to Muff Potter" (78). And an unnamed "belated citizen" comes "upon Potter washing himself in the 'branch' about one or two in the morning" and watches him as he "sneak[s] off" (78). One of these informants *could* be Joe, and his position as informant is further strengthened by his presence in the crowd gathered at the murder site.

When Potter, dragged to the site by the sheriff, protests his innocence, a voice from the crowd cries out, "Who's accused you?" It is at this point that Twain clearly labels Joe as the engine of the second betrayal: "This shot seemed to carry home. Potter lifted his face and looked around him with a pathetic hopelessness in his eyes. He saw Injun Joe, and exclaimed: 'Oh, Injun Joe, you promised me you'd never —'" (79).

Potter's heartbroken reproach, combined with the immediate and forceful presentation of Potter's knife by the sheriff, solidifies Joe as the ultimate Judas, an abject betrayer of one who has thought of him as a friend. At the least, Twain's narrative strategy strongly insinuates that Joe is *probably* the anonymous man who identifies the knife as belonging to Potter.

Twain continues to connect Joe with the essence of evil by crafting a scene that casts him as a "stonyhearted liar" who is somehow beyond the divine retribution that awaits the average mortal man (79). Since "God's lightnings" fail to descend "upon his head" during his slanderous testimony against Potter at the graveyard gathering, Tom and Huck conclude that "this miscreant had sold himself to Satan." (80) Their fear of coming forward to testify on Potter's behalf is exacerbated because it "would be fatal to meddle with the property of such a power as that" (80).

The boys' belief that Joe will somehow manage to escape hanging, even if one of them testifies against him, is borne out in the court scene when Tom finally follows his conscience and takes the stand in Potter's defence. In the middle of Tom's testimony, "the half-breed sprang for a window, tore his way through all opposers and was gone!" (150). Although rewards are offered and a search is conducted, "no Injun Joe was found" (152). Joe's ability to vanish completely causes Tom's fear to grow large. His nights become "seasons of horror" as Joe is further characterized as a kind of predatory vermin who "infested all his dreams, and always with doom in his eye" (151).

Although Tom "felt sure he never could draw a safe breath again until that man was dead and he had seen the corpse" (152), he forgets his fear of Joe for a time by embarking on a treasure-hunting adventure with Huck. However, his distraction is short-lived. While hunting for treasure in a "ha'nted house" (158), the two boys come upon Joe again. Disguised as a "deaf and dumb Spaniard," Joe is once again recognizable by his voice as he plots more nefarious deeds with his new partner in crime, a "ragged, unkempt creature" (162). True to form, and with a "wicked light flam[ing] in his eyes" (165), Joe emerges once again as something more than a common criminal. As had his previous crime, his new undertaking has the diabolical element of revenge. Since Joe and his partner, in their search for a place to conceal some of their ill-gotten gains, stumble upon the very treasure that Tom and Huck are looking for, Joe's partner assumes that now Joe "won't need to do that job" (165). Frowning, Joe informs his cohort that "You don't know me. Least you don't know all about that thing. 'Tain't robbery altogether — it's *revenge!*" (165).

After spying Tom and Huck's pick and shovel standing in the corner "with fresh earth on them," Joe becomes suspicious and decides to take the treasure to hideout "Number two — under the cross" (166). This mysterious second hideout turns out to be the very cave in which Joe will eventually meet his death. While the cave is real, as is the cross mark on its ceiling (Allen 130), the significance of Joe's association with the place of the cross transcends the practical imperatives of setting and atmosphere and becomes an allusion to Joe's mixed (or crossed) racial heritage: this cross represents the one that the town is bearing as a result of his chaotic presence and, possibly, reflects the notions of the mark of the cross as used by Robert Montgomery Bird in *Nick of the Woods: Or, The Jibbenainosay. A Tale of Kentucky*. The protagonist of Bird's novel, a well-known

Indian-slayer, consistently leaves an identifying mark on the bodies of his victims, "a knife-cut, or a brace of 'em, over the ribs in the shape of a cross. That's the way the Jibbenainosay marks all the meat of his killing" (64). Therefore, by associating Joe with a cross, Twain places an even greater emphasis on his antagonist's mixed racial heritage. He inverts the Cooperian preoccupation with "purity of blood" embodied by the character of Hawkeye in *The Last of the Mohicans* who "repeatedly insists that he is a 'man without a cross'" (Backus 265), and positions his Mixedblood antagonist as a marked man whose time within the novel is rapidly coming to a close. Twain also evokes the two thieves of the biblical crucifixion, placing Joe in the guise of the bad thief, a variety of anti-Christ, who deserves to die for the deeds he has committed and who will not obtain heaven, much less take part in a resurrection. Joe's death, when it comes, will be final, an irrevocable end to the chaotic force that he embodies as a disturber of the white racial order.

In "When the Fences Are Down: Language and Order in *The Adventures of Tom Sawyer* and *Huckleberry Finn*," Wayne Fields acknowledges that Tom Sawyer's world is one that "is dominated by fences," further noting that "Aunt Polly's white-washed fence . . . represents the care and maintenance of order to which the town is committed" (369). However, Fields neglects to address the perceived racial disorder that Twain seeks to fence in within the text. When Fields asserts that there are "*presences* which the town cannot so neatly keep in place," Injun Joe is not mentioned as one of these "disordering forces" (372; emphasis added), in spite of the fact that he is closely associated with each of the "presences" Fields does mention: the haunted house, the graveyard, and McDougal's cave. Joe's connection to each of these places is significant, as each site situates him deeper within an aura of abjection that functions as a variation on guilt by association. Each place frequented by Joe mirrors some aspect of his abjectified self. The graveyard, as discussed earlier, links Joe to the abjection of "decay . . . and corpse[s] . . . [and to the] society threatened by its outside[r]" in the form of the racial decomposition and pollution that the Mixedblood represents for Twain (Kristeva 71). The haunted house, like the graveyard, is also unkempt, overgrown with weeds, and filled with the "signs of decay" (162). Joe's presence within the house intensifies his association with the abject, while Twain's description of the house implies that a society inhabited by, and "overgrown" with, Mixedblood "weeds" is an "unkempt" society that has failed to keep its racial borders intact and is therefore in a state of decay and deterioration. Twain's perception of the depraved and decayed moral nature of the Mixed-blood becomes even clearer in the next episode.

When Huck follows Injun Joe to the Widow Douglas's farm in an attempt to discover the location of the mysterious hiding place, he discovers instead that the widow, a woman of great kindness and hospitality, is the intended target for Joe's new revenge. In the conversation that follows, Twain paints Joe with the precise and decisive strokes that mark him out as an animal entirely devoid of conscience or human feeling; an abject, immoral, and demonic entity driven by a lust for revenge and clearly deserving of the death that will eventually come to him:

> I don't care for her swag [money] — you may have it. But her husband was rough on me — many times he was rough on me — and mainly he was the justice of the peace that jugged me for a vagrant. And that ain't all. It ain't the millionth part of it! he had me *horsewhipped*! — horsewhipped in front of the jail, like a nigger! — with all the town looking on! HORSE-WHIPPED! — do you understand? he took advantage of me and died. But I'll take it out on *her*. (179)

The target chosen for revenge, a defenceless woman, the apparently innocent wife of the perpetrator of past injustice, sheds further light on Joe's aberrant character and interior deformation, as does the proposed act itself. And, once again, Twain demonstrates his belief in the unnatural and thoroughly degraded nature of the Mixedblood by playing him off against a partner who, although dishonest and degraded himself, nevertheless emerges as the "good thief" and remains above the particular brand of heinous revenge that Joe's depraved nature demands, because, as one of the townsmen later notes, "white men don't take that kind of revenge" (184). When confronted with the grisly details of Joe's plan to attack the widow, his partner in crime recoils and begs for her life:

> "Oh, don't kill her. Don't do that!"
> "Kill? Who said anything about killing? I would kill *him* if he was here; but not her. When you want to get revenge on a woman you don't kill her — bosh! you go for her looks. You slit her nostrils — you notch her ears like a sow!"
> "By God, that's —" (179)

Inhuman? Immoral? Indian? The reader is left to fill in the blank. What *does* the "good thief" think? Twain has Joe cut off the protestation in order to insert a further point of redemption for his partner in crime. As Huck later tells the Welshman, "The ragged one beg[ged] for the widder" (183). If the "good thief" reluctantly consents to go through with the heinous crime, it is only because he fears for his own life, and, in an ironic twist, he may also be motivated by the possibility of saving the widow's life. Says Joe:

> Keep your opinion to yourself! It will be safest for you. I'll tie her to the bed. If she bleeds to death, is it my fault? I'll not cry if she does. My friend you'll help in this thing — for *my* sake — that's why you're here — I mightn't be able alone. If you flinch I'll kill you. Do you understand that? And if I have to kill you, I'll kill her — and then I reckon nobody'll ever know much about who done this business." (179)

Although Huck is able to avert the attack on the Widow Douglas, Joe once again evades capture. It is Tom Sawyer who is fated to meet up with him again when he and Becky Thatcher become lost in McDougal's cave during a community picnic outing. After hours of searching along endless corridors for a way out, Tom hears voices, sees a "hand holding a candle," and gives a "glorious shout," only to discover that the hand belongs to Joe, disguised as a Spaniard: "Tom was paralyzed; he could not move. He was vastly gratified the next moment, to see the 'Spaniard' take to his heels and get himself out of sight. Tom wondered that Joe had not recognized his voice and come over and killed him for testifying in court. But the echoes must have disguised the voice. Without doubt, that was it, he reasoned" (197).

Nature, it would seem, is for the white man and against the so-called unnatural fruits of miscegenation that Joe represents, because it is a phenomenon of nature — the cave — that saves Tom from being murdered by distorting and disguising his voice. And it is the same cave that will ultimately bring about, and literally seal, Joe's doom.

Twain's earlier representation of Joe as a kind of societal vermin carrying the dis-ease of miscegenation resonates again when both Tom and Huck become sick following their last encounters with him. And it is this illness that prevents Tom from telling anyone that Joe is inside the cave until it is too late, thereby reinforcing the idea that Joe, as a Mixedblood, carries the seed of his own destruction within himself.

When the cave is sealed to prevent anyone else from getting lost in it, Mother Nature proves herself a terrible, pitiless parent capable of turning against her misbegotten progeny. The cave, the womb of the Great Mother herself, swallows Joe, refuses him nourishment, and finally reabsorbs her monstrous offspring, liberating the outside world from his unnatural influence. The cave is "a prison for the Indian . . . whose brotherhood is denied and whose demonhood is exaggerated" (Tracy 111–12); there is no way out for Joe. He is trapped there, just as he is trapped within the prison house of what Twain considers to be his abject Mixedblood nature. Buried alive in the cave whose labyrinthine twists and turns mirror the corridors of his own dark and twisted soul, "The poor unfortunate had starved to death" (202). Like the bad thief in the biblical crucifixion story, Joe cannot enter heaven; rather, he is consigned to hell in the form of the underworld cave, clearly a symbol of containment.

Ironically, the site of Joe's death becomes a place of pilgrimage. Tourists journey from far and wide to get a glimpse of "Injun Joe's cup," which "stands first in the list of the cavern's marvels" (202), the unholy grail of Twain's Mixedblood anti-Christ bad thief, a piece of hollowed-out stone placed on top of a broken stalagmite "to catch the precious drop that fell once every three minutes with the dreary regularity of a clock tick" (202), but which has failed to be Joe's chalice of redemption. When all is said and done, the "doom" that Tom dreams he sees in Joe's eye is Joe's own (151).

Often, what is not said in a novel has as much import as what is said. It is of no mean significance that no one laments Joe's passing, for Twain has constructed his Mixedblood antagonist as not only evil and undeserving of compassion or pity, but also as the quintessential man without a people. Throughout the novel, no mention is made of his community, no references are made of a father, mother, brother, sister, lover, or friend in connection with Joe. Rather, Joe moves through life as a disconnected shadow beast, existing on the fringes of human society without a place of his own. His funeral is as much a cause for celebration as his hanging would have been. If, indeed, as Fields asserts, the town of St. Petersburg "is a society where things [and people] have been assigned their proper places" (369), we have to ask where the Mixedblood's place is within it. Twain does not hesitate to answer that there is no place for him.

Joe, as "a being of abjection," functions as a kind of secularized "*pharmakos*, a scapegoat who, having been ejected [or destroyed], allows the city to be freed from [its racial] defilement" (Kristeva 84).

Clearly, his death stands as a sacrifice on the altar of racial purity, but in contriving it, Twain cleverly sees to it that no blood is shed. Indeed, Joe is "destroyed unintentionally by Judge Thatcher" (Smith 85), whose "presence provides constant reassurance that order is secure in St. Petersburg" (Fields 370), thereby strengthening the notion that the Mixedblood is doomed by nature to extinction. Although Twain's biologically deterministic argument is partially deconstructed by the fact that it was a white man who "sheathed" the door on the mouth of the cave "with boiler iron" and "triple-locked" it (200), the reader is nevertheless left with a lasting image of a thoroughly abjectified Joe sinking back forever into the moist dark earth that, according to the racist stereotypes of the nineteenth century, never really intended for him to live.

WORKS CITED

Allen, Jerry. "Tom Sawyer's Town." *National Geographic* July 1956: 120–40.

Backus, Joseph M. " 'The White Man Will Never Be Alone': The Indian Theme in Standard American Literature Courses." *Studies in American Indian Literature: Critical Essays and Course Designs.* Ed. Paula Gunn Allen. New York: MLA, 1983. 259–72.

Beider, Robert E. "Scientific Attitudes toward Indian Mixed-Bloods in Early Nineteenth Century America." *Journal of Ethnic Studies* 8.2 (1980): 17–30.

Bird, Robert Montgomery. *Nick of the Woods: Or, The Jibbenainosay. A Tale of Kentucky.* Ed. Curtis Dahl. 2nd ed. New Haven: College, 1967.

Brandon, William. *Indians.* 1961. Boston: Houghton, 1987.

Fields, Wayne. "When the Fences Are Down: Language and Order in *The Adventures of Tom Sawyer* and *Huckleberry Finn.*" *Journal of American Studies* 24.3 (1990): 369–86.

Kristeva Julia. *The Powers of Horror: An Essay on Abjection.* Trans. Leon S. Roudiez. New York: Columbia UP, 1982.

Nakashima, Cynthia L. "An Invisible Monster: The Creation and Denial of Mixed-Race People in America." Root, ed. 162–78.

Owens, Louis. *Other Destinies: Understanding the American Indian Novel.* Norman: U of Oklahoma P, 1992.

Petersen, Jacqueline. "Ethnogenesis: The Settlement and Growth of a 'New People' in the Great Lakes Region, 1702–1815." *American Indian Culture and Research Journal* 6.2 (1982). 23–64.

Root, Maria P. P., ed. *Racially Mixed People in America.* Newbury Park, CA: Sage, 1992.

Saldivar, Ramon. "Narrative, Ideology, and the Reconstruction of American Literary History." *Criticism in the Borderlands: Studies in Chicano*

Literature, Culture, and Ideology. Ed. Hector Calderon and Jose David Saldivar. Durham: Duke UP, 1991. 11–20.

Scharnhorst, Gary, ed. *Critical Essays on* The Adventures of Tom Sawyer. Critical Essays on American Literature. New York: Hall-Simon, 1993.

Scheik, William J. *The Half-Blood: A Cultural Symbol in Nineteenth-Century American Fiction*. Lexington: UP of Kentucky, 1979.

Smith, Henry Nash. "Discovery of River and Town." Scharnhorst 79–87.

Spickard, Paul R. "The Illogic of American Racial Categories." Root, ed. 12–23.

Tracy, Robert. "Myth and Reality in *The Adventures of Tom Sawyer*." Scharnhorst, ed. 103–12.

Twain, Mark. *The Adventures of Tom Sawyer*. New York: Penguin, 1980.

Savage Erotica Exotica: Media Imagery of Native Women in North America

Marianette Jaimes-Guerrero

1. The Pocahontas Perplex and Hollywood Cinema

Native American women have been portrayed in Hollywood cinema in images of "erotica exotica" — from the erotic "pagan nymphomaniac" to the picturesque erotic "Cherokee princess" to the objectified "Indian squaw."[1] These objectifying references parallel the titillating "whore" with the idyllic "madonna" projected onto women by the objectifying male. This essay operates within the critique of feminist and Native womanist theory regarding women in cinema and focuses on the representation of Native women as stereotypical celluloid images in early-to-present cinema. It is a denigrating portrait derived in significant part from early Eurocentric novels, and one that reflects xenophobia as racism and misogyny as sexism.

There is a strong connection between early literature that manifests a Native erotica exotica and later media and video imagery. I will also tie in these earlier literary portrayals of Native women with the contemporary stereotypical status imaged in Hollywood cinema using the mythologized story of Pocahontas. My conclusion emphasizes the ways in which Native women are resisting this denigration while asserting their more genuine sense of "beingness." These Native women are doing so in a variety of roles, including as educators, movie consultants, and spokespeople for their respective Native cultures. Today, there are also Native women journalists and cultural critics, as well as magazines on media, cinema, and the arts, most notably the Toronto-based *Aboriginal Voices*. It appears that movie scripts and cinematic imaging are about metaphors and need to be deconstructed layer upon layer — a process that is like peeling away the skins of an onion in order to get to the core of what motivates both racism and sexism, and to counter the Eurocentrism that permeates our Euro-American society.

In the context of both institutional sexism and racism in American cinema, there is a need for a particular emphasis on the representation, or lack of representation, of Native American women among other women of colour and ethnic cultures. Such practices both negate and exclude more authentic portrayals of these women, who find themselves easily appropriated into the general population of mainstream "white" women.

Today, Native women are having to contend with the Disney-produced Indian Barbie doll, the animated movie caricature of a childlike Pocahontas. Native critics of both genders have addressed this problematic imagery of Native women and how it affects young Native girls (Morrisseau 16–17). Rayna Green contextualized this back in 1975 as the "Pocahontas Perplex" within the colonialist legacy, which includes Eurocentric ethnographic interpretations. She describes the "perplex" image thus:

> She is young, leaner in the Romanesque rather than the Greek mode, and distinctly caucasian, though her skin remains slightly tinted in some renderings. . . . But when real Indian women . . . intruded . . . the perplex emerged as a controlling metaphor in the American experience. The Indian woman, along with her male counterpart, continued to stand for the New World and for rude native nobility, but the image of the savage remained as well. (17)

Green writes that this is not a new phenomenon, since Euro-American colonialists have always been intrigued by the Indian maiden as a vestal virgin. In fact, the chaste persona of a romanticized princess is an early symbol of a national icon for the United States (even before Uncle Sam). The colonial-era sculpture of this figure sits atop the Capitol Building. She has also been interpreted as a hybrid female with both Greek and Roman ornamentation, thought by many to be a composite of Indian royalty in the image of Native woman as romantic figure of womanhood. Her opposite, the demeaned squaw, can be perceived as parallel with the madonna and whore derived from Judeo-Christian biblical lore. Green adds that "The Mother Goddess and Miss Liberty peddle their more abstract wares as Indian Princesses, along with those of the manufacturer, and while she promises much she remains aloof" (19). Green also queries: "But who becomes the white man's sexual partner? Who forms liaisons with him? It cannot be the Princess, for she is sacrosanct. Her sexuality can be hinted at but never realized. The Princess' darker twin, the Squaw (therefore), must serve this side of the image, and again relationships with males determine what the image will be" (19). The reader will see how these sexual dynamics are played out in the cinematic illustrations depicted in this essay.

2. *False Images from Early Literature to Modern Media*

Beginning with the Spanish campaign for Christian imperialism and continuing on to American conquest and colonization, the Euro-American agenda in this "New World" created a Eurocentric mythology for the United States. The historical legacy of the United States is wrought from a savage genocide and imperialism that usurped the original claims of the early Indigenous peoples to this continent; that legacy is also wrought from the dispossession and disfranchisement of peoples of colour and Native cultures by the European usurpers who came as immigrants to the New World. This legacy continues to negate and denigrate the first inhabitants of this hemisphere, and Hollywood cinema can be seen as propaganda serving white America at the expense of its first inhabitants.

There is a need to compare our present with the past in these cinematic contextualizations using a process that involves deconstructing the mythology arising from Eurocentrism. That mythology has produced a xenophobic image making that is reflected in nationalist metaphors as well as images of a rapacious American society that is globalizing in its advanced stage of colonialism. This arrogance rationalizes the pathological and even predatory nature of a settler state and its Eurocentric mindset at the expense of the first inhabitants to these lands.

The question of Indian identity for many of us is also a Native response to the 1992 reexamination of the Columbian legacy from Euro-American conquest and colonization. Even before the 1992 "Columbus Quincentennial" acted as a catalyst, there was a continuing Indian resistance to this version of history, with Indian voices demanding to be heard in many contexts. Native American women have always rejected both the sexist and racist stereotypes that they have been subjected to since European contact; these were first manifested in early colonialist literature and ethnographies by predominantly male European and Euro-American authors. Regarding the Pocahontas legacy, Green remarks: "Whether or not we believe

[Captain John Smith's tale], and there are many reasons not to (one among them being that Pocahontas was only a child of ten years at the time of their first encounter), we cannot ignore the impact the 'rescue' story has had on the American imagination" (15). The popular legend goes that a young Indian princess saves Smith from being put to death by her people, eventually marrying him and becoming a Christian while teaching him what he needs to know in order to survive in the so-called New World. She later travels to England with him, and eventually dies in that foreign land, never seeing her people and homeland again. Yet, as Green adds, there are many versions of this legend, even among people from many different Western and northern European cultures. Therefore, the question becomes one of determining what is historical fact and what is Eurocentric mythmaking.

Since it is only recently that the American public has acknowledged the power of media to control our lives in more covert and subtle sociopsychological ways, it needs to be recognized that its systematic and systemic effectiveness in doing so has made us all, Indians and non-Indians alike, its products as well as its victims. In the journal of Christopher Colon (or Columbus), the messianic opportunist was ambivalent about whether he had found paradise among Native populations living as one with nature or a cannibal society. Rousseau and Voltaire considered the New World Indians to be "uncivilized heathens" compared to "civilized" Europeans. The intrigue surrounding these "primitive savages" led to Native people being exhibited at World fairs in their sparse clothing like two-legged animals in a zoo or a Barnum and Bailey circus; men, women, and children were coerced into performing "exotic pagan rituals."[2]

3. Root Perceptions of Racist and Sexist Stereotypes

The depiction of Native American women in early Hollywood cinema cannot be separated from the negative stereotyping of Indian men in these films. This is a major point that Native writer Richard Hill makes in an article entitled "Savage Splendor: Sex, Lies, and Stereotypes." My analysis links this stereotypical racism with sexism in the early imaging of Native American women in cowboy-and-Indian films. It also explores the dichotomy of the Native woman as squaw (or a similar derivative) or Cherokee-princess in the continued objectification that demoralizes Indigenous peoples of both genders.

In this context, the root perception of Native Americans as less than human has resulted in racism and sexism on the big screen.

The Eurocentric notions of male thievery and female sexual activity have been with us since 1492. When Europeans first encountered Indian men and women with little clothing on, sometimes dancing without inhibition, and watched the women bathing, the voyeuristic conquistadors and missionaries wrote down their titillating accounts in vivid detail in their journals and diaries. Native literary critic Dr. Kate Shanley's paper "Ceremonialism and Celluloid Indians" illustrates how Indian characters were used as erotic "Indian kitsch" at the expense of historical realism. Such stereotypes prevent any meaningful understanding of Native people as fully human or of their cultures as possessing indigenous wisdom.

In his 1504 *Mundes Novas: Letters to Lorenzo Pietro di Medici*, Amerigo Vespucci, the overrated mariner this country was named after, described Native women as lustful and promiscuous, and alleged that Indian males eventually become eunuchs as a result of their women's sexual rapaciousness. Similarly, a twentieth-century megamovie, *Little Big Man* (1970), shows a satisfied Dustin Hoffman taking turns with three Indian sisters in a teepee orgy. There has been recognition of what has been called a "sexual fluidity" among precolonial Native peoples since our ancestors did not have the same hang-ups as Judeo-Christian believers did. There is even documentation of "cross-gender females" among these cultural groups who were not denigrated or thought of as perverse (see Blackwood). Another extreme scenario is the anti-Indian movie *A Man Called Horse* (1970), which shows an aging Indian woman losing her mind and wandering off to die after her husband has died, the message being that she is now useless without him. The message is also that her people condone her suicide by neglect, but death for Native people does not have the finality that Christians fear. This film, therefore, depicts, at best, a modification and, at worst, a distortion of traditional gender roles in the context of matrilineal/matrifocal tribes and egalitarian Indigenous nations that respect their elders, both male and female, for their experience and wisdom.

There is also the ideal of Euro-American portrayals of motherhood; the sacrificing and even martyred pioneer woman prototype appears in many films. This is in contrast to the imagery of Indian women as cartoon characters, noted by Lahoma Burd of FAME. This is also exemplified by the Abbot and Costello movie *Ride 'Em Cowboy* (1942) in the kitschy depictions of "twin" Indian sisters —Sunbeam and Moonbeam. There are physical differences, since Sunbeam is the slender and therefore "pretty" one, while Moonbeam is big and supposedly "ugly."

The prevailing racism and sexism in American colonialism have European cultural origins; they are derived from the Anglocentric interpretation of biblical scriptures. This is particularly apparent in the colonialist puritan applications that developed from the theological roots of racism inherent in the Judeo-Christian traditions of patriarchy and New World imperialism. As an illustration, the scriptural contextualizations of "Man shall inherit the earth" and "Man shall have dominion over nature" (Gen. 1.30) imply European male domination of women and Natives in order to subdue the forces of nature that are traditionally attributed to both. In effect, the Bible promises that "If you diligently keep all [the Lord's] commandments . . . the Lord will drive out all these nations before you and you shall occupy the territory of nations greater and more powerful than you. Every place where you set the soles of your feet shall be yours" (Deut. 11.22–24). These biblical scriptures have been interpreted as justification for a Euro-American doctrine arrogantly proclaimed as "manifest destiny" and derived from a christian (as in white Anglo Saxon Protestant) agenda for a nationalism founded on a patriarchal and racialized colonialism.

According to feminist analysis, European women attempted to soften the aggressive manner of their male oppressors — fathers, husbands, and sons — in order to protect children and slaves as well as themselves; they did so by being tolerant of the male need for control and ownership. But this was evidently at the expense of their gender equality once patriarchy took hold. Such chauvinism did not occur in most documented Indigenous societies, especially the matrilineal nations. Yet, a patriarchal attitude is manifested by the early film *The Apache Kid* (1941), in which a dialogue between a young Indian man and a young Indian woman reflects the prevailing Eurocentric sexism:

> *Woman:* "I promise to be a good wife. And I will do only that which pleases you."
> *Man:* "And I can beat you. . . . You won't speak your mind on family matters?"
> *Woman:* "No, never!"

Hill presents a paradox in his article (cited earlier) when he writes, "The American male's (desire) for pretty Indian women had been used to symbolize that (some kind of) racial harmony could be possible" — in the movies, anyway. A case in point is *Broken Arrow* (1950), starring James Stewart as a man whose Indian wife is killed by the whites due to her "fatal attraction" to one of them (*Images*). Another non-Indian actor, Jeff Chandler, plays the woman's brother. The overall message of this sappy melodrama is that interracial blood mingling is not done; that is, dire consequences result from breaking miscegenation taboos. This could not be further from the truth among Native societies, since intermarriage/exogamy was encouraged as healthy, as were the adoption and naturalization of outsiders who wanted to become members of the nation. The novel on which this particular movie was based had a happier ending, one the movie's producers decided was unacceptable, so the Indian wife had to die for marrying a white man. Another Romeo-and-Juliet scenario in film is the Indian male killing himself when he is denied the love of a white woman who symbolizes forbidden fruit (*Images*). However, the most common scenario in early westerns was the savage Indian male pillaging, tomahawking, and raping the pioneer woman before killing her and her children; that is, if the pioneer husband and father is not able to come to the rescue first.

4. Mimetic Assumptions in Sexual Politics

On European male proprietary rights, Hill notes: "The white male had viewed the land, the trees, the minerals, the animals, and the Native women as his possessions" after he got the Indian male out of the way. Even though Hill covers a lot of ground in his article, and I agree with most of his analysis, it still originates in a predominantly Indian male perspective. He also remarks that "Sex has become such an essential part of most films that it is hard to separate stereotypes about Indian women from those of all women" (14). This indicates his failure to see the Native woman's perspective in his cinematic analysis; he perceives no difference between her sexist and racist objectification in the movies and that of her non-Native counterpart. This can be partly explained by the fact that few Indian women have found themselves on the big screen. However, the disparity between non-Indian women's roles and Indian women's stereotypes is clear when you compare, for example, a Euro-American ideal of woman-hood as portrayed by Olivia De Havilland opposite Errol Flynn as Custer in the 1941 film *They Died with Their Boots On* (*Images*). In this glorification of Custer, Anthony Quinn plays another caricature of an Indian, this time the historically factual and proud Lakota leader Crazy Horse. Movies of this genre are fabricated as American mythology, and even objects that are sacred to Indigenous peoples and their cultures are not exempt from distortion. One film shows the Apaches with the sacred pipe, although in reality these people did not have the tradition of the sacred pipe, and it is sacreligious to the Great Plains Indians nations to portray it as such. Hence, Indian cultures and people are trivialized by distorted representations of material culture.

The De Havilland/Flynn film perpetrates historical distortion as well: it highlights Custer and his "heroic" calvary in conflict with the wily Sioux; in fact, the Lakotas won the Battle of Little Big Horn. Furthermore, many now see Custer as an arrogant fool whose reckless ambition led to his own death. His brothers also died at Little Big Horn under his command, thus wiping out the Custer male line. Yet the film depicts Custer as an American hero rather than the foolhardy egomaniac he was.

Kate Shanley's work deconstructs this American mythology further by focusing on the notoriety of other American legends, such as Buffalo Bill Cody and his Wild West Shows, for which Indians including Sitting Bull, after his capture, were coerced into performing as showman's clowns. Director William Wellman's popular film *Buffalo Bill* (1944) is flagrantly fictionalized according to historical records. It depicts him as a "nice guy" instead of the derelict he was, and it reeks of the maudlin sentimentality of the times. A modern-day treatment (*Buffalo Bill and the Indians* [1976]) starring Paul Newman as Buffalo Bill and depicting Sitting Bull as the even more pitiful "vanishing Indian" was a flop at the box office because it did not uphold the myth of macho white hero and savage but beaten Red Man (*Images*).

Another illustration of this racist and sexist milieu can be found in the Canadian film *Black Robe* (1991), which portrays an Indian woman, in a key, suspenseful scene, "bending over backwards" to service a man. Her actions set him up for an escape, and she and her family do, in fact, get away, since her sexual prowess weakens the male guard who is holding them hostage. The woman's actions in this sensational scene are presented as custom instead of the means to survival. Native women, according to their own histories, have had more dignified means of empowerment than this movie depicts. This particular movie, therefore, insults the Native woman by depicting her as a whore with wily intentions to seduce the male. However, the thing that most intrigues me about *Black Robe* is its colour scheme: the missionized Indians among the Hurons are bathed in white light, while the "savage" Mohawks are cast in dark, ominous shadows; the troubled priests who are caught in the middle are cast in shades of grey. These men of God are also portrayed as having a strong faith, which is supposed to somehow justify their missionary zeal to convert the woodland Indians among the Hurons and Mohawks. A more realistic movie, *The White Dawn* (1974), involves a young Inuit woman, played by Nilak Butler, who commits suicide after her involvement with a white trader jeopardizes her relationship with her Inuit husband. In the finale, the entire Inuit community executes the trader and his companions because they have brought evil upon their people by disturbing their peaceful family relations.

It was early assumed by Europeans that Native American women, like European women, were male property in the prevailing Euro-American patriarchy as a result of a long history of male chauvinism and even a generalized misogyny. In the 1992 film version of Fenimore Cooper's novel *The Last of the Mohicans*, the white male saves his non-Indian woman from the hands of savage Indians. Despite an award-winning soundtrack and a performance by the enigmatic Indian activist Russell Means, who stars in a role that is secondary to that of leading man Daniel Day-Lewis, the film's script is pure romantic slop. Native women only exist as backdrop props, while both Indian and non-Indian men cavort with white damsels in distress (such as the one played by Madeleine Stowe) and try to survive in a war zone between the British and the French with American colonialists and Indian men as their protectors.

As these modern-day cases illustrate, Native women in Hollywood cinema are either erotic, exotic objects of lust or mere backdrop — if they are not altogether invisible. They are consequently never seen as fully complex human beings in the powerful societal spheres of cinema and other media. And it is only when Native women are able to tell their own stories, as producers and directors, as well as writers, scriptwriters, and actors, that there will be a change for the better. Then we will be able, authentically, to position our representation and translation in order to challenge our invisibility as well as the caricatures in media and cinematic stereotyping.

5. Appropriated Metaphors in All the World's a Stage

John Ford's *The Searchers* (1956), a popular and award-winning western, is a classic case of distorting history at the expense of Indians and their cultures, of manipulating history according to Eurocentric cultural perspectives in order to create an American colonialist mythology (*Images*). In this film, John Wayne plays a typically macho man in the frontier cowboy mode who becomes angry with his niece, played by Natalie Wood, after she has been kidnapped by Indians. When he finally finds her, in the course of a "heroic" rescue attempt, she has been adopted into the tribe and married to an Indian. She does not want to leave — which makes the xenophobic Wayne character very angry. During his search for his niece, he has come across some other young white women who have apparently gone crazy after being held captive by the Indians. To another white male who says "It's hard to believe they're white," Wayne makes this arrogant protest: "They ain't white, anymore!" He then proceeds to abandon them to their keepers. Later in the movie, this callous character laughs heartily when his young white male cohort kicks the heavyset Indian "squaw" who carries his packs for him down a ravine after she tries to sleep next to him in his bedroll. It is difficult to fathom a more blatant illustration of sexism and racism in cinema than this one — the denigration of a woman for being both an Indian and a "squaw," the "American hero's" object of scorn and ridicule.

There has never been a movie made of the real-life Cynthia Ann Parker, who at the age of nine was taken captive by the Comanches and later adopted into the nation. She married a Comanche leader, becoming a prominent member in the Comanche nation and mother to a daughter and two sons. One of her sons was the famous Mixedblood Comanche leader Quanah Parker, who had a lot to do with Indian and non-Indian peace negotiations during that period. But Cynthia Ann was eventually returned to her white relatives and society, and soon afterwards died of a broken heart; she had been torn from her Comanche family and the society to which she had come to belong. Actually, her story is one of several that inspired John Ford to produce, and John Wayne to star in, *The Searchers* — one of the most blatantly racist and sexist movies of this century (*Images*).

In a later film, *The War Wagon* (1967), Wayne plays opposite Kirk Douglas and several other male stars (*Images*). A "man's man," he aggressively inquires of an Indian chief: "Who do you ride with, the warriors or the women?" His acting roles, as these films exemplify, evidently reflect the concurrent racist and sexist attitudes of the time, attitudes that contributed to the containment of stereotypes about women and people of colour in general. The real-life Wayne actually received a Congressional Medal of Honor, even though he never did military duty outside of Hollywood movies. A case can be made that Wayne was a patriotic idealogue who actually played himself in all his movies until his eventual demise from cancer. (The disease was allegedly brought on by exposure to radiation at a nuclear testing site on a western movie set in the Nevada desert. His female costar, Susan Hayward, among others who were on that set, also died of cancer later in life.)

Hill points out that in Hollywood westerns Indian males have to be demoralized while degrading Indian women in order to appropriate both gender identities as European psychocultural projections. The film *A Man Called Horse* (1970) features the English actor Richard Harris as a European wanderer who becomes a "super chief" among the Indians. The message to movie-goers is, again, that a white man is superior to all Indians, including leaders.

6. On Practices and Politics in Hollywood Cinema

Soon after contact with the patriarchal leadership class of political and military-oriented Europeans, Native women began to be ignored in their traditional leadership roles. This was due to the prevailing sexism among the Europeans. Native women were not allowed to participate or be recognized in treaty negotiations between Indian nations and representatives of European powers. This had not always been the case; on the contrary, before European immigrants became Euro-American colonialists who took Indian lands for western "settlement" by deceit and force, French and some Dutch traders utilized and therefore valued Indian women as spokespeople, mediators, and translators. This sometimes even led to marriages that were encouraged by such business liaisons and that were seen as a political means to thwart European takeovers. Hence, such relations were regarded as mutually beneficial, and Indian women were held in high regard for holding valuable positions among their peoples (Weatherfield 19–36).

It can be surmised that the English more than any other group had more problems with Native women in positions of prestige and leadership.

197

In their disempowerment brought about by British chauvinism and patriarchy, the American colonialists carried these ideas of presumed female inferiority along with their racist beliefs and they set the tone for Indian-Colonist relations. Today, european-derived sexism prevails even in parts of the Indian world, between people who traditionally held beliefs and practices of mutual gender respect and even reverence among their members as many of the traditionally derived matrilineal/ matrifocal tribes can attest to today. (Jaimes-Guerrero, "Civil Rights")

Prior to this, it is well documented even by non-Indian anthropologists and other social scientists that Indigenous cultures of the so-called New World developed their societies with gender egalitarianism in balance with the natural world order as their guiding spirit.

As the Indian comedian Charlie Hill once said, Indians are not allowed to be contemporary, and this seems especially true today. There is a continuing mentality that fossilizes Indians in amber as relics of a vanishing breed (*Images*). One exception to this rule is the contemporary movie *Pow Wow Highway*, a satire of serious matters relating to Native spirituality. The film is one of the first cinema productions to have input from Indian actors in believable Indian roles. The cast of characters, which is not all Indian, includes a strong Indian woman who is framed and locked up in jail. She is played by Joanelle Nadine Romero. However, *Pow Wow Highway* has not gained the recognition it deserves from the non-Indian public despite the fact that it is very popular among Indians. The story is also especially noteworthy for its Indian humour, which non-Indians generally feel uncomfortable with. The novel on which the film is based is different from the actual script, which prompted the author to threaten to sue the movie's producers; yet this is one of those cases in which a movie script is actually an improvement upon the original work.

Another high-quality movie that did not make it big at the box office is *Geronimo*, starring the Cherokee Native actor Studi (who only got billed fourth in the credits) as the proud Apache "renegade." Even though it was good, at last, to see a present-day movie about the Southwest Indians — the Apache and Yaqui in what is now Arizona — the Native women in this film are, yet again, no more than silent props for the macho heroics of paternalistic whites and doomed Indians. Nonetheless, Studi, who also appeared in *The Last of the Mohicans*, should be commended for playing a believable, if stereotypically stoic, Geronimo. The TNT television production of the same story presents a more credible version of history, since in it the women emerge from the background; they actually have speaking roles — some are main characters. But it remains to be seen whether Native voices can truly be heard within these powerful media spheres, and this especially goes for women: Indians today are perceived as just another self-interest group rather than cultural nations in their own right.

Seasoned Native actress Joanelle Romero gave a testimonial presentation in Oklahoma at the International Indian Council, hosted by the Cherokee Nation, in the fall of 1993. She talked about how difficult it was for her to continue to obtain roles as an Indian woman since she does not have the required certification to claim her Pueblo ancestry. She is of Mestizo descent from the Southwest, and her home base is in New Mexico, a state that recognizes any Native person who is not from a designated "federally recognized" New Mexican pueblo as "quasi-Indian" at best. She also related this problem to the younger generations of Native peoples who are being defined out of their Indian heritage. This problem is a result of the very restrictive federal standards and regulations that are now being adopted by some tribes, such as "blood quantum" criteria for "race" formulations. I have researched and written about this controversy in Indian identity politics elsewhere (see "Some Kind of Indian"). I should note in this context of sociographic patterns that there is a fifty-percent rate of intermarriage in the Indian world among both men and women; yet, Native women tend to marry outside their tribe intertribally, while Indian men tend to marry white women. While it is only in recent years that this "blood quantum" issue has entered the social spheres of movies and literature, it has become an escalating problem that has more to do with power monopoly than issues of legitimacy. This divisive situation establishes a political factionalism that pits Indian against Indian in a time of diminishing resources and federal support. It is from within this sociopolitical context that Romero gives testimony as to how all this negatively affects others, not simply herself as a Native woman actress. Other Native women writers have written about the dilemma of Mixedblood women, most notably Louise Erdrich, Linda Hogan, and Leslie Marmon Silko (see Shaddock). I have referred to the novels of these Native women authors as "historical literature" in regard to their respective ethnographic storylines.

Another Native woman, Lois Red Elk, has summed up her days as a movie extra by explaining that she never had a name, just a prop role to play. And many Indian male roles were played by big name whites, with bit parts going to Mexican nationals who looked more the part than the whites did. Most secondary Indian-woman roles went to non-Indians as well: in *The Unforgiven* (1960), Audrey Hepburn plays a despised and confused Mixedblood caught between cultural and racial worlds due to racist attitudes. In this movie, which was directed by John Huston, Burt Lancaster stars opposite Hepburn (*Images*). The racist rationale for how movie actors and actresses were chosen for Indian parts was that non-Indians looked better and were better actors than Indian people. This seems ludicrous, but the star system had a lot to do with perpetrating the idea that white actors playing Indians were more likely to be box office draws than would unknown Indians. One director even went so far as to decide not to have one non-Indian actor, Chuck Connors of *Rifleman* fame, wear brown contact lenses when playing an Indian role; the blue-eyed actor has a strange, icy stare as he tries to play an Apache warrior.

It seems we can safely predict that Indians will once again be in vogue in American theatres, enjoying a popularity that swings like a pendulum. The last big cinema hit for Indian actors was Kevin Costner's *Dances with Wolves*, which garnered all the attention at the 1991 Academy Awards. The movie's popularity was partly due to the Lakota language that was in its script; this brought brief recognition to one of the older Indian women actresses in the film and allowed her to make a speech in her native tongue at the awards ceremony. This was reminiscent of the 1974 Academy Awards, when the enigmatic Marlon Brando, a generous ally of American Indian causes, failed to show up, and rejected his Oscar for *The Godfather*. This made very little impact other than earning him condemnation for politicizing the awards. His fellow actors were even heard grumbling that his actions were "in bad taste." Brando had sent a pretty Indian emissary, by the cute name of Sasheen Littlefeather, to make a controversial speech on his behalf. He may have been taken more seriously if he had chosen an older Indian woman, a grand-mother, an actress of long standing, to prove his point to the academy on that gala evening. Nevertheless, his supportive actions did gain him respect among Native Americans, including those who were not members of any activist movement.

The women depicted in Costner's *Dances with Wolves* again serve as backdrop, which seems to be our Hollywood plight. However, in comparison to *The Last of the Mohicans*, the Costner film does more justice to Native women's roles, since at least the women in it talk. There is also a very ambiguous secondary role of a white woman, played by Mary McDonnell, who is taken in by the Indians after being found alone; hence, she is not quite a captive. At the end of the movie, she rides off with the Costner character, but under ominous portents. This finale has an implied message that the two are racial outcasts, but not necessarily from the point of view of the Indians, who adopt outsiders as full members of their nations. As I have noted, among Indigenous peoples in precolonialist times, such barriers did not exist: the race construct was brought over by European societies, and it was indicative of Eurocentric racist attitudes that fuelled land-hungry calvary and settlers. This colonialist situation could have been made much clearer in *Dances with Wolves*, since the Costner character would evidently prefer to remain with the Indians. As for the woman, we are left unsure whether her newfound companion is one she would have chosen for herself. It is presumably fitting for the two characters to ride off to their fate together as they are both white.

Prior to acting in this film, Graham Green had an exceptional role in a Canadian-produced surrealist film called *Clearcut* (1992), which includes Native women characters and deals with Native resistance to deforestation that is resulting in ecological devastation. However, white audiences were, generally speaking, uncomfortable with this movie plot, since the persistent clear-cutters must finally face a fierce reckoning with the Natives. Exemplified by *Clearcut*, it becomes apparent that Native films made in Canada, for the most part, are more authentic vehicles for Aboriginal perspectives, and display more gender equity, than more glitzy American productions.

The somewhat pro-Indian film *Thunderheart* (1993) pays long-overdue attention to the environmental issues that are impacting on Indian lands today. Val Kilmer plays an urban-raised Mixedblood who becomes an FBI agent with a conscience; Sam Shephard is the bad agent. The plot involves the Kilmer character's search for his soul on a Sioux reservation. There is a strong woman character who was inspired by Anna Mae Aquash, a real-life Canadian Micmac woman. Aquash was found dead, with a bullet through her head, on the Pine Ridge Indian Reservation in South Dakota. She has since become a martyr of the American Indian Movement, which she joined after arriving in the United States. However, this fictionalized version of events and killings that occurred in the aftermath of Wounded Knee 1973 not only distorts the facts of what actually happened but also gives the impression that the only good Indian woman is a dead one. To this day, the killing of Aquash, a Native woman activist, remains a mystery. Her murderers are still at large. Suspects range, unofficially, from an FBI agent who threatened her to members of the movement itself. Despite its appropriation of the story of a real-life person, this movie is an improvement for Indians in film, and it is even more popular among Natives than the epic sagas illustrated in this essay. This is perhaps because it hits closer to home — meaning the reservation — in regarding contemporary problems and socio-political situations.

7. The Dominant/Subordinate Discourse from Feminist/Womanist Criticism

In the discourse on structures of domination and subordination, feminist critics of patriarchal cinema such as E. Ann Kaplan have had much to say about the pornographic imagery of American women in movies. Regarding basic patterns and mechanisms in Hollywood film periods, Kaplan outlines four eras defined by "the male gaze": 1) there was a rigidly circumscribed sexual and political ideology in the 1930s and 1940s; 2) the 1950s were an extension of this rigidity, and featured what Kaplan describes as "sexuality . . . splattered everywhere and nowhere recognized," noting Marilyn Monroe and Natalie Wood as female icons in this context; 3) the 1960s appeared less puritanical, but in the films of the 1970s there were more rape scenes; 4) the post-1960s era generated a feminist discourse that is still with us, and it is focused on gender differentiation and conflict as well as gay and lesbian alliances for "freedom of expression" (1–4).

But the issue of race and its attendant racism, with very few and obscure exceptions, have not been clearly addressed in American film to date. Such denial and avoidance denotes an ahistoricism and a myopic essentialism in the general treatment of women from other cultural groups. Hence, Indigenous conceptualizations of womanhood, motherhood, and sisterhood are not represented, and the female fetishism of Native erotica exotica as good object, bad object with its attendant semiotics among other women of colour is even more pronounced in a legacy of racism as well as the prevailing sexism in colonialist America. Today, racism and sexism are just as rampant in Hollywood cinema and other media, and we are all products as well as victims of its coercive ideological impact on fantasy life. This nonrepresentation or misinterpretation can, therefore, be appropriately termed "institutional racism and sexism" in the societal spheres of American myth-making and propaganda. It is only in international and Third World cinema that the issue of race and its attendant racism, in the context of European imperialism and Euro-American colonialism, are being intensely analysed and synthesized. These concerns are especially evident in the current work of Brazilian, Caribbean, and Israeli cinema critics, among others in the broader inter-American and international arena. These critics deconstruct the Eurocentrism that fuels imperialism and the colonization of Others — women and Natives, ethnic minorities and Third World peoples worldwide (see Shohat and Stam).

I return to Rayna Green's analysis of Native women's subordinate imaging for representation and subaltern positioning as a national mythos. Green enhances her treatise on what she calls the "perplex": "In this movement from political symbolism (where the early Indian woman defends America) to psychosexual symbolism (where she defends or dies for white lovers), we can see part of the Indian woman's dilemma. To be 'good,' she must defy her own people, (even) exile herself from them, and become white, and perhaps suffer (even) death" (18). Green illustrates in song lyrics what can be referred to as "martyr mythology," stating that "Such songs add to the exotic and sexual, yet maternal and contradictorily virginal image of the Indian Princess, and are reminiscent of the contemporary white soldier's attachments to 'submissive,' 'sacrificial,' 'exotic' Asian women (as in an 'Other' female species)" (18). Concludes Green:

> The Indian woman is between a rock and a hard place. Like that of her male counterpart, her image is freighted with such ambivalence that she has little room to move (but she could add, unlike Indian men, as a result of the double whammy of racism and sexism). He, however, has many more modes in which to participate though he is still severely handicapped by the prevailing stereotypes (and has to compete with "males" for Indian parts). They (Indian women and men) are both tied to a definition by relationship with white men, but she is especially burdened by the narrowness of that definition. Obviously, her image is one that is troublesome, to all women, but tied as it is to a national mythos, its complexity has a special piquance. (20)

Thus, she speculates,

> Perhaps the Princess had to be removed from her powerful symbolic place, and replaced with the male Uncle Sam because she confronted America with too many contradictions. As a symbol and reality, the Indian woman suffers from our needs, and by both race and sex stands damned. . . . The Native American woman, like all other women, needs a definition (I would say a conceptual reconfiguration) that stands apart from that of males, both red and white. Certainly, the Native woman needs to be defined as Indian, in Indian terms . . . for a humane truth. (21)

Decolonization must also counter and challenge the myopic imagery that lends itself to literary stereotyping and celluloid pigeonholing, still a chronic problem. From a Southwest Native woman's perspective, this negation could also be called a "Malinche complex," since the problem affects many Native women of Mixedblood heritage (as Romero illustrates). The legend goes that Malinche became the mistress of Fernando Cortez, the conquistador who conquered the Aztec/Mixtecas in the fifteenth century, after serving as his most valued interpreter between her people and the Spanish. In some circles, she is blamed for being the symbolic mother of the Mixedblood races, since she consorted with the enemy as his "whore." This is yet another complex that blames the woman, another saint-or-sinner duality. From a Native womanist vantage point, such a sociopsychological dilemma is a racist as well as a sexist one, and it is all part of Indian identity politics. It also impacts upon Native women more than men, since women are more likely than men to lose their tribal status if they marry outside their tribal group.

The 1994 TNT television production *Lakota Woman*, based on the autobiography of Mary Crow Dog (coauthored by Richard Erddoes), comes close to addressing Native-women-focused issues. It is a sad story of a Mixedblood Indian woman who is still searching for herself in the aftermath of several violent relationships with men, volatile Indian-movement activism, bouts of alcoholism, self-loathing, and a destructive lifestyle. Both the book and the movie end in a hopeful recovery. However, this author has since changed her name in order to write another book about who she was before she was Mary Crow Dog. She had the same coauthor for that book, and it is alleged she has since criticized him for manipulating her in both projects. It is interesting to note that Jane Fonda had a lot to do with getting Crow

Dog's story told by TNT, but not without problems. It is also rumoured that Fonda is interested in doing the biography of Anna Mae Aquash, who was a friend of Crow Dog. However, since this Native woman's murder is still unsolved, obstacles have been presented by Natives as well as federal authorities that may prevent it from ever getting to the screen.

8. As a Subaltern Alternative for Native Representation

Several Native American women are involved in acting and countering the imagery of Native women that has prevailed since the days of silent pictures. For example, some are involved with the American Indian Community House in New York, a casting service for Indian actors. Others are also raising funds for important media productions, including radio ones, and are working to present the Native American perspective of women in a more balanced light. Their individual successes are evident in the music and enterprises of Buffy Saint-Marie, who, among other achievements, has narrated television shows for children (*Sesame Street*) and written award-winning movie scores (*Atla*). One of my favourite theatre groups is the Spider Woman Theater, which is headquartered in Brooklyn, New York, and composed of three Native sisters. These delightful entertainers are just as enjoyable offstage as they are on. Their satirical skits are about their real-life relationships, and much of their success comes from knowing how to laugh at themselves while ribbing the world and those who take themselves too seriously. Their humour is contagious. When I first met them, I recalled the archetypal Native women characters in Leslie Marmon Silko's intense novel *Almanac of the Dead* (1991). Such successes, of course, have not come easily, due to lack of access to the media as a vehicle of hegemony to the American public. Yet another group with the primary purpose of countering Indian stereotypes by producing films about Native Americans by Native Americans is the Native Voices Public Television Workshop at Montana State University. The negative imaging of Native men and women in cinema can lead to low self-esteem. This theatre group processes human feelings through a kind of dramatic therapy; novice actors are encouraged to act spontaneously.

Native women are having to deal with the double negation of sexist and racist stereotyping. But the issues go beyond just the creation of caricatures, since the power of media has also led to our cultural appropriation and even cultural genocide in the "cinema art" of propaganda and mythmaking by Euro-Americans. Indians, the first inhabitants of this hemisphere, are still around; we continue to resist these sociopsychological atrocities and work towards a more authentic portrayal of our cultures. Native cultures are landbased, and they recognize the powerful imaging of archetypes derived from prototypes in what is being called "geomythology." In the precolonialist arena, images of Native women were more prominent and prevailing — what I refer to as "feminine organic archetypes" (for example, Buffalo Calf Woman among the Lakota; Sky Woman among the Abenaki; Corn Daughter among the Hopi; Yellow Woman among the Southwest Pueblos), but this theme is outside the scope of this paper (see Jaimes-Guerrero, "Native Women").

Recently, I attended the twenty-third-annual American Indian Film Festival, held in San Francisco for *Aboriginal Voices*, the Toronto-based Native magazine. At this gala event, I had the opportunity to hear Native women who act (they wish to remain anonymous), and some producers, talk about how difficult it is for them to make a living in Native cinema, since roles are few and stereotypical. One Native actress stated that it is not easy for her to get roles because she does not conform to the Disney Pocahontas look. Another said that she could not get roles when she used her Indian last name, but when she anglicized it she was able to get bit and secondary parts. When it became trendy to have an Indian name, she changed it back, even though it limits her acting opportunities. Such cases indicate how little things have changed for Native women in film since Lois Red Elk's days. This seems to be the state of Native acting, and it indicates that things will get worse in this age of profit- and power-driven media. Hollywood movies are still all about image making and persona rather than, and even at the expense of, acting ability or narrative substance. In this arena, it is evident that for Native women it continues to be more difficult than it is for Native men, no matter what level of a production they are working on.

A 1996 issue of *Aboriginal Voices* contains a special feature entitled "A Woman's Eye," which profiles four Native women who are rising exemplars as a result of their respective achievements in Canadian-based Native cinema. These women are Alanis Obomsawin, producer of Native documentaries (*My Name Is Kahentiiosta*); Loretta Todd, who won an award for *Forgotten Warriors* (1996), which deals with Indian veterans of World War II; Sandra Sunrising Osawa, an independent producer for commercial television (*Lighting the Seventh Fire*); Shelly Niro, a storyteller turned filmmaker (*Honey Moccasin*) who uses Indian humour.

In 1996, I attended the Sundance Film Festival, of Robert Redford fame, at Park City, Utah. Sundance is the only film festival that even recognizes an emerging Native cinema, but still Native movies were excluded that year from mainstream audience screening, a result of the pigeonholing of Native cinema that perpetuates existing stereotypes. However, I was pleased to be involved in reviewing the Native debuts. One of these was a short film called *Borders*, a poignant Canadian work about citizenship featuring a Native woman in the lead role. There was also *Follow Me Home*, by a San Francisco Native production team; it received a standing ovation. In this special multi-ethnic movie with a mostly male cast, a black actress plays a role crucial to the storyline.

9. Towards the Future: A Native Womanist View of "Indigenous Education"

Today's mainframe of American pop culture is also a vehicle for global homogenization; yet it is becoming apparent that we are living in a time when people are increasingly aware of the forceful impact of media (cinema, television, video) on society. Media has become a powerful vehicle that especially denigrates groups that are subcultural to the American mainstream mythology. This is evident in the subordinate vantage point of the psychocultural images that Euro-Americans project onto American Indians through the American media. This treatment is deemed important in the rethinking of this negative representation of Native women in media spheres and in its interpretation within this dominant discourse from a subaltern vantage point. Writing from the perspective of a Native American woman positioned as a cinema critic, I have intended with this essay to provide a more comprehensive understanding of cinematic illustrations, as well as a behind-the-scenes look at how sexism and racism go hand in hand in the subjugation and longterm colonization of Indigenous peoples as manifested in the denigrating stereotypes that correlate with socioeconomic factors in the gender/racial/class hierarchies that have been institutionalized in American society.

At this juncture, it remains to be seen if things will improve regarding Native women's positioning and/or representation or iconography and our own reinterpretation of composition as mise-en-scène in the powerful arena of media production. In this reexamination, it is essential for women from marginalized cultures to include the extra-cinematic setting for discourse on: 1) cultural assumptions of the mythmakers, authors, directors, and producers in cinema; 2) the politics of the period; 3) the institutional racism and sexism that have been entrenched in the media up to the present. There also needs to be, as a fourth essential criterion, an international dimension to what has been termed a "subaltern perspective." Such factors even have the potential of defying the force that protects this powerful and elite media sphere, a defiance predicated on perceiving the dominant culture as hegemonic in terms of the struggle of marginal sociocultural groups to achieve political power. In this context, then, Native peoples, with women and men everywhere, need to find ways and means to revolutionize this power sphere, known as media, for their own ends and in terms of Indigenous survival, preservation, and resistance to Euro-American appropriation, exploitation, and cultural genocide. Yet, at the same time, we must never lose sight of the fact that there is a line to be drawn between media-produced fantasy versions of our more genuine life ways (what amounts to yet more Hollywood kitsch) and the traditional knowledge bases that describe our real-life Indigenous existence.

Consequently, it is going to take more representation by Indian actors/actresses, scriptwriters, directors, and producers to hold this powerful sphere accountable and to debunk Native stereotypes created for crass commercialism. It is going to take constant vigilance and indigenizing education in schools and colleges, as well as alternative activist agendas, to utilize media for more liberating struggles that challenge those who would maintain the racist and sexist status quo. However, it is a struggle that we, women and men, Natives and non-Natives, need to engage in every day of our lives. We cannot afford to ignore this need for the sake of younger generations. Abstract materialism in animated and celluloid imaging is a denigration of the human spirit, and our collective resistance to it, to the enterprise of human commodification, will not be easy. But this resistance is necessary, since much is at stake as a result of the corporate fascism that prevails in the United States. It is a social system that is also globalizing, and its only purpose is to increase the wealth and privilege of elite capitalists in what is being a called a "new world order."

Yet, as we fight to rein in the oppression and greed of our destructive times, a more inclusive Indigenous movement is opening to the human spirit, one that demands a decolonized agenda in Indigenous education as the world becomes a global village. Those who partake of this Indigenous movement can envision a future that recognizes the significant contributions Native cultures can make in bringing the world's people together, especially the once-revered Native women, the clan mothers, who were accorded authority. Hence, those who can harness media and technology for these greater humanitarian ends will hold our society accountable, ensuring that the present will be the vehicle for a more hopeful, egalitarian future.

NOTES

[1] A variation of this paper was presented at a conference entitled Goodbye Columbus: Rethinking Media and Representation, Society for the Humanities, Cornell University, in April 1992. In addition, a much shorter version entitled "Hollywood's Native American Women" was published in the spring/summer 1993 issue of *Turtle Quarterly*.

[2] The films and interviews cited in this paper are part of *Images of Indians in Film*, a five-set series produced by Phil Lucas and Robert Hagoplan, funded by KCTF Seattle, Humanities for the Arts, the Corporation for Public Broadcasting, and the Lilly Foundation. The series was narrated by the late, great Indian actor Will Sampson of *One Flew over the Cuckoo's Nest* and *The Fisher King*, among other notable movies. The fourth set, *Heathen Indians: The Hollywood Gospel*, is highlighted for its excerpts of Native Indian women in Hollywood cinema. Lucas is also credited with a song called "False Images," which inspired the title of an earlier version of this essay.

WORKS CITED

Blackwood, Evelyn. "Sexuality and Gender in Certain Native American Tribes: The Case of Cross-Gender Females." *Signs: Journal of Women in Culture and Society* 10.1 (1984): 27–42.

Crow Dog, Mary, with Richard Erddoes. *Lakota Woman*. New York: Grove, 1990.

Green, Rayna. "The Pocahontas Perplex: The Image of Indian Women in American Culture." *Massachusetts Review* 16.4 (1975): 698–714.

Hill, Richard. "Savage Splendor: Sex, Lies, and Stereotypes." *The Turtle Quarterly* (1992): 14–23.

Jaimes-Guerrero, Marianette. "Civil Rights versus Sovereignty: Native American Women in Life and Land Struggles." *Feminist Genealogies, Colonial Legacies, Democratic Futures*. Thinking Gender. Ed. M. J. Alexander and C. Talpade Mohanty. London: Routledge, 1997.

———. "Native Women, Kinship, and Sacred Traditions." Unpublished essay. 1994.

———. "Some Kind of Indian." *American Mixed Race: The Culture of Microdiversity*. Ed. Naomi Zack. Lanham, MD: Rowman, 1995. 133–53.

Kaplan, E. Ann. *Women and Film: Both Sides of the Camera*. New York: Routledge, 1983.

Morrisseau, Miles. "Disney's Disgrace." *Aboriginal Voices* 2.3 (1995): 16–17.

Romero, Joanelle. Presentation. International Indian Council. Waggoner, OK, Sept. 1993.

Shanley, Kathryn. "Ceremonialism and Celluloid Indians: The Cinematic Eye." Cornell University. Ithaca, 27 Mar. 1992.

Shohat, Ella, and Robert Stam. *Unthinking Eurocentrism: Multiculturalism and the Media*. New York: Routledge, 1994.

Silko, Leslie Marmon. *Almanac of the Dead*. New York: Simon, 1991.

Vespucci, Amerigo. *Mundus Novas: Letter to Lorenzo Pietro di Medici*. 1504. Trans. George Tyler Northup. Princeton, NJ: n.p. 1916.

Weatherfield, J. McIver. "Women (and a Few Good Men) Who Led the Way." *Native Roots: How the Indians Enriched America*. New York: Crown, 1991. 19–36.

When the Good Guys Don't Wear White: Narration, Characterization, and Ideology in Leslie Marmon Silko's Almanac of the Dead

JO-ANN THOM

Like many contemporary Indigenous writers, Leslie Marmon Silko subverts the rhetorical practices of European colonizers in order to advance Indigenous attitudes and ideas.[1] Following Susan Rubin Suleiman's definition, one can say that Silko's *Almanac of the Dead* (1991), like her earlier works *Ceremony* (1977) and *Storyteller* (1981), is an ideological work in that it tries "to persuade [its] readers of the 'correctness' of a particular way of interpreting the world" (1). *Almanac* is subversive in that the ideology it tries to persuade readers to consider and accept is one that runs counter to that of the dominant society.[2]

In *Almanac of the Dead*, several antithetical belief systems coexist and sometimes merge, most noticeably in beliefs surrounding the nature of reality. Silko implicitly argues that realism is not a means of reflecting reality, but, rather, a means of interpreting it. Readers see that a fictional world that seems realistic according to the belief systems of one culture might seem unrealistic or even fantastic according to the belief systems of another. This attitude towards realism in literature allows Silko to give voice to Indigenous peoples and to reflect our beliefs about the nature of reality. Because belief systems are not innocent and transparent, however, a better term, *ideology*, is needed to discuss these systems.

Because definitions of the term *ideology* are as diverse as the many belief systems they represent, I have found it useful to consolidate several definitions in my examination of *Almanac*, Silko's largest and, in many ways, most opaque narrative. I apply to *Almanac of the Dead* three definitions of ideology, which agree on the basic nature of ideology but emphasize slightly different aspects of the term. Susan Sniader Lanser, in *Fictions of Authority*, uses the term "to describe the discourses and signifying systems through which a culture constitutes its beliefs about itself, structures the relationships of individuals and groups to one another, to social institutions, and to belief systems, and legitimates and perpetuates its values and practices" (5n7). Catherine Belsey, in "Constructing the Subject, Deconstructing the Text," discusses the psychological aspects of ideology and argues that "ideology is both a real and an imaginary relation to the world — real in that it is the way in which people really live their relationship to the social relations which govern their conditions of existence but imaginary in that it discourages a full understanding of these conditions of existence and the ways in which people are socially constituted within them" (46). Sacvan Bercovitch, in "The Problem of Ideology in American Literary History," discusses how the dominant society in America uses ideology to protect its interests and to vanquish competing ideologies, but Bercovitch implies that competing ideologies coexist despite efforts at synthesis:

> In the broad sense in which I use the term here (in conjunction with the term "America"), ideology is the system of interlinked ideas, symbols, and beliefs by which a culture — any culture — seeks to justify and perpetuate itself; the web of rhetoric, ritual, and assumption through which society coerces, persuades, and coheres. . . . The American ideology suggests something almost allegorical — some abstract corporate monolith — whereas in fact the American ideology reflects a particular set of interests, the power structures and conceptual forms of modern middle-class society in the United States, as these evolved through three centuries of contradiction and discontinuity. So considered, "America" is not an overarching synthesis, *e pluribus unum*, but a rhetorical battleground, a symbol that has been made to stand for diverse and sometimes mutually antagonistic outlooks. (635–36)

Because each contains some element necessary to further my examination, I have tried to synthesize these definitions.

For the purposes of this essay, I have used the language of narratology in my discussion of ideology, which I have defined as the set of ideas, beliefs, and discourses that every society uses, first, to preserve itself by prescribing the individual's role in relation to her own society and to all things that comprise her world and, second, to perpetuate itself by convincing its members that its way is the correct way of perceiving the universe. Although countless ideologies exist in the world today, each encourages its adherents to imagine that its way is the right way and to evaluate all other ideologies according to their similarities to and differences from it. Most ideologies have difficulty coexisting with others because they perceive different ideologies as threats. Even the most passive ideology constitutes a threat because its very existence calls into question those beliefs that comprise other ideologies. To preserve themselves, then, all ideologies must be, to some degree, intolerant or they will not be able to perpetuate their existence. Many ideologies are aggressive because eliminating or converting those who maintain disparate ideologies ensures their own preservation. The ideology that the European colonizers brought to the Americas was aggressive in this way, and its victims were the Indigenous peoples.

Like all of Silko's works, *Almanac of the Dead* attempts to subvert the ideology of the European colonizers. In *Almanac*, Silko examines the colonization of the Americas and the resistance that the colonizers still encounter. Through the discourse of its multiple narrators, *Almanac* argues that the Americas have been both a physical and a rhetorical battleground for the last five hundred years. Within the text itself, the rhetorical battle rages on in the form of a moral treatise on the nature of good and evil. The narrative contains many complex and contradictory characters who function as representatives of the social classes to which they claim membership. Each one represents a point on the moral continuum of the text. *Almanac* subverts the dominant ideology by showing readers America through the eyes of the Indigenous peoples.

Like Silko's earlier works, *Almanac of the Dead* contains a set of ideological propositions; however, *Almanac* is bigger in both size and scope than Silko's earlier works, and its lessons are more complex. To understand *Almanac*'s many lessons, readers must accept that there is a treatise on good and evil implicit in the narrative. Like the lessons of many stories in the oral tradition of the Indigenous peoples of the Americas, *Almanac*'s lessons are not easy to grasp. Following in this tradition, the narrative perplexes readers in pursuit of its meaning by leading them along false trails and confounding them with dead ends. *Almanac* is, indeed, an exercise for the wits. *Almanac*'s narrator, in her construction of character, exploits narrative strategies to convey and conceal simultaneously the moral treatise on good and evil contained within the narrative.

Almanac is narrated by a multitude of often unrelated character-focalizers with no one central protagonist, and its implied author —

the entity that selects the data comprising the narrative (see Booth) — and its narrators fuse together so that we find it difficult to determine how we are influenced and by whom.[3] Furthermore, although *Almanac*'s narrator may encourage us to align ourselves with any character, we soon discover that she is misleading us and that she views all the characters with a kind of scorn that only varies in degree. As a result, readers find themselves alienated from the characters and denied any real point of entry into the narrative.

In the first chapter of *Almanac*, the narrator manipulates focalization so that we align ourselves with the character Seese, so that we sympathize with her and we accept her interpretation of characters and events. To this end, the narrator begins the chapter using external focalization to describe a strange scene.[4] Although the scene takes place in a kitchen, what occurs there is the antithesis of domesticity. An old woman, Zeta, is dyeing her clothes "the color of dried blood"; two men, Ferro and Paulie, are cleaning "pistols and carbines"; and another old woman, Lecha, "is concentrating on finding a good vein for Seese to inject the early-evening Demerol" (19). Zeta blends her voice with Lecha's to describe the scene in the kitchen: "No food anywhere. Pistols, shotguns, and cartridges scattered on the kitchen counters, and needles and pills all over the table. The Devil's kitchen doesn't look this good" (20). The narrator is an external focalizer standing outside the scene. Although she supplies a small amount of background information, she does not penetrate the characters' consciousness nor does she evaluate their actions. The narrator functions merely as an impartial reporter and offers readers no easily penetrable point of entry into the world of the narrative.

When focalization shifts to Seese, however, she assumes the role as guide to the world of the narrative and fosters an intimate relationship with readers by sharing her inner life with us. As a result of this intimate relationship, we are predisposed to trust her and to sympathize with her. Because she is the first character to open herself to us, to share her memories and her fears, we tend to consider her the heroine, to compare other characters to her, and to judge them, as we did Tayo in *Ceremony*, according to their relationship with her. Bal points out that:

> Character-bound focalization (CF) can vary, can shift from one character to another. In such cases, we may be given a good picture of the origins of a conflict. We are shown how differently the various characters view the same facts. This technique

can result in neutrality towards the characters. *Nevertheless, there usually is never a doubt in our minds which character should receive most attention and sympathy.* On the grounds of distribution, for instance the fact that a character focalizes the first and/or the last chapter, we label it the hero(ine) of the book. (105; emphasis added)

The narrator uses character-bound focalization to encourage us early in our reading to consider Seese as *Almanac*'s heroine. However, after book 4, Seese vanishes; when she reappears, her importance is diminished and she no longer resembles a heroine. As a result, we must seek out other characters with whom we can align ourselves and through whose perceptions the narrative will become intelligible.

Although the narrator treats all characters with apparent neutrality, she uses Seese, in the first four books of the text, to establish a set of norms against which readers may judge other characters as good or as evil. Upon entry into the world of the text, each reader brings a set of moral standards, which for many readers are the standards of white, middle-class, North American society. Although not all readers accept the premises on which mainstream society bases its standards, most readers certainly understand what those standards are, and although contradictory ones exist, they are not, in this society, the norm. Almost all readers understand that the dominant society privileges forces that bring forth life over ones that cause death. *Almanac* exploits readers' knowledge of the dominant society's moral code while blurring the boundaries between good and evil.

According to mainstream society's standards, Seese, a drug addict, a prostitute, and a weak woman, is a character few readers would admire. However, through her focalization of Seese's inner life, the narrator covertly champions her as a life-force character by emphasizing both her heterosexuality and her role as a mother. By drawing our attention to Seese's heterosexuality, the narrator implies that if she were not a heterosexual she would be a death-force character. The narrator relates Seese's memory of her first encounter with Zeta, the elderly Mixedblood gunrunner, who we learn mistakenly suspected her of being her sister Lecha's lesbian lover. Then, the narrator emphasizes her role as a life-giver by revealing that she is a well-intentioned and relatively good mother for having given up cocaine to search for her missing son. Seese resists her addiction (which the narrator considers a death force when used for amusement rather than for ceremonial purposes) and has "weaned herself down to glasses of burgundy and fat marijuana cigarettes" (22). The narrator exploits the readers' familiarity with the values of mainstream society to encourage us to favour Seese, as a life-giver, over other characters who do not manifest this quality. Despite Seese's obvious shortcomings according to this same value system, the narrator, in her characterization of Seese, establishes the textual norms for good.

Characterization of Beaufrey, the aristocratic pornography czar, contrasts sharply with that of Seese because Beaufrey is a death-force character. The narrator employs narrative strategies that make it clear that readers should approve neither of him nor that segment of society of which he claims membership. The narrator does not accord Beaufrey the privileged position of first focalizer, as she does for Seese, and focalization does not shift to Beaufrey until book 4 of part 1. Instead, the narrator effects her initial characterization of Beaufrey through Seese's memories of him. These memories not only supply us with our initial information about Beaufrey, but also imply an assessment of his character. By labelling Beaufrey "David's faggot lover" (22), the narrator capitalizes on mainstream society's deep-seated prejudice against homosexuals and insinuates that, because of his sexual preferences, he cannot be a life-giving character. Furthermore, the narrator draws upon Seese's memories of Beaufrey to stigmatize him as a death-force character. Seese remembers that Beaufrey, knowing the full extent of her addiction, gave her a kilo of cocaine as "a 'go-away' present" that she believes he intended as "a suicide kit" (22). Because readers already sympathize with Seese, we are predisposed to accept her assessment of Beaufrey and to dislike any character who means her harm. In the first four pages of the text, then, the narrator establishes both Seese's and Beaufrey's characters as binary opposites that constitute the opposing poles of the moral continuum of the text. Granted, the moral continuum seems to be a lopsided one, according to the standards of the dominant society, because Seese has enormous character flaws. However, she is no more flawed than any other character in the text and substantially less than most.

Throughout part 1, the narrator uses Seese's memories to characterize Beaufrey. As Seese remembers her life in San Diego with David, Beaufrey, and Eric, she offers plausible explanations for Beaufrey's actions. His behaviour during her first pregnancy leads her to conclude that he is jealous of her relationship with David and is insecure about his own. Beaufrey encouraged her to have an abortion, and nightmares of him standing "near the bed holding a white porcelain basin" still haunt her (52). To her, Beaufrey's behaviour clearly demonstrates that he loves David and does not want to share him. When she becomes pregnant a second time and refuses to have an abortion, she interprets Beaufrey's anger as a sign of his reluctance to share David's love with her and the child. The narrator draws on Seese's memories of another character to support Seese's characterization of Beaufrey as an insecure, aging homosexual. Until focalization switches to Beaufrey, readers must trust Seese's memories for information.

Beaufrey plays a prominent role in Seese's memories because she suspects him of being partly responsible for the disappearance of her baby, Monte. She believes that, when fleeing the country with David, Beaufrey "had taken Monte or hired someone to take Monte, but then something terrible had gone wrong" (44). Seese suggests that Beaufrey is capable of facilitating events that could result in death. It is not until much later in the text that the narrator reveals that Seese has naïvely misunderstood Beaufrey completely. Only when focalization shifts to Beaufrey himself do we realize how wrong Seese's explanations are; she does not suspect the extent of Beaufrey's depravity. Thus, we see that the narrator has led us down a false trail by encouraging us to rely on someone who does not understand the situation. We learn that Seese has misinterpreted Beaufrey's actions in a number of significant ways, not because she is an unreliable narrator who deceives us intentionally, but because she is naïve, someone who is basically good and not familiar with this level of evil.

First of all, Seese believes that Beaufrey hates her because he considers her a rival for David's affections and that his hatred for her arises from his love for David. Beaufrey, however, is not in love with David. Although having sex with David amuses him, Beaufrey regards their relationship as part of a larger game: "The idea of the game was to permit gorgeous young men such as David to misunderstand their importance in the world. . . . Beaufrey loved the theatre. Players such as Eric or David and the cunt [Seese] were a dime a dozen; Beaufrey was the director and author; he was the producer" (537). Monte's kidnapping is merely one of Beaufrey's real-life theatrical productions in which David and Seese unwittingly take the lead roles. Not only does the kidnapping furnish Beaufrey with the power to hurt "the cunt," it allows him to manipulate David's emotions for his own amusement. Always a pragmatist, Beaufrey has the child killed when the infant's needs begin to interfere with his own sexual ones. He harvests Monte's organs in order to sell them, and films the entire procedure for further profit.

Although Seese and Beaufrey function mimetically in that both are complex characters that resemble actual people, they neither develop nor change during the course of the narrative. Instead, they function thematically to represent the social groups to which they belong. James Phelan explains: "Thematic dimensions are traits, taken individually or collectively, viewed as dramatizations of ideas or as representative of a whole class of people. . . . In works that strive to give characters a strong overt mimetic function, thematic functions develop from thematic dimensions as a character's traits and actions serve to demonstrate, usually implicitly, some proposition or propositions about the class of people or the dramatized ideas" ("Thematic Reference" 358). The narrator's attitude towards Seese and Beaufrey reveals her attitude towards the classes that they represent. In class, as in character, Seese and Beaufrey are situated at opposite poles.

Through her characterization of Seese, the narrator exposes the alienation that distinguishes the working and middle classes of American society. She describes how Seese, having grown up in a military family, has her life disrupted by constant moves and frequent separations. Her mother, lonely and bitter, divorces her father but marries another military man who is just like him, and the cycle of displacement continues. Neither Seese nor her parents have any ties to family or location. The narrator uses Seese's memories of her childhood to stress that, like many people in North American society, especially those of European descent, the members of her family are isolated and without history, roots, and community. Seese finds this life intolerable, and leaves to seek something better, but all she finds is the dubious camaraderie of life on the street.

Through her reporting of Seese's memories, the narrator traces a series of desperate attempts to find her place in the community, attempts that culminate in the birth of Seese's son. The narrator suggests that Seese's inability to achieve a sense of belonging results from her inability to see her place in the larger community. Seese cannot understand that the defects in her life mirror the defects in her society, and that the defects in the larger society result from its historical evolution. While typing an old almanac for Zeta's twin, Lecha, Seese is presented with an opportunity to understand, but she can do nothing but retreat in fear. The almanac, displaying no pity for frail human emotions, grants her a vision of her son and his fate, but Seese can only react in anger and return to cocaine to hide from her pain. Like her drugs, the almanac has "an almost narcotic effect on her" (592). Raised in the typical American nuclear family, a social institution that strives to be independent and self-contained, Seese finds herself alienated within a larger community of lost people and believes that "she had no one left, nothing to live for with Monte gone" (595). Although the narrator uses Seese at the beginning of the text to establish the opposition between life and death forces and to set the standard for goodness, her dominant trait, in the end, is her ineffectuality. Thus, she becomes a mere appendage to Lecha because she cannot understand where she is and because she has nowhere else to go.

The narrator uses Beaufrey's characterization to demonstrate certain propositions about the aristocracy, the social class to which he claims membership. The narrator insinuates that Beaufrey's individual selfishness, his callousness, and his avarice represent the selfishness, callousness, and avarice of the European aristocracy that colonized the Americas. Beaufrey contends that certain of his character traits are a natural result of his aristocratic lineage, and he believes that other blue bloods share similar features. For example, the narrator draws our attention to the traits that Beaufrey has in common with his childhood hero, Albert Fish — a child molester and a cannibal directly descended from a family that arrived on the *Mayflower*. Both lack sensitivity; both lust for the forbidden; and both believe themselves above the law of the common masses. By linking Beaufrey with Albert Fish and the European aristocracy, the narrator indicts an entire class for crimes against humanity. Beaufrey as an expert in depravity is almost incredible. The narrator ensures that his deeds are of the sort that offend even the most liberal reader. Beaufrey not only revels in his evil, he celebrates it without remorse. Because Beaufrey sets the standard for evil within the text, we are compelled to compare other characters to him, especially other aristocrats. Unlike Seese, Beaufrey has a very definite understanding of his place in history, and although he focalizes only two short sections of the text, the narrator uses him, and by implication the colonial aristocracy, to exemplify evil.

The narrator uses her characterization of Serlo to support both her characterization of Beaufrey and her argument that the colonial aristocracy is evil. At first, Serlo seems an unimportant character, merely a member of Beaufrey's entourage, but when the narrator shifts focalization to him, his character becomes fully realized. Like their colonial forefathers, Serlo and his allies fear the black and brown peoples of the world, and in an effort to save themselves and their class they destroy both humanity and the Earth herself. Like Beaufrey, Serlo is a death-force character in that he rejects the life-giver role of both women and Mother Earth. The narrator reveals that Serlo learned his attitudes from his grandfather, who "had looked far into the future and had seen that reproduction needn't involve the repulsive touch and stink of sex with a woman" (547). Following in this tradition, Serlo unites with a group of like-minded aristocrats who apply modern technology to improve what they believe are weaknesses in the natural order. The narrator underscores the hubris in Serlo's — and by implication the aristocracy's — attitude to creation. Serlo's group believes that it can even replicate the life-giving function of the Earth and plans to steal what it needs to escape the poor masses of black and brown people and to preserve the prevailing social hierarchy. In case its other strategies fail, the group aims to create "Alternative Earth modules," which "would be loaded with the last of the earth's uncontaminated soil, water, and oxygen" (542).

The narrator parallels Serlo's rejection of the Earth with his rejection of women to stress both his own and the aristocracy's role as destroyers. Serlo uses scientific jargon to justify his belief in thinking that there is "a strict biological order to the natural world; in this natural order, only *sangre pura* sufficed to command instinctive obedience from the masses" (549). Yet for all their scrambling to survive, Serlo and his peers realize that not only do they belong to an endangered species that is unable to evolve, but they have also lost the little that was good and honourable in the attitudes of their colonial forefathers. Serlo thinks: "Yellows, browns, and blacks, let them slaughter one another. The agenda was concerned with survival, not justice. The old man had taught Serlo years before that to kill a man was unjust in the first place, so why bother about rules of 'fair play'"? (546). In these ways, the narrator insinuates that Serlo and his aristocratic compatriots are in a state of moral and physical devolution, which will inevitably lead to their extinction.

Although not all of *Almanac*'s villains claim direct links to European aristocracy and colonialism, those links still exist. Leah Blue, for example, is a real estate mogul with a typically imperialistic attitude towards the Earth. To her, the Earth is a potential source of financial gain, not a source of life. By shifting focalization to Leah, the narrator reveals that, like the Europeans who colonized the Americas, Leah considers the land an antagonistic force, an untamed wilderness that she must civilize. She believes that if she dislikes the landscape of the desert, her money gives her both the power and the right to alter it. Thus, she makes plans to replicate Venice in the heart of the Arizona desert. However, to realize her "grand scheme" Leah must drill deep wells that will access saline water, which will then pollute the surface water (375). So by drilling the deep-water wells necessary to create Venice, Arizona, Leah commits a symbolic rape of Mother Earth. Still, many readers would not consider her attitude a hubristic one or her actions criminal because big business and its development is, after all, highly revered in the world outside the text.

To support her indictment of Leah and to convince readers of both Leah's villainy and the villainy of the landholding social class that she represents, the narrator situates her among an assemblage of characters whose actions are morally reprehensible according to the standards of mainstream society. Leah's husband, Max, for instance, belongs to one of the most infamous of European criminal organizations, the Mafia, and works as a hit man for corrupt government agencies. Through his connections, Leah is able to obtain the legal consent necessary to begin construction of her city. An associate of Max's, Judge Arne, anxious to curry the favour of the notorious Max Blue, sets a legal precedent — which will ultimately legalize Leah's deep wells — by dismissing the water-rights case of a group of Nevada Indians against a similar real estate developer.

To undermine any credibility that Arne might possess in the eyes of readers who respect the judiciary, the narrator recounts in detail his sexual routines, which are perverted according to mainstream morality. The narrator stresses that Arne's perversions, like Serlo's, are part of a tradition that has been passed down through the generations. Arne's grandfather, like Serlo's, teaches him to seek unnatural outlets for his sexual appetites and to reject the life-giving role that he, as a male, could play. While Serlo's grandfather teaches him to embrace the "sterile, prewarmed stainless steel cylinders used for the artificial insemination of cattle" (547), Arne's grandfather teaches him the pleasures of copulating with domestic animals. By detailing Arne's legal and sexual perversions, the narrator not only attacks him, but she also vilifies his profession, his class, and his associate, Leah Blue. Realizing that some readers might consider Leah a successful businesswoman who succeeds in a male-dominated profession rather than a villain who perpetrates crimes against the Earth, the narrator launches an oblique attack against her that undermines her character by making her guilty of associating with characters who are unquestionably despicable. As a result, the narrator strengthens the link, which she begins to construct in her characterization of Serlo, between crimes against humanity and crimes against the Earth.

The narrator's treatment of the Indigenous characters differs radically from that of the other characters in the text. The narrator allows those Indigenous characters who resist the colonial aristocracy to grow when they begin to understand the roles they must play in the continuing Indigenous resistance to colonialism. It is not until the text nears its end that the narrator reveals that *Almanac*'s true heroes and heroines are the Indigenous peoples who grow and change by developing an understanding of the history of the Americas and of their place in it. At the beginning of the text, Zeta and her associate, Calabazas, claim to be exercising their resistance by smuggling drugs and artefacts from Mexico into the United States. Both recognize that the American and Mexican governments have stolen Indian land and murdered Indian people, and both claim that they smuggle in retaliation. They call themselves subversives because they refuse to recognize the border between the United States and Mexico. Like the villains, these characters learn their attitudes and behaviours from their ancestors. Remembering what her grandmother Yoeme would say, Zeta asks, "How could one steal if the government itself was the worst thief?" (133).

Yet Zeta is not the champion of the people that she claims to be. The narrator situates her on an isolated ranch with only her adopted son and her employees around her. Zeta has little contact with anyone; she is especially isolated from the people for whom she professes to be fighting. Furthermore, at the beginning of the narrative Zeta can only "recite Yoeme's arguments" without truly understanding them, and calls her grandmother's legal theories "crazed" (133). She smuggles, although she knows that her grandmother does not consider the smuggling of artefacts a true act of resistance because "Old Yoeme had made a big point of shaming those who would sell the last few objects of the people who had been destroyed and worlds that had been destroyed by Europeans" (128). Initially, the narrator suggests that Zeta and Calabazas are not true revolutionaries because their actions benefit only a few and their main goal is material gain. Rather than using the profit from her smuggling to help her people, Zeta invests it in gold and guns, which she hoards in an abandoned mine shaft on her property. Similarly, Calabazas does little with the earnings from his schemes that really benefits his people. Granted, he employs his in-laws, but not out of concern for their welfare. Calabazas is a cynic who "had always had the philosophy it was better to put in-laws to work for you. . . . It made the prospect of betrayal less likely" (238). For the most part, Calabazas's money either goes back into his business or is used to provide his employees with drugs and alcohol. Although both Zeta and Calabazas have been educated by the elders, they either ignore or reject the history of the people and think only of themselves. At *Almanac*'s beginning, the narrator gives no indication that these characters are capable of change and provides little information to distinguish them from the villains.

Towards the end of the text, however, the narrator reveals that both Zeta and Calabazas are not static characters, that they are capable of change. Zeta is first prompted to change when she sees her adopted son devastated by his lover's murder at the hands of the police. Until the moment that she sees Ferro in the throes of grief, Zeta has never been a real mother to him. Although she has taken care of his physical needs, she has ignored his emotional ones, treating him as a burden rather than a person. When Ferro's anger over Jamey's death turns to plans for vengeance, Zeta fears for his life and realizes that she does indeed love him. Her priorities change, and she turns into the mother that she has never been in spirit. Her eyes open, and although she has never brought life into this world, she becomes a life-force character whose change in outlook generates a change in action. She kills Greenlee, the racist gun dealer whom she has tolerated for years. She attends the International Holistic Healers Convention along with Calabazas, something that neither of them would have considered doing in the past. Her sister, Lecha, is amazed at this change in behaviour and concludes that "the earth must truly be in crisis for both Zeta and Calabazas to be attending this convention" (719).

Through their contact with the like-minded people they meet at the convention, Zeta and Calabazas begin to see that they are a small part of a larger movement rather than isolated individuals carrying out futile acts of subversion. As a young man, Calabazas rejected the knowledge of the old ones, but now "he had been listening to his loco lieutenant, Mosca, who had wild stories about a barefooted Hopi with radical schemes, and new reports about the spirit macaws carried by the twin brothers on a sacred journey north accompanied by thousands of the faithful" (719). The discussions that occur at the conference both put into perspective the knowledge that Zeta and

Calabazas received as children from their grandparents and update it. Zeta and Calabazas learn that the story of the people is not a relic of the past, for as long as it endures in the memories of the people it lives. The narrator demonstrates that Zeta and Calabazas can change only by understanding that they are part of the people, part of the land, and part of the story.

Although the narrative begins with Seese occupying the position of primary character-focalizer, Zeta's Laguna handyman, Sterling, emerges as a character of equal magnitude because he is both the second character-focalizer and the last. Unlike the other characters whom the narrator introduces through Seese's memories and perceptions of them, Sterling is neither sinister nor enigmatic. When Seese sees him working on Zeta's ranch, she remarks to herself, "Sterling looks too harmless to be working here. He is graying and chubby and brown. His eyes look a little lost and sad. He rakes the pebbles and smaller rocks, and she can tell he knows how to appear busy when there is nothing to do. He sees her looking at him and gets bashful, looking down at the rocks he is raking" (22). Through Seese's interpretations of Sterling's demeanour, the narrator suggests that Sterling is a benign character. Still, the narrator reveals that Sterling is not a life-giving character, nor does he contribute to his community. His alienation from that community begins when he is very young. His parents die, and he leaves the reservation to attend the Indian boarding school. When he grows older he does not return; he instead chooses to isolate himself from both the Laguna people and the rest of society. By electing to live alone and refusing to marry, Sterling implicitly rejects life. Yet he minimizes the consequences of his decision, thinking that "His main trouble with marriage was that he was not used to telling anyone else what to do. . . . He was very happy going along on his own. He liked the simple life with his magazines, visits home to his old aunts, and the occasional vacation to Long Beach to ride the big roller coaster" (86). Sterling's choices are unacceptable according to the values of the text, and his story is didactic because events conspire to teach him a lesson. The narrator suggests that Sterling's exile from Laguna is an indirect result of his choices. When the tribal council accuses him of crimes against the people, he finds that because he has isolated himself from his relatives and because he has no wife and no children, no one steps forward in his defence. After spending his life believing that he can remain uninvolved in life, Sterling learns that he has deluded himself.

The events of the entire narrative have a profound effect upon

Sterling. Because the narrator focalizes the final two chapters through Sterling's perceptions, most readers tend to interpret all previous information with its effect on Sterling in mind. The narrator emphasizes that throughout his life Sterling has ignored much of the history of his people, which is available to him through the Laguna oral tradition, and has instead accepted the piecemeal history presented in popular detective magazines such as the *Police Gazette*. When the stone snake appears on the Laguna reservation, Sterling's life changes. A Hollywood movie crew films the snake and prompts the tribal council to banish Sterling, while the appearance of the snake itself calls into question the history that Sterling has chosen to embrace. Although he tries not to, Sterling spends much of his time at Zeta's ranch trying to make sense of the events that have occurred in the last few years of his life. In the final chapters of the text, when he starts to understand that he, too, is a part of history, he becomes a dynamic character. He regrets the choices that he has made, and "tried to remember more of the stories the old people used to tell; he wished he had listened more closely because he vaguely recalled a connection the giant snake had with Mexico" (759). When he returns to the reservation, the narrator stresses how his appearance, his behaviour, and his understanding of his life's story have changed. Returning to the history of the Indigenous peoples enables Sterling to understand his life and enables him to hope for change.

Narration of *Almanac*'s dynamic characters differs from that of its static ones in that it contains not only the voice of the narrator and the character focalizer, but also the voices from the characters' past. The narrator demonstrates that as long as the old stories continue to live in the minds of the characters they continue to exist, and as a result affect both character and plot. Zeta, Calabazas, and Sterling — all dynamic characters — eventually look to the stories from their youth to supply answers to the problems of the present. Whether they live in this world or in the land of the dead, their ancestors are ready to guide them through the stories. The narrator implies that although each character has the ability to choose good or evil much of what that person does is determined by the deeds of his or her ancestors. Despite their past transgressions, the Indigenous characters have the potential to be good because they come from good people. Still, being an Indigenous person does not guarantee that a character will be good, even if that character has access to the old stories. The villains we have examined function both mimetically, in that they create the illusion of unique and believable individuals, and thematically, in that they represent their social class. Because all are wealthy, white landowners, the narrator seems to be delivering a message about the villainy of the colonial aristocracy. But the narrator does not reduce the conflict between good and evil to one of brown against white. Indeed, she spends all of part 2 and a significant portion of part 4 exploring the villainy and colonial mentality of a prominent group of Indigenous characters.

Like the other characters who are capable of growth and change, Menardo learns the culture and the stories of the Indigenous peoples through the oral tradition, but Menardo is neither dynamic nor good. His grandfather, a descendant of the Maya from Chiapas, shares with him the predictions of the ancestors who foresaw the approach of the catastrophic times that followed the Indigenous peoples' first contact with Europeans, "The time called Death-Eye Dog" and "The Reign of Fire-Eye Macaw" (257). Menardo's grandfather teaches him the Mayan belief that "The only true gods were all the days in the Long Count, and no single epoch or time of a world was vast enough or deep enough to call itself God alone" (257–58). However, Menardo's world is full of contradictions, and his grandfather is not his only influence. Menardo attends a school run by Catholic brothers. Here "one of the teaching Brothers" gives the students "a long lecture about pagan people and pagan stories," and the older boys call Menardo "Flat Nose" (258), a racist term they reserve for Indians. Only when this happens does he realize that "the people the old man called 'our ancestors,' 'our family,' were in fact Indians. All along Menardo had been listening to the one who was responsible for the taunts of the others" (259). As a result, he shuns his grandfather and rejects his heritage, hoping to pass for "one of the *sangre limpia*" by claiming that a boxing accident has caused his nose to be flat (259). The narrator uses Mendardo to demonstrate that the battle between good and evil in the text is not purely a racial one.

Like the other villains, Menardo functions mimetically, in that he seems to be a plausible character, and thematically, in that he represents a particular social group. The group to which Menardo belongs comprises Indigenous people who reject their heritage and adopt the ways of the colonizers. The narrator demonstrates how, from the moment he first claims that his nose was broken in a boxing match, Menardo's compulsion to divorce himself from his Mayan roots influences every aspect of his life. He faces discrimination and humiliation to accumulate a fortune, which he hopes will elevate his social status. He marries a woman whose family members consider themselves better than he is and who have reminded her, "every day since she was three years old, that her great-great-grandfather on her mother's side had descended from the conquistador De Onate" (269). Determined to escape his roots, Menardo becomes a financial success, a man who is " 'self-made' . . . which meant here was a man of darker skin and lower class who had managed to amass a large fortune" (277). His business is insurance, and he insures against both natural disasters and man-made ones, especially those triggered by the Indigenous people who are rebelling against the oppression of the colonial system. He claims to insure against losses from "thieves calling themselves 'revolutionaries' and 'the wave of the future'" (261). But rather than emphasizing the role Menardo plays in oppressing his people, the narrator downplays his crimes against humanity and emphasizes, instead, how pathetic he is. The narrator treats Menardo sympathetically in comparison to the aristocratic characters of European ancestry, and saves her most severe condemnation of Indigenous characters for Menardo's compatriots in El Grupo, the ruling elite of Tuxtla Gutierrez.

The narrator treats the villainous Mixedbloods who belong to El Grupo in a different way than she does any other characters in the text by employing tactics that resemble those used in the oral tradition of American Indigenous peoples. Rather than creating distinct individuals, she devises generic characters distinguishable only by occupation. Thus El Grupo's members could be any governor, any police chief, any judge, or any former ambassador residing in Mexico or any South or Central American country. The governor could be any politician whose actions and words contradict each other. Like all of El Grupo's members, the governor, in difficult economic times, concludes that "the Mexican economy is a sinking ship. . . . He will embrace Mexico and love her, but his money goes to a safe place" across the border (331).

Likewise, the police chief could be any public official intoxicated with the power he wields over life and death and who justifies his videotaping of the interrogation and torture of prisoners because the videotape is an "official record" that he believes can "educate the people about the consequences of political extremism" (344, 342). The narrator uses an ironic tone to divulge that the police chief lies not only to others but also to himself. She explains that he is compelled to watch, over and over again, a videotape of his junior officers whipping a young whore who has "hard upturned breasts" because he must evaluate their interrogation techniques, not because he finds it sexually stimulating (341). These characters illustrate the corruption of an upper class that rationalizes its unscrupulous actions by claiming to be acting in the best interests of the state. All members of El Grupo rationalize their actions by arguing that "Theirs is a business of the most serious nature: they govern the many; all the more reason they had to fortify, even indulge, themselves in every way" (330). Their very identities, however, are lies because they deny their mixed ancestry. Characterization of El Grupo members differs from that of other villains because with it *Almanac*'s narrator does not make yet another surreptitious attack on the many generations of colonial aristocracy. Instead, she mounts a direct frontal attack on those Indigenous people who venerate the colonizers and emulate their behaviour.

In *Almanac of the Dead*, Silko both describes the rhetorical battle for the minds of the Indigenous inhabitants of the Americas and participates in it by trying to persuade readers to accept the subversive ideologies present within the text. *Almanac* has a definite ideological agenda in that it tries "to persuade [its] readers of the 'correctness' of a particular way of interpreting the world" (Suleiman 1), a way that both champions the belief systems of Indigenous peoples and challenges them to adapt and survive. In *Almanac*, Silko proposes an ideology that is more syncretic, perhaps, than those in her earlier works, but she situates it in a novel that, to many, would seem anything but optimistic. To many readers, especially the descendants of the European colonizers, this work may seem apocalyptic in its forecasting of the destruction of contemporary society in the Americas. Based on the prophecies of the Maya, the Aztec, and the Inca, *Almanac* predicts that the colonizers' culture, vulnerable to attack from within and without, will soon vanish because of its greed, a greed that has led to crimes against humanity and against Mother Earth. It predicts that Indigenous peoples will play a significant role in the next American society and anticipates that much of the Americas will be populated by an assortment of Mixedbloods of all combinations.

NOTES

[1] This article is an adaptation of chapters 1, 4, and 5 of my master's thesis, University of Regina, 1994.

[2] Silko would probably agree that her works are subversive. In an interview with Laura Coltelli, she says art is a more effective vehicle to bring about social change on behalf of Indigenous peoples than political

confrontation like that employed by the American Indian Movement: "Certainly, for me the most effective political statement I could make is in my art work. I believe in subversion rather than straight-out confrontation" (147).

3 For the sake of convenience, I will refer to this fusion as "the narrator."

4 Mieke Bal says that "When focalization lies with one character which participates in the fabula as an actor, we could refer to *internal* focalization. We can indicate by means of the term *external* focalization that an anonymous agent, situated outside the fabula, is functioning as the focalizer" (105).

WORKS CITED

Bal, Mieke. *Narratology: Introduction to the Theory of Narrative*. Trans. Christine van Boheemen. Toronto: U of Toronto P, 1985. Trans. of *De theorie van vertellen en verhalen*. 2nd ed. Muiderberg: Coutinho, 1980.
Belsey, Catherine. "Constructing the Subject, Deconstructing the Text." *Feminist Criticism and Social Change*. Ed. Judith Newton and Deborah Rosenfelt. London: Methuen, 1985. 45–64.
——. *Critical Practice*. London: Routledge, 1980.
Bercovitch, Sacvan. "The Problem of Ideology in American Literary History." *Critical Inquiry* 12 (1986): 631–53.
Booth, Wayne C. *The Rhetoric of Fiction*. 2nd ed. Chicago: U of Chicago P, 1983.
Lanser, Susan Sniader. *Fictions of Authority: Women Writers and Narrative Voice*. Ithaca: Cornell UP, 1992.
——. *The Narrative Act: Point of View in Prose Fiction*. Princeton: Princeton UP, 1981.
Phelan, James. "Character, Progression, and the Mimetic-Didactic Distinction." *Modern Philology* 84 (1987): 282–99.
——. "Thematic Reference, Literary Structure, and Fictive Character: An Examination of Interrelationships." *Semiotica* 48.3–4 (1984): 345–65.
Silko, Leslie Marmon. *Almanac of the Dead*. New York: Simon, 1991.
——. *Ceremony*. Markham, ON: Penguin, 1977.
——. "Leslie Marmon Silko." With Laura Coltelli. *Winged Words: American Indian Writers Speak*. Ed. Coltelli. Lincoln: U of Nebraska P, 1990. 135–53.
——. *Storyteller*. New York: Arcade, 1981.
Suleiman, Susan Rubin. *Authoritarian Fictions: The Ideological Novel as a Literary Genre*. New York: Columbia UP, 1983.
Thom, Jo-Ann. "Study of Narrative Voice, Discursive Authority and Ideology in the Works of Leslie Marmon Silko." MA thesis. University of Regina, 1980.

Beginner's Mind:
Learning to Read the
Ghost Dance Songs

CHARLOTTE HUSSEY

Recently, while delivering a paper on Margaret Sam-Cromarty at a writer's retreat for the alumni of a well-known American MFA program, I was appalled at my colleagues' lack of interest in this East James Bay Cree poet's work. Only four people showed up, while numbers flocked to such topics as "How to Get More Humour in Your Poetry" or "Prozac, Mood Swings, and the Contemporary Poet." Finally, an apologetic friend admitted she found Native writing flat and inaccessible. She just couldn't relate.

Unlike her, I have taught on Cree, Algonquin, and Mohawk reserves — an initiation that has led me to approach Native texts and culture with what Zen poet Margaret Gibson calls a "beginner' mind" — as when: "Suddenly I hold everything / I know, myself most of all, / in question" (90). Such a mind requires a sort of never-ending readjustment to things — blizzards that strand you in remote, northern communities, or that sleep-inducing lesson plan (the one that worked so well down south) that must be overhauled completely on the spot. Often I have prayed for John Keats's *"negative capability"* — in order to face the inevitable "uncertainties, mysteries, doubts, without any irritable reaching after fact and reason" (62). This desire to face what makes one uncertain and, at times, "irritable" leads me to say something about the way I had unconsciously structured this essay. While editing it for publication, I suddenly realized that its end — the place of greatest emphasis — did not stress the vitality of "a continuing tradition" that Creek/Cherokee critic Ward Churchill points to in the Ghost Dance Songs (162). Rather, it emphasized what is less threatening to whites — that tone of lamentation and despair that expresses the underside of Native assertion and prophecy. Before the final rewrite, I had ended this text with a song that portrays the saintly Native who, in spite of his or her poverty, offers up a prayer "for every living creature" (Mooney 316)! Was this my bid to be forgiven for what my forebears had done to Native peoples?

Thus, with a kind of reverential bafflement, I offer up this, my socially constructed reading of a Native classic — the messianic Ghost Dance Songs. In so doing, I want to apologize to Native readers for my blind spots while, at the same time, inviting non-Natives, like myself, to read a highly undervalued and misunderstood discourse. According to Churchill, the spirit of the Ghost Dance continues to be a primary source of inspiration for contemporary Native poetry. As such, it encourages a "call to active resistance" (164), and a "continuous assertion of Indianness" (165). The Ghost Dance Songs, then, are as important to our understanding of Native literatures as Wordsworth's *The Prelude* is to our study of English poetry.

Do my American friends dismiss Native texts because they feel indicted by them? And, do they disregard the Ghost Dance Songs because the communal chant rhythms found in such traditional oraliture have dwindled away to all but a ghostly whisper in contemporary mainstream poetry? Some chantlike reverberations do occur in the biblical cadences of Whitman, the near tribal catalogues of Ginsberg, and the curses and beats of the mean-streets poetry of Imamu Amiri Baraka (LeRoi Jones). But in most contemporary poems, as critic Andrew Welsh points out, one finds "the Image rather than a rushing rhythm; the precision of careful thought rather than repetition, catalogue, or incantation; autonomy . . . rather than *participation mystique* of the communal voice" (187).

In our postindustrial culture, we too often dismiss Native discourse because our literati espouse a poetics of self-expression. As Native literary critic Paula Gunn Allen explains:

> The purpose of Native American literature is never one of pure self-expression. The "private soul at any public wall" is a concept that is so alien to Native thought as to constitute an absurdity. The tribes do not celebrate the individual's ability to feel emotion, for it is assumed that all people are able to do so, making expression of this basic ability arrogant, presumptuous, and gratuitous. Besides one's emotions are one's own: to suggest that another should imitate them is an imposition on the personal integrity of others. (174)

In his book *Roots of the Lyric: Primitive Poetry and Modern Poetics*, Welsh stresses that we must consider the communal chant an important source for our modern lyric poem. One of the examples he alludes to but does not develop in detail is the Ghost Dance Songs. And, although unwisely calling the chant a "primitive" genre, Welsh does offer an instructive definition.

For Welsh, one characteristic of the chant is that its "words are strongly controlled by rhythms derived from music and dance" (162). For example, parallelism and repetition create strong, regular cadences to steady a dancer's steps. And often these incantatory rhythms supersede the precision of a chant's meanings. This can be seen in the following Arapaho Ghost Dance Song, where sounds, such as the *"He'eye'!"* act primarily as rhythm markers:

> O, my children! O, my children!
> Here is another of your pipes — *He'eye'*!
> Here is another of your pipes — *He'eye'*!
> Look! thus I shouted — *He'eye'*!
> Look! thus I shouted — *He'eye'*!
> When I move the earth — *He'eye'*!
> When I move the earth — *He'eye'*! (Mooney 206)

Welsh writes that the chant's hypnotic rhythms act as "a public power which joins together the members of a society" (165) addressed in these quoted lines as the "O, my children! O, my children!" Although tribal members undoubtedly possess a wealth of information about the society that inspired these Ghost Dance Songs, whites like myself continue to rely on such accessible documentations as those compiled by Irish immigrant and pioneer ethnologist James Mooney. Employed by the Bureau of American Ethnology, Mooney went west in the late 1880s to study the Ghost Dance phenomenon. The bureau also instructed him to assess the dreaded possibility of another Sioux uprising like that of the Minnesota and Santee Sioux that took place between 1862 and 1864 (Champagne 44). Highly sympathetic to these dispossessed Plains tribes whose plight was not unlike that of his own disinherited Irish forebears, Mooney spent some twenty-two months collecting songs and other ethnographic data not only from the Sioux, but also from other Siouan speakers such as the Omaha, Crow, and Winnebago (*Native Tribes* 66, 32). He also collected Ghost Dance Songs from such Caddoan peoples as the Pawnee and Wichita, from the Algonkian bands of the Arapaho and Cheyenne, as well as from the Shoshonean-speaking Comanche, among other Plains peoples (*Native Tribes* 66, 85).

To further complicate our growing bafflement, Mooney, our source for Plains culture in the late nineteenth century, is obviously a white ethnographer. Having worked with a number of unnamed Native informants, he offers us at best a rough translation of the Plains peoples' dialects and ways. Nevertheless, his detailed documentation is still regarded by many as one of the primary sources of information about the Ghost Dance phenomenon. Clearly, Mooney's research delineates white civilization's violent encroachment upon these prairie peoples. The Siouan-speaking tribes, for example, had reigned supreme on the Great Plains for centuries, ruling territories stretching "from Minnesota to the Rocky mountains and from the Yellowstone to the Platte" (Mooney 69). "Millions of buffalo to furnish unlimited food supply," continues Mooney, "thousands of horses and hundreds of miles of free range made the Sioux, up to the year 1868, the richest and most prosperous, the proudest, and withal, perhaps, the wildest of all the tribes of the plains" (69).

Railroads, emigrant settlements, and buffalo-hunting whites began swallowing up Native land and laying waste to their game supplies. "By the late 1880s," reports *The Native North American Indian Almanac*, "there were only about one thousand buffalo left" (Champagne 47). And, by 1868, some of the Sioux and Cheyenne chiefs had signed the Treaty of Fort Laramie (Champagne 45), which relegated them to a reserve "which embraced all of the present state of South Dakota west of the Missouri River" (Mooney 69). The gold discovered in the Sioux's "Paha Sapa" (Champagne 45), or sacred Black Hills, led to "the Custer war and massacre" in 1876 and resulted in the Sioux's loss "of one-third of their guaranteed reservation, including the Black hills" (Mooney 70).

Commissioner of Indian Affairs Morgan, in his 1891 annual report to the American secretary of the interior, describes the Sioux's dismal state at the time of the Mooney study:

> Within eight years from the agreement of 1876 the buffalo had gone, and the Sioux had left to them alkali land and government rations. It is hard to overestimate the magnitude of the calamity, as they view it, which happened to these people by the sudden disappearance of the buffalo and the large diminution in the numbers of deer and other wild animals. Suddenly, almost without warning, they were expected at once and without previous training to settle down to the pursuits of agriculture in a land largely unfitted for such use. The freedom of the chase was to be exchanged for the idleness of the camp. The bound-

less range was to be abandoned for the circumscribed reservation, and abundance of plenty to be supplanted by limited and decreasing government subsistence and supplies. Under these circumstances it is not in human nature not to be discontented and restless, even turbulent and violent. (qtd. in Mooney 70)

The Sioux, along with numerous other disinherited Plains peoples, began to seek solace in the messianic promises of the prophet Wovoka (Mooney 2), whose Paiute name meant "the Woodcutter," and whose English one was "Jack Wilson." Wovoka possessed the same strong medicine as had his father, Numuraivo'o, "who could make rain and was 'bulletproof.'" Wovoka soon set about reviving the Ghost Dance Movement that another Paiute elder, Wodziwob, had started in 1870 (*Encyclopedia* 700–01). Wovoka told the Plains tribes who sought his council to abandon the futility of the warpath for his Ghost Dance religion. He asked them to lay down their war clubs and take up such mystical weaponry as the rituals and songs inspired by his night dreams and trance visions.

"During the solar eclipse of January 1, 1889," Wovoka received "his Great Revelation," a vision that became the cornerstone of his ministry. Stricken with fever, he allegedly died and ascended to heaven, where his deceased ancestors "lived." After they welcomed him enthusiastically, he met with God, who gave him certain instructions along with these "twin-powers: control over the natural elements, and the political status of the co-presidency of the United States" (*Encyclopedia* 700).

Returned to Earth, Wovoka promptly told his people that God wanted them to stop fighting the whites and to resume practice of "the traditional Round Dance" (*Encyclopedia* 700). If they followed this council, all their dead ancestors, reaching back to the beginning of time, would reawaken. Amassing as spirit armies, they were to arrive in our world accompanied by earthquakes, hurricanes, tornadoes, and other natural disasters. As his predecessor Wodziwob had promised, the cataclysmic return of these ancestral spirits would destroy white North America. Natives who carefully followed Wovoka's ritual prescriptions would sleep through this three-day apocalypse, awakening to "the restoration of the game and the return of the old-time primitive life" (Mooney 4). And, in this longed-for utopia, all born-agains "were to be white" (Mooney 4)!

In 1890, the Office of Indian Affairs banned the Ghost Dance, and the Seventh Cavalry brutally ended the Native resistance movement affiliated with it when they massacred some "three hundred Indian men, women and children" at Wounded Knee. Disturbed by how the Sioux had distorted his words to violent ends, Wovoka soon stopped his public proselytizing, but quietly continued his shamanic practices. He did offer to assist President Wilson during World War I "by freezing the Atlantic and sending Indians over to fight the Germans with ice." Finally, he predicted that an earthquake, signalling his ascent to heaven, would rock the Smith and Mason Valleys of western Nevada that had been his lifelong home. On 29 September 1932, Wovoka, the "weather prophet," died at the age of seventy-four. Three months later, the earthquake occurred (*Encyclopedia* 49, 701, 702).

Let's return now to 1889. It was the height of the Ghost Dance craze. While Wovoka was causing rain to fall on drought-stricken fields and rivers to ice over on hot July days (*Encyclopedia* 700), the rhythms of his Paiute songs were galvanizing a people, as Welsh sees the chant doing. Reinterpreted by the more warlike Siouan tribes, these traditional round-dance chants were forging a religious alliance based on the promised restoration of Native supremacy.

Given that the chant usually serves to rally members of an already somewhat homogenous society, Welsh explains that it draws on "the shared knowledge" of a group (175). Gunn Allen, while theorizing about literature in general, points to the fact that a particular genre, be it a lyric poem or a chant, "is a facet of a culture. . . . [A]nd its purpose is meaningful only when the assumptions it is based on are understood and accepted" (173). These Ghost Dance Songs, as we shall see, are founded on many cultural suppositions not immediately intelligible to someone unaccustomed to Plains Native ways. Mooney says the songs containing "special tribal mythologies, together with such innumerable references to old-time customs, ceremonies, and modes of life long since obsolete, make up a regular symposium of aboriginal thought and practice" (201). This Kiowa refrain shows that Wovoka's resurrection theology was not a new idea for the Plains peoples:

> I shall cut off his feet,
> I shall cut off his feet;
> I shall cut off his head,
> I shall cut off his head;
> He gets up again, He gets up again. (Mooney 320)

The song refers to a custom whereby if one kills a buffalo, one must leave behind its feet and head from which a new animal will spring.

This practice of displaying carcass tokens stems from a need to show respect for the dead animal, as well as from a belief commonly held across Native America that when a species, such as the buffalo, becomes scarce, it is not endangered but has chosen to disappear beyond the "horizon or in caves" in order to restore itself (Mooney 163). Thus, the ritual display of carcass parts mentioned in the preceding song was meant to encourage the buffalo's return.

The following Arapaho song also speaks of a practice based on a legend common to many North American Aboriginal groups:

> The sacred pipe tells me — *E'yahe' eye!*
> The sacred pipe tells me — *E'yahe' eye!*
>   Our father — *ya he' eye!*
>   Our father — *ya he'eye!*
> We shall surely be put again (with our friends)
> *E'yahe'eye!*
> We shall surely be put again (with our friends)
> *E'yahe'eye!*
>   Our father — *E'ya he'eye!*
>   Our father — *E'ya he'eye!* (Mooney 207)

Mooney reports at length about the ritual importance of "the *seicha*," or sacred flat pipe. A "medicine keeper" passes it "sunwise" around a prayer circle (208). Its smokers automatically associate the *seicha* with a well-known creation story in which Turtle swims up from the depths of the void, a bit of Earth resting upon its back. This piece of mud metamorphoses to become the Earth's landmass, symbolized by the *seicha* or sacred stone pipe.

As one can see from these two examples, non-Natives would have difficulty connecting such sparsely epigrammatic Ghost Dance chants to the Plains rituals and legends that underlie them. Karl Kroeber explains that most Native songs are never complete in themselves, "each depending," he writes, quoting Frederick Burton, "upon something external, a story or ceremony." Kroeber offers this Papago explanation: "the song is very short, because we understand so much" (105).

Jeffrey Huntsman, in his essay "Traditional Native American Literature: The Translational Dilemma," also emphasizes the need to understand the living situation from which an oral text comes, especially in relation to "the more close-knit, more systematized societies" (89). For example, to appreciate fully the following Arapaho song one needs to understand how it encodes the social rituals of a close-knit hierarchy:

> Little boy, the coyote gun —
> Little boy, the coyote gun —
> I have uncovered it — *Ahe'e'ye'*!
> I have uncovered it — *Ahe'e'ye'*!
> There is the sheath lying there,
> There is the sheath lying there. (Mooney 234–35)

Mooney writes that this song "has to do with an interesting feature in the sociology of the Arapaho and other prairie tribes." The "coyote men," a caste of middle-aged bachelors, acted as "pickets or lookouts for the camp." They often faced grave dangers armed with a "coyote gun," or "club decorated with feathers and other ornaments and usually covered with a sheath of bear gut" (235).

Based on tacitly understood Plains lore and learning, these Ghost Dance Songs imply or point to things rather than describe or explain them. This may help clarify why there is an absence of metaphor and simile, the predominant tropes of Eurocentric literature, in such oraliture. Kroeber writes: "Let us observe how rare in any form of Indian literature are metaphoric figures, similes, for instance, being so unusual as at times to be touchstones for an inaccurate translation" (103). Instead, Native discourse relies primarily on what Western poets would call synecdoche (Kroeber 104; Krupat 231), a trope in which the part usually stands for the whole. Examples of synecdoche appear in this Sioux chant:

> I know, in the pitfall . . .
> I know, in the pitfall . . .
> It is tallow they use in the pitfall,
> It is tallow they use in the pitfall. (Mooney 242)

The parts "pitfall" and "tallow" stand in for the whole, an elaborate eagle-trapping procedure. A solitary and fasting hunter would dig out, then roof over, a "pitfall" in which to await his sacred prey, baiting it with "tallow" stripped from buffalo ribs (Mooney 243–44).

The following also contains two instances of synecdoche: "The buffalo head — *Yä'hä'yä'*! / The half buffalo —" (Mooney 273). Again, such parts as the "buffalo head" and the "half buffalo" symbolize the whole, a Cheyenne-Arapaho "Crazy Dance called

Psam." In this healing ritual, participants often donned a robe consisting of "the upper half of a buffalo skin, the head portion, with the horns attached, coming over the head of the dancers" (Mooney 273). In another song, synecdochic "fruit," a part of the Great Plains harvest, signifies the abundance given to the whites by the now regretful spirit father, who will soon take back his gift:

> My children, when at first I liked the whites,
> My children, when at first I liked the whites,
> I gave them fruits,
> I gave them fruits. (Mooney, 209)

Noted American critic Kenneth Burke writes that synecdoche builds relationships of association by convertibility between its terms, while metaphor constructs those of association by comparison. I. A. Richards defines metaphor as a trope fuelled by tensions, juxtapositions, or even a collision of "disparate and hitherto unconnected things" (240). And C. Day Lewis concurs, describing it as a "collision rather than the collusion of images" (72). Examples of such a collision can be found in the following stanza from Sylvia Plath's poem entitled "Wuthering Heights," where sheep, who seem to be more in the know than the poet, are compared to clouds, and their eyes, even more surprisingly, to mail slots that reduce the alienated speaker to "a thin silly message":

> The sheep know where they are,
> Browsing in their dirty wool-clouds,
> Gray as the weather.
> The black slots of their pupils take me in.
> It is like being mailed into space,
> A thin silly message. (167)

Unlike the jarring surprise of Plath's metaphor comparing sheep eyes to a mail slot, a synecdoche results in a much smoother energy flow between macrocosm and microcosm that manifests as a seamless recapitulation of part for whole. An excellent example of synecdoche appears in this excerpt from Sioux medicine man Lame Deer's discussion of the cosmological significance of an old, sooty stewing pot:

> What do you see here, my friend? Just an ordinary old cooking
> pot, black with soot and full of dents.

It is standing on the fire on top of that old wood stove, and the water bubbles and moves the lid as the white steam rises to the ceiling. Inside the pot is boiling water, chunks of meat with bone and fat, plenty of potatoes.

It doesn't seem to have a message, that old pot, and guess you don't give it a thought. Except the soup smells good and reminds you that you are hungry. Maybe you are worried that this is dog stew. Well, don't worry. It's just beef — no fat puppy for a special ceremony. It's just an ordinary, everyday meal.

But I'm an Indian. I think about ordinary, common things like this pot. The bubbling water comes from the rain cloud. It represents the sky. The fire comes from the sun which warms us all — men, animals, trees. The meat stands for the four-legged creatures, our animal brothers, who gave of themselves so that we should live. The steam is living breath. It was water; now it goes up to the sky, becomes a cloud again. These things are sacred. Looking at that pot full of good soup, I am thinking how, in this simple manner, Wakan Tanka takes care of me. (Fire 171–72)

Here in this metamorphic soup, bubbling water transmutes into sky; fire into sun, meat back into its animal forms, while the stew's rising steam merges with the living breath of all beings and turns, as well, back into clouds journeying across the sky. Lame Deer's pot of simmering beef provides us with a near cosmological vision of the recurrent flow of synecdochic parts into wholes, cycles within cycles, rhythmic, continual, "an incredibly complex matrix of interpenetrating connections in which a small effect may lead to a large one" (Dunn and Scholefield xxxiv).

The worldview from which metaphor comes appears to be a more piecemeal one. Kroeber, who draws on Monroe Beardsley's notion "of metaphor as 'a poem in miniature' " (134), sees this trope existing as a self-contained, smaller poem within an equally self-sufficient larger text (104). Examples of these smaller poems-within-a-poem can be found in British poet Craig Raine's "A Martian Sends a Postcard Home." Here, a young Martian tries to describe our alien planet to the folks back home:

Mist is when the sky is tired of flight
and rests its soft machine on the ground:

then the world is dim & bookish
like engravings under tissue paper.

Rain is when the earth is television.
It has the property of making colours darker.

Model T is a room with the lock inside —
a key is turned to free the world. (1)

Used by Raine to explain such Earth phenomena as "mist," "rain,"
"the world," and the "Model T," these metaphors exist as small yet
self-contained lyric statements. The fact that each metaphor appears
as a separate couplet further reinforces its sense of momentary
enclosure.

Synecdoche, on the other hand, is much more open-ended:

Given this contrast between poem as isolated artifact and poem
as means by which energizing power flows between man and
world, divine and natural, individual and cultural community,
it does not seem unreasonable to suggest that the vivid, original
metaphor crucial to our poetry, and central to our critical
theorizing, may not be essential to *poeticité*, but may be a
phenomenon of our culture. (Kroeber 108)

Kroeber's preceding comment rang true to me when I recently went
to the small subarctic community of East Main, Quebec, to offer a
creative writing course to a group of Cree literacy teachers. They
quietly discussed my definition of a metaphor among themselves in
Cree, gave it a lot of thought, and then, as a group, unequivocally
resisted my instructions. They refused point blank to create metaphors to describe the butchering and preparation of game for a feast.
"Our animals are sacred," they told me. "We can't speak of them in
that way." Did they fear that my metaphor exercise might demean
their animals, turning sacred totems into cartoonish Wiley Coyotes?
"We were brought up not to lie," one of them politely explained.
Does our metaphor — a trope foreign to East James Bay Cree oraliture
— appear as a sacrilegious lie produced by the collision of hitherto
unconnected things? Does it rupture the flow of sacred parts into the
immense cosmological matrix?

If, as Kroeber (104) and Beardsley (144) have pointed out, a
metaphor is a small, self-referential poem contained within a larger

art object, then according to the mainstream practice, such an object must first be published singularly in a literary magazine before being collected into a book, along with other equally self-sufficient texts. Thus, a poem and its metaphoric tropes appear to stand alone, while a synecdoche contrastively amalgamates into a synthesis of composite parts. Gunn Allen explains that a Native ceremony contains "compositional elements," such as "songs, prayers, dances, drums, ritual movements, and dramatic address." Such elements do not exist as separate artistic statements, but relate "to one another in various explicit and implicit ways, as though each was one face of a multifaceted prism" (178).

More polarized and dialectic, a metaphoric bias struggles instead to unite separate, individuated things. If synecdoche stems from a close-knit world of tacit assumptions, then metaphor springs from a more culturally diverse one that encourages not only self-expression, but also self-questioning. Susan Mitchell, in "Experience Falls through Language like Water through a Sieve," encourages her mainstream students to insert five or more metaphors in the draft of a poem in order to discover "what we can't articulate, but feel pressured to say" (51). Metaphor, for Mitchell, abets the "pure self-expression" that Gunn Allen finds "so alien to Native thought" (51). Here, Mitchell counsels her creative writing students to use metaphor as a tool to help "write ahead of our understanding." She continues: "Then it becomes our job to understand what we have written, and with that new understanding write the poem further and deeper. Simile and metaphor require a new way of thinking where the writer leads with unconscious or irrational thought processes, then waits for conscious thinking to catch up" (52).

Such process writing allows one to "clarify, define, and explain" (Mitchell 52), to describe, compare, and contrast. Taken to an extreme, such analytic modes of thought lead to a sort of hubris or presumption that they can be used to decipher the meanings of the vast universe completely. For example, contemporary Mesquakies poet Ray A. Young Bear subtly pokes fun at our querulous, Eurocentric mind-set in the following:

> Who is there
> to witness the ice
> as it gradually forms itself
> from the cold rock-hard banks
> to the middle of the river?

Is the wind chill a factor?
Does the water at some point
negotiate and agree to stop
moving and become frozen?
When you do not know the answers
to these immediately you are afraid,
and to even think in this inquisitive
manner is contrary to the precept
that life is in everything:
Me, I am not a man;
I respect the river
for not knowing its secret,
for answers have nothing
to do with cause and occurrence.
It doesn't matter how early
I wake to see the sun shine
through the ice-hole;
only the ice along
with my foolishness
decides when
to break. (183)

Here, in a poem that contains no metaphors, Young Bear questions the role of the witness who focuses primarily on factors and negotiations. He, himself, does not try to fathom the river's particular intelligence. His manhood does not depend on being able to explain away the river's fickle power to break up ice when and where it chooses. Subverting the scientist's propensity to theorize about causes and their effects, Young Bear prefers to replace the word "effect" with "occurrence." Like certain of the "new" chaos advocates, he suggests that events occur with less predictability than traditional science once anticipated. Preferring not to force metaphors onto the natural phenomena that surround him, Young Bear may well be cajoling readers to stop our interminable intellectualizing and learn some basic survival smarts: respect the river's icy caprice.

Be this as it may, metaphor, given its ability to assimilate disparate things, will undoubtedly remain the central trope of our Eurocentric literature. It will do so because its mainstream readership is heterogenous in comparison to the more homogenous audience of a Native oral performance. As discourse theorist Paul Zumthor explains:

In principal, if not in fact, the oral message is up to public consumption: writing, in contrast, isolates. This notwithstanding orality functions only in the midst of a limited sociocultural group: the need to communicate that sustains it does not spontaneously look towards universality, whereas writing split between so many individual readers, buttressed on abstraction, moves freely only at the broad, social level, if not at the universal. (28–29)

We have seen how Native chants rely on synecdoche rather than metaphor to confirm a communal identity. Affirming group solidarity in this way, chants often develop around a common theme — "the journey of The Visionary, a man who travelled with the gods, learned the ceremonial from them, and brought back its powers of healing and fertility" for the good of all (Welsh 170). This definition describes the Ghost Dance ceremonies perfectly. Their repetitively hypnotic cadences abetted participants on their travels to a shadowy spirit realm. Mooney places the Arapaho spirit world, for example, "in the West, not on the same level with this earth of ours, but higher up, and separated also from it by a body of water" (233). Ghost dancers, both men and women, performed a dragging, near-broken-footed step of lamentation in the hopes of entering an oceanic trance state typified by a loss of individuality. Often a medicine man whirled sacred crow and eagle feathers and/or a handkerchief in front of their eyes. This mesmerization continued until their bodies began shaking violently or became rigid. Then they would drop, unconscious, to the ground, remaining there undisturbed for minutes or even hours (Mooney 198–99). In this altered state, a dancer undertook "the journey of The Visionary" (Welsh 170). He or she would fly to the spirit world to procure his or her own Ghost Dance Song — a song that could heal its composer and others as well.

Mooney cites numerous examples of this visionary journey motif. In the following Arapaho chant, a dreamer rides on a whirlwind to meet deceased relatives:

Our father, the whirlwind
Our father, the whirlwind —
By its aid I am running swiftly,
By its aid I am running swiftly,
By which means I see our father,
By which means I see our father. (Mooney 219)

And in this song, the crow, messenger from the land of the dead, is offering to guide the dancer on a vision quest:

> The crow is circling above me,
> The crow is circling above me,
> The crow having come for me
> The crow having come for me. (Mooney 234)

A Pit River refrain points to the Rockies' snowy peaks and beyond to the Milky Way, the spirit road traversed by wayfaring seekers. In spite of its simplicity, this chant must have been powerful when intoned under the myriad, lucent constellations illuminating the prairie night sky:

> The snow lies there — *ro'rani'*!
> The snow lies there — *ro'rani'*!
> The snow lies there — *ro'rani'*!
> The snow lies there — *ro'rani*!
> The Milky Way lies there,
> The Milky Way lies there. (Mooney 289)

Like Welsh, Zumthor likens the chant to a journey. He writes that, in general, oral poetry does not emphasize an Aristotelian sense of proportion and measure, but rather *"mouvance"* (202). A chant concentrates on progress, on the movement of a current episode. Oral time, Zumthor adds, is "fleeting" (102), what with its lack of description, perspective, and strong sense of closure. Via repetition, recurrence, and the interweaving of numerous threads, as in a Navajo tapestry, the oral becomes "'inscribed' in the fleeting nature of the voice" (Zumthor 113). Thus, Ghost dancers repeated their brief texts, round upon round, as if to incise them into a canyon or mesa such that the geography itself became a sacred script.

We already have seen many examples of *mouvance*, or, as Welsh calls it, "mythological action," in these Ghost Dance Songs (178). Writing in the 1970s, Welsh could not foresee that he might be taken to task in the 1990s by Canadian literary critic Penny Petrone for his use of the word *myth* in relation to Native texts. Petrone writes that non-Native readers usually consider myth to be but a fiction. Native oraliture defies the Eurocentric tendency to classify things in terms of such binary oppositions as myth and history, or fiction and fact. Welsh does avoid such extreme polarization, showing preference instead for a bipolar continuum. Here he describes ceremonies joining: "a continuing rhythm and community, both of which 'stretch unbrokenly through the ages and on interminably into the future.' 'Now as at all times,' Yeats said: *'sa'a narai,'* the Navahos say. . . . [This movement] joins the rhythms of time and human experience to continuing rhythms of eternity" (178).

For Welsh, the chant moves along a continuum extending from history towards eternity. In his view, this lyric genre approximates a fluid and continuous intermingling of past, present, and future tenses. The following Ghost Dance Song seems suspended in such a continuing lyric moment of radiant simultaneity. Here, the dreamer is visiting — or has visited — the spirit world where people are *still* making the pemmican that he is *still* using:

> The pemmican that I am using —
> The pemmican that I am using,
> They are still making it,
> They are still making it. (Mooney 242)

The following chant refers to knowledge found in some of "the oldest traditions of the Cheyenne [who] locate their former home at the headwaters of the Mississippi in Minnesota" (Mooney 269). Here, the dreamer stands at the eternal site of tribal origins:

> My children, my children
> Here is the river of turtles,
> Here is the river of turtles
> Where the various living things,
> Where the various living things
> Are painted their different colours,
> Are painted their different colours,
> Our father says so,
> Our father says so. (Mooney 269)

These repetitions serve to suspend the onrush of time. The repeated "Our father" not only creates a reverential tone, but also alludes to the prophet Wovoka, the "spirit" fathers and grandfathers, and to such elemental elders as Crow, Eagle, Thunderbird, Four Winds, and so on. All of these beings, combined with "my children, my children," accrue to a present plenitude encompassing past, present, and future generations, totemic turtles, elemental forces, and many other "various living things" painted in "their different colours."

Here is a final favourite that illustrates the omniscient lyric present:

> I hear everything,
> I hear everything.
> I am the crow,
> I am the crow. (Mooney 245)

Crow, the great totemic father of the Caddo peoples, is expressing his omnipresence throughout all of time. Crow is hearing everything simultaneously. And, as a friend and hot-air ballooning aficionado once pointed out to me, "High up in the air like a crow, you can hear forwards and backwards over great distances."

The continuous present of the chant is not always a pacific one. Welsh mentions a type characterized by "a rushing movement, the feeling of events sweeping down on us, for which prophecy is especially suitable" (184). Many Ghost Dance Songs simulate this headlong rush. Some were doubtlessly inspired by the ever restless elements sweeping across the Great Plains. Many also stem from the cataclysmic tumult of history that was causing the late-nineteenth-century demise of Native civilizations in the Americas. In many such chants, one feels a great gust of wind, which "makes the head-feathers sing" (Mooney 214). In others, awesome yet beneficent whirlwinds circle around, stirring "the willows . . . the grasses" (291), and shaking the tent flaps. This urgent chant would call up the prophesied maelstrom of elements to destroy white civilization: "Fog! Fog! / Lightening! Lightening! / Whirlwind! Whirlwind!" (Mooney 291).

In this song, a whirlwind rushes down, raising clouds of dust:

> There is dust from the whirlwind,
> There is dust from the whirlwind,
> There is dust from the whirlwind,
> The whirlwind on the mountain,
> The whirlwind on the mountain,
> The whirlwind on the mountain. (Mooney 292)

In another such refrain, a tornado roars over a mountain, making the rocks ring (292). Often crows, eagles, thunderbirds, and actual dancers fly or circle about. Dice are rolled, songs resonate, while the Earth itself rises, trembles, and hums, suggesting the prophesied arrival of the Messiah, the spirit hosts, and the new world.

This Crow Nation song represents the tumultuous approach of millennial forces and summarizes the underlying hopes of the Ghost Dance religion:

The whole world is coming,
A nation is coming, a nation is coming.
The Eagle has brought the message to the tribe.
The father says so, the father says so.
Over the whole earth they are coming.
The buffalo are coming, the buffalo are coming,
The Crow has brought the message to the tribe,
The father says so, the father says so. (Mooney 307)

Here, the totemic Eagle and Crow outride the vanguard to announce the oncoming herds of resurrected buffalo and spirit armies.

Unfortunately, the underside of such hopeful prophecy is lamentation and despair, for, as Welsh points out, "prophecy is also lament and the two are tied to the sense of community" (185). Alicia Ostriker, in a recent talk entitled "*Howl* Revisited: Allen Ginsberg and Prophetic Lamentation," spoke about how the Book of Jeremiah, which inspired *Howl*, is both a "literature of catastrophe" and a "vehicle for survival." Written at the end of the Jewish monarchial period during the destruction of Jerusalem, Jeremiah's prophecies promised a new covenant for the Jews who were fleeing into exile, as were the Plains Natives of the late nineteenth century. Wovoka's prophecies and the Ghost Dance Songs that they inspired became a similar "vehicle for survival" that oscillates, as does the Jeremiah, between the pathetic and the sublime, between catastrophe and its transcendence. Mooney writes that dancers who sang the following often wept openly:

Father, have pity on me,
Father, have pity on me;
I am crying for thirst,
I am crying for thirst;
All is gone — I have nothing to eat,
All is gone — I have nothing to eat. (Mooney 226)

And, this vision of a sweat lodge stirs up sad longings for lost ways:

When I see the *thi'äya*,
When I see the *thi'äya*

Then I begin to lament,
Then I begin to lament. (Mooney 231)

Finally, I will close with this elegantly stark Kiowa Ghost Dance song, whose generosity of spirit towards the suffering of all sentient beings reminds one of the compassion often expressed by the late-eighteenth-century haiku master Issa:

Heye'heye'heye'Aho'ho'!
Heye'heye'heye'Aho'ho'!
Because I am poor,
Because I am poor,
I pray for every living creature,
I pray for every living creature.
Ao'nyo! Ao'nyo! (Mooney 316)

I hope I have underlined some of the textual differences that might at first perplex a mainstream reader of these Ghost Dance Songs. Not only does their reliance on synecdoche rather than metaphor challenge our textual expectations, but also their grounding in communal ritual, music, and dance, and their close-knit worldview of tacit assumptions can initially try our patience. If, though, we approach these messianic songs with a beginner's mind, their sparsely epigrammatical surface will soon begin to reveal the visionary contours of a vitally resistant text. And, if we persist, we will soon realize that during our short, turbulent stay on this continent, we have, through our naïvety, been too quick to relegate this Native classic to the margins of our literary canon.

WORKS CITED

Beardsley, Monroe. *Aesthetics: Problems in the Philosophy of Criticism.* New York: Harcourt, 1958.

Burke, Kenneth. "Four Master Tropes." *A Grammar of Motives.* New York: Prentice-Hall, 1945.

Champagne, Duane, ed. *The Native North American Almanac: A Reference Work on Native North Americans in the United States and Canada.* Detroit: Gale, 1994.

Churchill, Ward. "Generations of Resistance: American Indian Poetry and the Ghost Dance Spirit." *Coyote Was Here: Essays on Contemporary Native American Literary and Political Mobilization.* Ed. Bo Scholer. Aarhus, Denmark: Seklos, 1984. 161–79.

Day Lewis, C. *The Poetic Image*. London: Cape, 1947.

Dunn, Sara, and Alan A. Scholefield. Introduction. Dunn and Scholefield, eds.

——, eds. *Poetry for the Earth*. New York: Fawcett-Columbine, 1991.

Encyclopedia of North American Indians. Ed. Frederick E. Hoxie. New York: Houghton, 1996.

Gibson, Margaret. "Beginner's Mind." *Beneath a Single Moon: Buddhism in Contemporary American Poetry*. Ed. Kent Johnson and Craig Paulenich. Boston: Shambhala, 1991. 89–90.

Gunn Allen, Paula. "The Sacred Hoop: A Contemporary Indian Perspective on American Indian Literature." *Symposium of the Whole: A Range of Discourse towards an Ethnopoetics*. Ed. Jerome Rothenberg and Diane Rothenberg. Berkeley: U of California P, 1983. 173–87.

Huntsman, Jeffrey F. "Traditional Native American Literature: The Translational Dilemma." Swann 87–89.

Keats, John. *The Life and Letters*. Ed. Lord Houghton. London: Dent, 1954.

Kroeber, Karl. "The Wolf Comes: Indian Poetry and Linguistic Criticism." Swann 98–111.

Krupat, Arnold. *The Voice in the Margin: Native American Literature and the Canon*. Berkeley: U of California P, 1989.

Fire, John [Lame Deer], and Richard Erdoes. "The Meaning of Everyday Objects." *Symposium of the Whole: A Range of Discourse towards an Ethnopoetics*. Ed. Jerome Rothenberg and Diane Rothenberg. Berkeley: U of California P, 1983. 171–72.

Mitchell, Susan. "Experience Falls through Language like Water through a Sieve." *The Practice of Poetry: Writing Exercises from Poets Who Teach*. Ed. Robin Behn and Chase Twichell. New York: HarperCollins, 1992.

Mooney, James. *The Ghost Dance Religion and the Sioux Outbreak of 1890*. Ed. Anthony F. Wallace. Chicago: U of Chicago P, 1965.

The Native Tribes of North America: A Concise Encyclopedia. Ed. Michael G. Johnson. New York: MacMillan, 1994.

Ostriker, Alicia. "*Howl* Revisited: Allen Ginsberg and Prophetic Lamentation." National Poetry Foundation Conference, University of Maine. Orono, 22 June 1996.

Petrone, Penny. *Native Literature in Canada: From the Oral Tradition to the Present*. Toronto: Oxford UP, 1990.

Plath, Sylvia. "Wuthering Heights." *The Collected Poems*. New York: Harper, 1981. 167.

Raine, Craig. "A Martian Sends a Post Card Home." *A Martian Sends a Post Card Home*. Toronto: Oxford UP, 1979. 1.

Richards, I. A. *Principles of Literary Criticism*. New York: Harcourt, 1926.

Sam-Cromarty, Margaret. *James Bay Memoirs: A Cree Woman's Ode to Her Homeland*. Lakefield, ON: Waapoone, 1992.

Swann, Brian, ed. *Smoothing the Ground: Essays on Native American Oral Literature*. Berkeley: U of California P, 1983.

Welsh, Andrew. *Roots of the Lyric: Primitive Poetry and Modern Poetics*. Princeton: Princeton UP, 1978.

Young Bear, Ray A. "The Reason Why I Am Afraid Even Though I Am a Fisherman." *Poetry for the Earth*. Dunn and Scholefield, eds. 183.

Zumthor, Paul. *Oral Poetry: An Introduction*. Trans. Kathryn Murphy-Judy. Minneapolis: U of Minnesota, 1990.

Memory Alive: An Inquiry into the Uses of Memory in Marilyn Dumont, Jeannette Armstrong, Louise Halfe, and Joy Harjo

JEANNE PERREAULT

Memory as a distinct meta-sense transports, bridges and crosses all other senses. Yet memory is internal to each sense, and the senses are as divisible and indivisible from each other as each memory is separable and intertwined with others.

— Nadia Seremetakis (*The Senses Still* 9)

It's like saying "world." Memory is the nucleus of every cell; it's what runs, it's the gravity; the gravity of the Earth.

— Joy Harjo ("A Laughter" 138)

In this essay, I undertake preliminary exploration of the role of memory, with its intimate relations to speech, history, and the sacred, in the poetry of Marilyn Dumont, Joy Harjo, Louise Halfe, and Jeannette Armstrong. Kenneth Lincoln observes that the "fulcrum" of First Nations literature is a "sense of relatedness" in which "tribe means ancestral history . . . an ever present religious history, not 'back there' in time, but continuously reenacted, even as it changes form" (8). But even as I read these words, nodding in agreement, I realize that the complexity and subtlety of such an integrated intellectual, social, and spiritual context is far from my range of experience. The ways *knowing* works in this view of history, the vagueness of "*sense*" in the "sense of relatedness" Lincoln describes, is perplexing. Only through codes of memory could the link of history and presentness find a way into voice. N. Scott Momaday declares, perhaps metonymically, that he is aware of "the memory in [his] blood" as an aspect of his relationship to the Native parts of his heritage (qtd. in Krupat, *Voice* 13). With pronounced authority, white scholar Arnold Krupat refutes Momaday's statement. In Krupat's words, "there is no gene for perception, no such thing as memory in the blood."[1] Krupat prefers the view that Native authors are "gifted individuals shaping a subtle and complex tradition" (*Voice* 12, 13). While one may agree with Krupat's more recent view that the important role of memory in Native literature should be examined comparatively rather than as "some sort of unique and autonomous expression of Native American culture" (*Turn* 48n17),[2] understanding what that role is — indeed, its variety and complexity — is essential. To stage a simple dichotomy between the two positions — one that memory is "ever present," "ancestral," and religious, *embodied* in Native literature, and the other that there is "no such thing as memory in the blood" — might make for a good ideological argument,[3] but it will not help in understanding the variety and complexity of memory as it appears in various Native writings.

Rather than turn to the long European philosophical discussion of memory, I will rely on First Nations theorists. Lee Maracle bases time itself on memory, and memory on the community. Maracle explains "the structure of time of First Nations cultures" in this way: "To claim lineage memory and juxtapose it with current memory is to articulate the most sacred of one's entire thought from the beginning to the present and is intended as future memory" (88). Like Momaday, Maracle seems to refuse the vision of the artist as an independent, gifted individual. Similarly, American poet Joy Harjo (Creek) has several times referred to the "responsibility" of remembering ("Ancestral Voices" 41; "Circular Dreams" 61), and the charge of this responsibility seems to appear as a strong force for many Native writers.

Memory is, necessarily it seems by conventional definition, a representation of what can no longer be directly experienced. It is often all we seem to have of the painful and elusive shimmer that divides the now from the then, the anguished slippage of life always dumbly or sharply undoing itself as it is done. Maracle's assertion of "lineage memory" shapes the ideas of mind and recollection along different lines from these commonplace notions of what constitutes memory. In her explanation, experience need not be individual, personal, specific to enter memory; indeed, the word "lineage" suggests bloodlines, a heritage of body that leaves its trace in mental effects, images, memories. For her, the personal and immediate past (which is how I read "current memory") and the collective past available through the lineage memory of a people coalesce, but this phenomenon is not simply a given. As I read her, Maracle emphasizes the necessity of *claiming* that communal memory, actively, purposefully, and imaginatively, "juxtaposing it" with "current memory." Most importantly, these acts are in the realm of the articulated. What is being articulated moves beyond the everyday and into what has always been "the most sacred" of thought. It is this dimension of the sacred that is carried through time and is "intended" to be passed on as "future memory."

Joy Harjo uses memory "to retrace the past not as an inducement to curl inwards on oneself, as if it were a point in time without escape route, but rather as a dynamic process to reaffirm ancient heritages and proceed forward on a path of constant renewal" (Coltelli 9). Bringing memory and history together in the process of retracing the past, the poet brings a personal process and a social one together. To evade the linearity of metaphors of "path" and the closure implied in circles and a "curl inwards," Laura Coltelli emphasizes Harjo's image of the spiral. The "proceeding of memory" thus "spirals down the tip [of a vortex] while simultaneously expanding toward the future" (9). Harjo, Armstrong, Dumont, and Halfe each provide distinct stagings of memory and its workings, as I will examine later, and each participates in developing the diverse ways memory can be conceptualized and imaged to indicate its function in cultural discourses.

I wish to lay these assertions of the multiple nature and function of articulated memory alongside Roland Barthes's brief discussion "the Discourse of History."[4] Barthes refers to the "breaks in silence" that inaugurate historical discourse and claims this as the linguist's well-known "performative opening" of speech. Barthes makes this performative opening of historical discourse a "solemn act of foundation" based on a poetic model, the "*I sing* of the poets." But it is equally as provocative that he claims a "sacred" character for this breaking of silence. In reference to the anxiety of breaking silence, Barthes insists that the inception of speech is "so difficult," "or, so sacred" (130). Although it is, I think, safe to suggest that what Maracle means by "sacred" and what Barthes intends by it will diverge in significant ways, I will offer Barthes's sense of the goal of historical statement: Barthes explains that "the entrance of the speech act into historical statement . . . has as its goal not so much to give the historian a chance to express his 'subjectivity' as to 'complicate' history's chronological time by confronting it with another time, that of discourse itself" (130).

253

The introduction of the speaker, the human voice, and its audience is subsumed in the assertion of "discourse itself" as a kind of Platonic figure existing in an abstraction that makes the polarity between the individualist "subjectivity" of the historian and the mechanics (or technology) of discourse. The goal, as Barthes imagines it, is to complicate historical time. He goes on to explain, "the presence, in historical narration, of explicit speech-act signs tends to 'de-chronologize' the historical 'thread' " (130).[5] Barthes, here with the metaphor of thread, suggests not only that narration makes its stitched pattern, but also that events themselves (and Barthes here does make a claim for the real, however elusive) are linked, threaded through the needle of time. The "de-chronologizing," the effect of explicit speech acts in historical narration, "restore[s], if only as a reminiscence or a nostalgia, a complex, parametric, non-linear time whose deep space recalls the mythic time of the ancient cosmogonies, it too linked by essence to the speech of the poet or the soothsayer" (130–31).

Alongside Maracle's statement, Barthes's ideas are provocative. The speaker of the past is in poetic and mythic mode (which may be Barthes's "sacred" mode) as the essential disturber of linearity, restoring what has been lost, bringing the past to the service of the future; so too is that speaker in Maracle's claim. In Barthes's argument, however, "de-chronologizing" the "thread" of history brings into play nostalgia (with its connotation of sentimentality and self-indulgence) or "reminiscence" — another word evoking misty pleasantries. Nadia Seremetakis's study of perception and memory criticizes this conventional understanding of nostalgia: "This reduction of the term confines the past and removes it from any transaction and material relation to the present; the past becomes an isolatable and consumable unit of time. Nostalgia, in the American sense, freezes the past in such a manner as to preclude it from any capacity for social transformation in the present, preventing the present from establishing a dynamic perceptual relationship to its history" (4). Seremetakis offers another way to understand nostalgia, linking it with memory through its roots in Greek thought:

"*nostalghía*" is the desire of longing with burning pain to journey. It also evokes the sensory dimension of memory in exile and estrangement; it mixes bodily and emotional pain and ties painful experiences of spiritual and somatic exile to the notion of maturation and ripening. In this sense, *nostalghía* is linked to the personal consequences of historicizing sensory experience which is conceived as a painful bodily and emotional journey . . . *nostalghía* is thus far from trivializing romantic sentimentality. (4)

Seremetakis, here, refers to nostalgia (or *nostalghía*) as having a geographical element: one must have travelled in space as well as time for the longing to have developed. For First Nations peoples, "exile" is more fraught. Place, land, home are often the same as they were before contact or invasion, but irrevocably different. Memory is the most effective weapon against exile that is not geographical but nonetheless in effect. While Seremetakis emphasizes the pain of loss in *nostalghía*, she does recognize the link of "spiritual and somatic" experience to the "notion of maturation and ripening."

Maracle allies, in ways similar to Seremetakis, linear, processual (and thus implying "ripening" or "maturation"), and complex (or nonlinear) time with speech, and thereby makes memory an active and empowering present reality in itself. The spiritual exile that Seremetakis records, however, is therein resisted by memory, even refuted. The assertion of a positive, even developmental or evolutionary, aspect to the embrace of memory links this "classical" (in the Greek connections) view of memory with those of Lee Maracle, Joy Harjo, Jeannette Armstrong, Marilyn Dumont, and Louise Halfe. In part, I will be looking to these poets to understand the way memory sings in the blood, or indeed, to see if this is a helpful way to think cross-culturally.[6]

Marilyn Dumont's first collection of poems, *A Really Good Brown Girl*, takes its title from her prose poem "Memoirs of a Really Good Brown Girl." This volume of personal lyric narrative, of moments of insight, and of social critique most often embeds memory in the body rather than in an explicit articulation of memory's force or function. In "Half Human/Half Devil (Halfbreed) Muse" (51), for example, the visiting muse comes in violence, and for the poet "no sound, no sound" escapes as the mechanistic (shutting off / a dripping faucet") and bestial ("dog / gnawing bone") force takes over. From "giving up to giving over" — the central, one-line stanza — the muse becomes a dance (or a dancer) with a "drum rattle / gangly movement, offbeat . . . blood / paint, ochre skin, ash smell." The muse figure seems to rise out of a tribal memory that is not containable in mere images but inhabits and "overtakes" the poet's body. Dumont does not say, explicitly, that the "half human / half devil (halfbreed) muse" is a remembered force. Her title and her tone instead suggest some comic or ironic thrust: "a herd of rattles overtakes me" is an image that should make us aware that this muse might have a powerful trickster aspect.7 Nevertheless, the only place of sound in the poem is that of the drum rattle, "pebbles encased trapped / in sound, pebbles rasp / against thin dry skin." In the drum rattles sound becomes possible and required. This muse will neither stay contained in memory, nor will it leave the past behind. As the poet is overtaken, she becomes able to speak.

Several pieces in the volume, including "The White Judges," appear to work directly from the rich detail of personal memory and family history, with a twist of the surreal that evokes both the child's sensibility and the adult's sharp vision. "The White Judges" (11–12) opens with straightforward declarative descriptions of the family home, "an old schoolhouse," where "all nine kids and the / occasional friend slept upstairs." The information is solid, plain, unemotional: a setting and a context that includes "our walls high and / bare except for the family photos whose frames were crowded / with siblings waiting to come of age, marry or leave." Only in the last line of the first stanza-paragraph does Dumont shift into another consciousness: "At supper / eleven of us would stare down a pot of moose stew, bannock and tea, / while outside the white judges sat encircling our house." The prose breaks here and the next line stands alone: "And they waited to judge" (no punctuation). The image of the encircling judges is a powerful one, suggesting dogs or wolves resting on their haunches waiting to pounce, or a group of bullies or predators that will evoke memories of fear from many children. Who has not been in such a circle? That Dumont positions us in the physical space of the home, the family circling the stew pot, the judges circling the house, makes an almost filmic visual effect: the one an easy reality, the other a strange vision of predation, judges white (and, in my mind's eye, black-robed, male, grey-headed, intense, and staring) and waiting.

The poem traces the moments of vulnerability recalled with a visceral, sensual immediacy that makes the haunted, hunted feeling a kind of peripheral vision in which the "white judges" are intermittently perceived but never forgotten. They wait until the moments of exposure, identifying or specifically marking moments, occur. Each section repeats how the "white judges" "waited till." From the eating of moose stew, "waited till we ate tripe / watched us inhale its wild vapour . . . watched us welcome it into our being . . . swallow its gamey juices / until we had become it and it had become us"; to the charity boxes of clothes dug through with first reluctance then excitement — "a box transformed now / into the Sears catalogue." Joy, nourishment, desire, intimacy, all make the family vulnerable.

It is these moments for which the "white judges" wait. Dumont describes the "twilight" when her father and older brothers "would drag a bloodstained canvas . . . onto our lawn" and "my mother would lift and lay it in place / like a dead relative, / praying, coaxing and thanking it," and, as she skinned and carved, "talking in Cree to my father and in English to my brothers." The image of a suburban lawn lies incongruously alongside the work of carving and skinning, made more difficult in the "truck-headlight-night." The mother's work here is a matrix that is spiritual with prayers and acknowledgement of the animal's gift, cultural as she speaks in two languages to the different generations, and profoundly traditional as the beast is treated with reverence, "like a dead relative." While the younger children drift into sleep, "bellies rested in the meat days ahead," the mother's role is woven into the whole of the twilight scene; she takes on her tasks without emphasis. The unspoken implication is that the family too, like the judges, has been waiting until twilight to do this work. The younger children's comfort in the murmured voices (Dumont is always "we" in reference to the children) makes a sharp contrast to the grim faces of the watching judges. The "sensory dimension of memory" (Seremetakis 4) is inflected here by the mixture of that which is precious always shadowed by the relentless and patient gaze of the "white judges."

The watchers "wait till the guitars come out" and the family members dance holes into their socks; and in the last stanza "wait till a fight broke out." The repetitions and costs of everyday life are invoked as Dumont describes the effect of the fight:

> and the night would settle in our bones
> and we'd ache with shame
> for having heard or spoken
> that which sits at the edge of our light side
> that which comes but we wished it hadn't
> like "settlement" relatives who would arrive at Christmas and
> leave at Easter.

The rhetorical repetition in which the judges would wait until something "would" happen (whether of pleasure or wretchedness) leaves the implications open: that point is the moment a judgement would occur — and the judgement would be made. The white judges would judge and "shame" would rise — not for an action or a wrong-doing but for an awareness, "for having heard or spoken / that which sits at the edge of our light side." Here, the Métis acceptance of "our light side," the white side, is deeply conflicted. I read these lines as indicating that judgement (the purview of the white judges) has been picked up and brought into the family, into the centre of the circle. Shame, then, is the result of having brought the judges' gaze to speech — indeed, to any acknowledgement at all. The inevitability of this revisitation is made familial, the simile bringing the shame home, like other relatives who come and won't go away.

It is possible to see this memory as a "recovered utopian feeling, alterity and cultural procreation" that bears itself against official history and carries the sensory memory with it (Seremetakis 10), but the edges of the circle of this consoling gathering of recollections are always drawn by the attentive judges. The "utopian feeling" of childhood memory is removed from even a remote nostalgic senti-mentality by those avid eyes. The recurring events that embed cultural identity and familial congruence are inappropriately set off from everydayness and charged with the assessment of difference and its meaning. The relation of "white judges" to white readers is ambig-uous. We (all readers) are invited to judge the judges and to experience the circle from the inside of that ring of eyes. If our histories provide a mirror for us reflecting our place in that circle of judges, then another set of memories is put into play, and with those memories may come a degree of comprehension, a revised awareness. Dumont's concern here, of course, is not to examine the white judges but to provide a trope for the existence and effects of poverty, cultural specificity (Cree and English), dislocation (the lawns, the city neigh-bours), and the marking of racial difference and pain — with the word "white." Racism is figured in the hungry attention of the judges and the shame felt when that vision is brought home.

In "Breakfast of the Spirit" (*A Really Good Brown Girl* 41), Dumont brings another aspect of memory to language. In this delicate poem, the strangeness and familiarity of self-knowledge touch in the most intimate ways, being "things that are / like nothing else is." The familiar senses of one's ("your") body — "the smell of your own scent / taste of your own skin" — the familiar returns of the natural world — "the force of spring water" — are indeed "familiar," but they are also new, surprising, strange in the ways that "the sound of chickadees

/ in a stand of mute spruce" with the weight of silence lifted is always a surprise, always utterly right. The comfort of these images, with their careful placing of "you" in your own body and your own quiet spruce world, is distressed in the second stanza, where these images are brought to bear on another familiarity:

> familiar as the ripple in your throat
> waiting for your voice to return
> from the sealed-off jars of memory
> released now to feast on the preserves
> after you've slept so long
> tasted now, at the celebratory breakfast of your awakening. (41)

The intimate tensions of sleeping and waking, silence and speech, hunger and feasting all pivot on the homely image of memory as a jar of preserves carefully saved for the moment of need. It is from this source that voice comes, and it is this store that nourishes. Individual memory may be suggested here, but the celebration and the "spirit" whose fast is broken in the title, "Breakfast of the Spirit," suggest another kind of remembering, one that is as personal as one's own body and as impersonal as nature. Dumont does not abstract the *idea* of memory in this poem. Instead, she alerts us to the cost of amnesia and presents that forgetting as a place of hunger and of sleep. Memory, then, is the source of nourishment, the site of awakening, and the content of spiritual celebration.

Jeannette Armstrong's treatment of history and memory also participates in the evocation of the sacred. While Roland Barthes might be accused of sentimentalizing the historian (speaking of his essential links to "poet or soothsayer"), we find in Armstrong's short poem "History Lesson" a rather sharper enactment of the speaker of history (*Breath Tracks* 28–29). Here the "de-chronologizing" works not just as a manifestation of the speech act in "paper time" (Barthes 130), but also as a collapse of sequence with a return, at the end of the poem, to consequence. In this poem, Armstrong brings together the most mundane elements of everyday life in contemporary Canada — the Rice Crispies "snap, crackle, pop" advertisement, known to every Canadian child; or the pollution of rivers by "flower power laundry detergents" — and aligns them with the deadly destructive forces of Seagrams whisky. And, of course, smallpox, priests, Mounties, and miners are all jumbled together as Armstrong concludes with a devastating, and surprisingly compassionate, indictment of the colonizer.

"Civilization," we are informed, in a blunt parody of the grade school history lessons we have all had, "has reached the promised land." Working from the assumption that we know the story — no question about who "Christopher" is — this "history lesson" is not about events as they follow each other in some logic of causality. The "mob" — whether its members are "shooting each other / left and right" (we can't ignore a political jibe here), swelling rivers with "flower powered zee," or bringing "gifts / Smallpox, Seagrams / and rice crispies" — is enacting an impulse of apparently mindless triviality, greed, and destructiveness. This stands in distinct contrast to the implication of lineage, order, significance of "whole civilizations / ten generations" that are facing mutilation. Time is compressed here. A single blow can damage those "ten generations." The poem is in the present tense until the foreclosure in the last stanza: "Somewhere among the remains . . . is the termination" of a "long journey / and unholy search." It is in this last stanza that Armstrong's "lesson" makes its point beyond that of "de-chronologizing":

> Somewhere among the remains
> of skinless animals
> is the termination
> to a long journey
> and unholy search
> for the power
> glimpsed in a garden
> forever closed
> forever lost

The moment beginning this history is still happening; it is still bursting out of the belly of Christopher's ship, and the moment of "termination," when the animals are all skinned and the generations mutilated, is contained in another moment, one out of historical time altogether: that is, the ongoing moment of ejection from the garden of Eden, the biblical master narrative of Western culture, the narrative that feeds not just religion but also psychoanalysis and politics (the socialist golden age of perfect equality before private property appeared), the narrative of irrevocable loss, and the tormenting promise of restoration.[8] The lesson of history that Armstrong gives us here is not a single or simple one: not only is history not the past, and not past, it is also not explainable in merely material or social terms. In contrast to the usual evocation of losses undergone by

Aboriginal peoples, Armstrong looks at the losses suffered by the Europeans. Europeans' loss of a spiritual power, the loss of a moment of perfect harmony, "glimpsed in a garden / forever closed / forever lost," makes their search an unconscious one. Armstrong asserts that the Europeans do not know what they have lost and cannot know what they (or we) are seeking. With this blindness, this amnesia, in place, the Europeans cannot know what the poet knows: that "somewhere among the remains," a "termination" to an "unholy search" might be found. The requirement is a looking backward, a facing of their own spiritual loss — another kind of remembering. The inevitable desolation of the mob that burst from Christopher's ship is spiritual, but the effects of their violent and chaotic hunger are material and unending. The needs of Europeans may be spiritual but, Armstrong asserts, as long as the search itself is "unholy" the "power / glimpsed" in that garden will elude them. Memory, in other words, is an essential human requirement. Its absence creates brutal violations, stupid destruction.

Another kind of history lesson appears in Armstrong's "Threads of Old Memory" (*Breath Tracks* 58–61).[9] "[H]istory is a dreamer," she says, and the articulation of that dream makes it come into being, as she winds her threads of old memory through the skeins made available to us by Maracle's notions of lineage memory, current memory, and future memory. Armstrong affirms her belief in those connections, linking blood and memory, but affirming the power of language to make other bonds possible. This recollection requires a search for the right words, the "sacred words" that can be "spoken serenely in the gaps between memory / the lost places of history / pieces mislaid / forgotten or stolen." This claiming of a whole history and a people in the process of "becoming" from the "imaginings of the past" seems linked closely with Maracle's "lineage memory" articulated through "current memory" leading inexorably into a "future memory." But blood, or lineage, itself will not carry the weight of memory for Armstrong. The narrative linking the gaps requires more than blood. Memory, it seems, does not flow easily in "the blood" but must be wrestled or invited into being through language.

Louise Halfe's collection *Bear Bones and Feathers* also wrestles memory into existence. Halfe's poems refute an image of individual or tribal history as a location of simple sustaining recollections or harmonious unities of humans and nature. For Halfe, the grand-mothers (*Nòhkomak*, more than one grandmother; *Nòhkom*, my grandmother; or *Nòhkom àtayohkàn*, grandmother of the legends)[10] are remembered from childhood, beings who are the stuff of memory itself. Together these grandmothers seem to encode a range of the cultural and personal meanings of memory for Halfe. They are not uniformly comforting presences. In "Nòhkom Àtayohkàn 1" (10) and "Nòhkom Àtayohkàn 2" (11), we find the contrast even in the figure of the grandmother of the legends. In the first of these poems, the images of the grandmother of the legends are formed of nature: hair of brome, face soft leather cut through with ravines. The nourishing promise of this figure and the hunger of the speaker are explicit: "I want to cup / your breast, a starving suckling child"; and the address is personal, the plea fully trusting: "Old one with laughing eyes / wrap me in blanket grass . . . Ground my wandering feet." In "Nòhkom Àtayohkàn 2," another element appears, and this grandmother figure shows another force. From the poem's opening lushness, "Your flaming flowers / spread on my breast," the speaker observes depletion: "I've watched life / blossom and fade from / your eyes." Death images — "you've folded flies / between your lips" — combine with other blossom figures — "welcomed the swirl of drinking hummingbirds." The effect of this aspect or dimension of the grandmother of the legends is not the endless life of the evergreen "sweet pine" of "Nòhkom Àtayohkàn 1." The speaker here says

You have left me spent
lying open, dying
beneath the sun.

You, breathless,
sightless
beneath the snow.

If the "me" and the "I" speaking in this poem are understood to be the lyric subject, which the poem suggests, then the passionate life force of both the ancient grandmother and the speaking woman/poet are exhausted, "spent," if not yet dead then dying, if not dying then "breathless, / sightless." Whether under the sun or under the snow, the "I" of the poet and the "you" of the grandmother of legends cost each other everything in their encounter. These poems, with their links to the past, to legends snared in and by memory, carry a deliberate contradiction. Neither aspect of the *Nòhkom Àtayohkàn*

— a fundamental trope, if you will, of memory itself — can be forgotten or evaded; both have their effects in the present, one nurturing, the other totally challenging.

Similarly, the human, personal grandmother, Nòhkom, carries multiple implications and associations. A presence of power or medicine, "Nòhkom, Medicine Bear" (13–14) is described in the present tense. She is hardly a figure of memory, yet her existence does not seem confined to the moment. The conflation of "A shuffling brown bear / snorting and puffing" and "Nòhkom, the medicine woman / alone in her attic den / smoking slim cigarettes" brings human and beast together in a unity or connection whose intelligibility is wholly dependent upon cultural context. The bear and the woman are one being, yet each, in this poem, keeps its distinctiveness. She wears a red kerchief on her head, her skirt drapes over "her aged beaded moccasins," and when her work is complete, she "drapes her paws on the stair rails," leaving her "medicine power / to work in silence." The poem's references to secrets, to the darkness, the silence, all contribute to the doubleness of this poetic image. Halfe understates the mystery of how bear and woman can be one being, offering it as a given, and emphasizes the other mystery, the power of knowledge, of the herbs and roots and songs, the work of healing "troubled spirits," and, most profoundly, the power of silence for the medicine to gather its force for its "work." This Nòhkom can be claimed as grandmother, but the force of the figure and the acts seems to stand outside time or personal memory.

A very different representation of Nòhkom appears in "Off with Their Heads" (15–16). In this poem, Halfe sharply dispels the benevolent aura of the past, the delicate taste of memory, and any lingering illusions about inevitable and quintessential respect for nature's creatures by all Aboriginal people at all times. What is left is the image of deliberate cruelty and its effects on the child watching:

Nòhkom
used to take the
visiting tomcats
and ever so gently
wrap a snare wire
around their necks.

From the clothesline
we'd watch the cats

kicking, scratching,
clawing

until

they hung

limp. (15)

I read this careful shaping of line and stanza, the emphatic, ironic "ever so gently," and the chilling "used to," indicating the commonness of this practice, as the wish of the poet to convey quite precisely the events of this torture. The child ("I") would later "go and examine / the stiffs." The use of the word "stiffs" — a kind of hard-boiled detective story word — must be intended here to undercut the grotesque image of the cats' struggle for life; yet, the next stanzas describe the "lifeless eyes . . . foam around their / mouth land-salt / on a dry lake," the eager flies and beetles, and, most vividly, the child herself:

Cat stench
filled my nostrils.
I'd stumble away
clawing the invisible snare
for fresh air.

The identification of the child with the cats and the horrific surrealism of the "invisible snare" are underscored in the last stanza:

Nòhkom would sit at the window
with a cup of tea
puffing her pipe
staring at the tomcats.

The contemplative figure of the old grandmother with her pipe stands in almost bizarre contrast to the wilful and pointless cruelty enacted. Part of the dread conveyed by the poem is the sense of repetition: the child's curiosity and terror, repeated as the torture is repeated; the children unable to stay away from the scene of desperate suffering; the curiosity about death; and the (other) final mystery — What is the grandmother *seeing* when she stares at the dead cats? This is memory that does not seem to fulfil wishes for connection with a powerful heritage; the link of past with present evokes a sense of recurring panic, a scene of horror, and, finally, an inexplicable silence — that of death and of the grandmother's gaze.

For Halfe, with memory comes "voice," a truth indicated only in the title of "Crying for Voice" (6). Memory lives "inside marrow" (6), and to get at it is to go through a process of detailed dissection, clearing passages, purifying and replacing some aspects of self. Each stanza of this poem identifies a necessary action in the speaker's quest for voice: "I must pull frog," and "pry its webbed feet / from snails in / my throat." Weasel will be invited to untangle braids, the "brain / eyes and tongue" of duck, rabbit, and fish must be boiled and consumed. Finding voice requires pulling out as well as taking in. Frog and tapeworm must be removed to make room for "fresh blood"; Bible and tripe must be boiled and boiled and boiled to cook up this "soup"; and she will "Suck marrow from tiny bones" to "fill the place / where frog left slime." The last stanza treats memory with ambivalence:

> I'm fluttering wind
> tobacco floating
> against my face
> mosquitoes up my nostrils
> swatting memories
> inside marrow.

The spiritual association of tobacco and wind, and the comic discomfort of mosquitoes up the nose, mix uneasily with the floating image of "swatting" — memories are like mosquitoes here, an irritation, but "inside marrow"? The absence of a subject doing the swatting — the stanza implies the "I" — contributes to the free feeling, the "fluttering" and "floating" that "I" has achieved. The marrow sucked from tiny bones may or may not be the marrow holding memories. What is clear in this poem is the turning of inside to outside, and outside to in (that is, other and self shift and shift again), of the openings of throat and gut and intestine, the clearing out of innermost spaces and deepest places, and, most of all, the emptying and filling in a long process of finding voice.

In "Bone Lodge" (3), Halfe bonds with the creature world, asserting her connection in a profound unity:

> I'm meat and bones,
> dust and straw,

caterpillars and ants
hummingbird and crow.

Of these I know
in the bones of the lodge.

The "bones" are central to her image of embodied and spiritual life
and the centre of the bone is its marrow.[11] In Halfe, memory is seldom
abstracted from the active voice of the poem speaking its engagement
with the permeable animal, spiritual, earthly, and embodied life of
the female subject. The specific memories and the evocation of legend
and spirit world experience come together to produce memory as
praxis, a full blurring of the categories of memory that Maracle
establishes and an indication of the ways Joy Harjo's trope of the
spiral might work.

I will close this preliminary consideration of memory with a reading
of Harjo's "Skeleton of Winter" (30–31). In this poem, memory is an
"other-sight" that the speaker ("I") attempts to achieve. She has
remained "silent / as a whiteman's watch / keeping time." The image
of the alien disconnected circularity of the "whiteman's watch," that
way of "keeping time," gags Harjo's speech, but the figure is a simile,
and the link between her silence and herself is not integral. Rather,
the implication is one of waiting. And though "It is almost too dark
/ for vision," the speaker finds that she has not lost the possibility of
sight or of speech. It is memory that allows sight despite darkness
("and still I see"). To figure memory as a seeing is to suggest, as
Armstrong does, that amnesia is blindness, but she does not limit
memory to a single sense. As Seremetakis (in the opening epigraph)
asserts, memory is a "meta-sense" with the power to bridge and cross
all other senses.

In "Skeleton of Winter," Harjo makes all the senses part of memory:
"And sound is light, is / movement. The sun revolves / and sings."
This time is neither dark nor silent. With the "other-sight" visions of
dances and births, ancient symbols are seen to be "alive." The female
body of the speaker takes in viscerally the vision and its effects: "A
tooth-hard rocking / in my belly comes back." The labour pains of
memory bring sound, "echoes," to consciousness: "something echoes
/ all forgotten dreams, / in winter." The implication here that return,
echo, revolution are all in play, all part of what is to be seen and seen
again, takes memory utterly out of a fixed place. The last stanza
delivers the insight gained from "other-sight":

I am memory alive
                not just a name
but an intricate part
of this web of motion,
meaning: earth, sky, stars circling
my heart
                centrifugal. (31)

Harjo invites a connection between individual identity (a name) and cosmic sensibility. The "meta-sense" is not merely sensory. The lines are ambivalent: everything works in centrifugal relation to the heart — or the heart ("my heart," she says) circles the whole web of motion, the web of meaning. To say "I am memory alive" is to say memory lives in me; I live in memory; memory and I are one being, and memory (that wild abstraction) is essential to identity in its narrowest (the personal name) and its widest (cosmic) implications. Again, we see that Barthes's historian, in "de-chronologizing," coalesces with the poet. Barthes suggests, as I mentioned earlier, that this act of speech "restores" nonlinear time — and the gift of that time is "a deep space" that "recalls the mythic time of the ancient cosmogonies" (130–31). I do not want to belabour Barthes's flight of poetic speech or insight too crudely. But when, in an interview with Bill Moyers, Harjo responds to Moyers's observation that Harjo herself is "memory alive," and Harjo says, "We *all* are" (49), Harjo seems to push the link that memory and speech makes between historian and poet into a realm of "the sacred" that is culturally inclusive. This is not to suggest that differences — cultural, historical, personal, genetic[12] — do not matter, nor that they do not make both meaning and matter. The cultural inclusivity that I read in Harjo's "we *all* are [memory alive]" is more a kind of possibility and a responsibility. The "Breakfast of the Spirit" that Dumont celebrates, or the demanding search that Armstrong requires, the sucking of bone marrow that brings Halfe to her truth — all these speak to memory and from memory. The *idea* of memory and the content of memory come together and (as Ferron sings) they come apart. Those specific points and moments are what give memory its weight, and the force of memory is what holds us, individually and culturally, to our Earth ("gravity," says Harjo). Finally, then, speaking to Krupat's view that there is no memory in the blood: Why not? You will find it everywhere else, if you look for it.

¹ Given that new genes are being identified all the time, I am not sure how Krupat could be quite so certain of this, even on the biological level. Readers may be interested in Thomas King's antiessentialist stance on the issue (see, for example, the introduction to *All My Relations*).

² Krupat is making an urgent plea for the development of a responsible critical language that "might mediate" between Native American and other fiction, an informed comparative criticism that would not "foreclose possibilities of understanding" but would allow "cross-cultural translation or ethnocriticism" that would deepen our understanding of all literatures. See his chapter "Postcolonialism, Ideology, and Native American Literature" in *The Turn to the Native* for a full discussion of these views.

³ Jodi Lundgren takes up aspects of these questions in "'Being a Half-Breed," an important article on "racial and cultural syncreticity" in which she examines the emphasis various Métis writers (Culleton, Campbell, and Maracle) place on culture rather than "race."

⁴ This appears under the general heading "From History to Reality" in *The Rustle of Language* (127–40).

⁵ I am taking Barthes out of context and his own argument is tending elsewhere — nevertheless, his assertions are provocative.

⁶ When I gave a version of this paper in Bombay, with an emphasis on the debates staged by Krupat and Momaday on the possibility of "memory in the blood," I was disconcerted to observe how much of a nonissue it was to the Indian scholars I was addressing: of course there was memory in the blood — too obvious to argue about. This was a highly corrective experience for me in that it revealed to me my assumption that the scientific perspective would be one held by most academics (although even that science could be debated: genes are not all identified are they?) and has helped me shape this essay in more complicated ways. I owe the women of SNDT (the Women's University) my thanks for their helpful comments.

⁷ Kimberly Blaeser's comic poem about being mistaken for her mother ends with the arch and pointed query, "Wonder if I'm what they call living history?" ("Living History"). She is, of course, mocking the revisiting of the "vanishing peoples" notion that some current critical positions seem to articulate.

⁸ Leslie Marmon Silko has somewhere asked, "What can you expect of a people whose own God has kicked them out?" Kimberly Blaeser has examined revisionist treatments of Bible stories in Native literature in "Pagans Rewriting the Bible."

⁹ I have discussed this poem elsewhere at greater length and with different focus (see "'Speaking to Newcomers'").

¹⁰ Halfe generously provides a glossary of the Cree words and phrases that she uses.

[11] Examining anthropological practice and implication, Seremetakis looks at Greek exhumation, during which "the sensory presence of the dusted bones of the dead reawakens the memory of past commensal exchanges with the dead. Ignited by the collective memories invested in the bone as emotive artifact, the exhumers create a commensal ritual grounded on material substances" (37). The materiality of this study limits its direct use for my reading of Halfe, but the figurative reverberations are strong.

[12] Does this mean racial? I do not know, and the differences and similarities among these poets and poems have not told me.

WORKS CITED

Armstrong, Jeannette. *Breath Tracks*. Stratford: Williams-Theytus, 1991.

Barthes, Roland. "The Discourse of History." *The Rustle of Language*. Trans. Richard Howard. New York: Hill, 1986. 127–40.

Blaeser, Kimberly. "Living History." *The Colour of Resistance: A Contemporary Collection of Writing by Aboriginal Women*. Ed. Connie Fife. Toronto: Sister Vision, 1993. 44.

——. "Pagans Rewriting the Bible: Heterodoxy and the Representation of Spirituality in Native American Literature." *Ariel* 25.1 (1994): 12–31.

Coltelli, Laura. "Introduction: The Transforming Power of Joy Harjo's Poetry." Coltelli, ed. 1–13.

——, ed. *The Spiral of Memory: Interviews/Joy Marjo*. Ann Arbor: U of Michigan P, 1996.

Dumont, Marilyn. *A Really Good Brown Girl*. London, ON: Brick, 1996.

Halfe, Louise. *Bear Bones and Feathers*. Regina: Coteau, 1994. 3.

Harjo, Joy. "Ancestral Voices: Interview with Bill Moyers." Coltelli, ed. 36–49.

——. "The Circular Dream: Interview with Laura Coltelli." Coltelli, ed. 60–74.

——. "A Laughter of Absolute Sanity: Interview with Angels Carabi." Coltelli, ed. 133–39.

——. "Skeleton of Winter." *She Had Some Horses*. New York: Thunder's Mouth, 1983. 30–31.

King, Thomas. Introduction. *All My Relations: An Anthology of Contemporary Native Fiction*. Ed. King. Toronto: McClelland, 1990. ix–xvi.

Krupat, Arnold. *The Turn to the Native: Studies in Criticism and Culture*. Lincoln: U of Nebraska P, 1996.

——. *The Voice in the Margin: Native American Literature and the Canon*. Berkeley: U of California P, 1989.

Lincoln, Kenneth. *Native American Renaissance*. Berkeley: U of California P, 1983.

Lundgren, Jodi. "'Being a Half-breed': Discourses of Race and Cultural

Syncreticity in the Works of Three Métis Women Writers." *Canadian Literature* 144 (1995): 62–77.

Maracle, Lee. "Skyros Bruce: First Voice of Contemporary Native Poetry." *Gatherings: The En'owkin Journal of First North American Peoples* 2 (1991): 85–91.

Perreault, Jeanne. "Speaking to Newcomers in Their Language." *Open Letter* 9.2 (1995): 29–36.

Seremetakis, C. Nadia. *The Senses Still: Perception and Memory as Material Culture in Modernity*. Chicago: U of Chicago P, 1994.

Contributors

MARGERY FEE teaches postcolonial literatures, Canadian literature, and First Nations writing at the University of British Columbia. Her most recent book, with Janice McAlpine, is *Guide to Canadian English Usage* (Oxford UP, 1997); she has published on Indigenous writers Jeannette Armstrong, Beatrice Culleton, Keri Hulme, and Mudrooroo Narogin.

AGNES GRANT is the editor of *Our Bit of Truth: An Anthology of Canadian Native Literature* (1990), as well as the author of *James McKay: A Metis Builder of Canada* (1994) and *No End of Grief: Canadian Indian Residential Schools* (1996). She coauthored *Joining the Circle: A Practitioners' Guide to Responsive Education for Native Students* (1993) with LaVina Gillespie. She teaches Native studies and education courses at Brandon University for the Brandon University Northern Teacher Education Program (BUNTEP) and Program for Educating Native Teachers (PENT). As well, she has written numerous articles on Native literature and Native educational issues.

MARIANETTE JAIMES-GUERRERO is of Native and Mestiza descent. Her heritage is rooted in the Southwest, the Yaqui/Opata of Arizona, where she was born, and the California Mission bands (Juaneno) in southern California. She is currently an associate professor of women's studies, College of Humanities, at San Francisco State University. Prior to moving to California, she was a visiting professor at Arizona State University, School of Justice Studies, where she taught on Native environmental issues. She was also instrumental in developing the American Indian studies program at the University of Colorado at Boulder. Jaimes-Guerrero has published in anthologies and texts, in the interdisciplinary field of ethnic studies that is cross-cultural for comparative research and with a gender-specific focus on Native American women and early Indigenous peoples. She is the editor of the internationally award-winning *The State of Native America* (South End Press, 1992), now in its second printing. She has been a recipient of numerous grants and fellowships, primarily in the area of "the politics of identity." She is a former fellow at the Society for the Humanities, Cornell University (1991–92); and the Humanities Research Centre, Australian National University (1996). She is also a board member and a reviewer for *Aboriginal Voices*, a Native media magazine headquartered in Toronto. She is currently working on her fourth book, tentatively titled "Native Womanism: Exemplars of Indigenism," as well as her first book of poems, "Native Genesis."

CHARLOTTE HUSSEY is a poet and a Social Sciences and Humanities Research Council doctoral fellow at McGill University. Her book of poems, *Rue Sainte-Famille*, was published in 1990 by Véhicule Press. She currently teaches creative writing and study skills for the Office of Native and Inuit Education at McGill.

HARTMUT LUTZ earned his teacher's diploma in Kiel (1969), his Ph.D in English from the University of Tübingen (1974), and his post-doctoral "habilitation" from the University of Osnabrück (1985). He has taught in Britain, the United States, Canada, and Germany. His publications include *William Goldings Prosawerk* (1975), *"Indianer" und "Native Americans"* (1985), *Minority Literatures in North America* (with Wolfgang Karrer, 1990), and *Contemporary Challenges: Conversations with Canadian Native Authors* (1992), as well as numerous articles on Native American studies and Canadian women's literature. He is the founding editor of a bilingual series on minority writers, OBEMA, and has helped to publish Native authors in German. Since 1994, he has been a full professor of American and Canadian studies at the Ernst-Moritz-Arndt Universität Greifswald in northeastern Germany.

RON MARKEN has been teaching English and Irish literature at the University of Saskatchewan for over thirty years. He has published on the poetry of Yeats, Hardy, and Hopkins, as well as on the work of contemporary Irish poets Muldoon, Ormsby, Johnstone, Murphy, and Hewitt. For six years, he edited *The Canadian Journal of Irish Studies*. In 1997, he concluded eighteen months as acting head of the Department of Native Studies at the University of Saskatchewan.

PATRICIA MONTURE ANGUS (Mohawk) currently resides at the Thunderchild First Nations with her family. She is an associate professor in the Department of Native Studies at the University of Saskatchewan, and teaches in the areas of law and justice. She is author of numerous articles on First Nations, and her first book is entitled *Thunder in My Soul: A Mohawk Woman Speaks*.

JEANNE PERREAULT is associate professor of English at the University of Calgary. She is coeditor (with Sylvia Vance) of *Writing the Circle:*

Native Women of Western Canada (1990), and coeditor (with Joseph Bruchac) of *Critical Visions: Contemporary Native Writing and Writers*, a special issue of ARIEL (1994). She is the author of *Writing Selves: Contemporary Feminist Autobiography* (1995). Currently, she is examining the racializing of whiteness in white women's texts. Other articles on this topic appear in *Colour*, a special issue of *West Coast Line* (1995), and *Reading Canadian Autobiography*, a special issue of *Essays on Canadian Writing* (1996).

PATRICIA RILEY is a literary critic and writer of Cherokee and Irish descent. She currently teaches Native American literature and other literatures in the English department at the University of Idaho. In addition to being the editor of *Growing Up Native American*, an anthology of fiction and nonfiction, she has published a number of poems, short stories, and critical essays.

ARMAND GARNET RUFFO's work is strongly influenced by his Ojibway heritage. He is the author of a collection of poetry, *Opening in the Sky* (Theytus, 1994); and a creative biography, *Grey Owl: The Mystery of Archie Belaney* (Coteau, 1997). His latest play, *A Windigo Tale*, will be workshopped by Native Earth Performing Arts Inc.; a short story will appear in an anthology of Anishnabe writing to be published by the University of Minnesota. His last essay on Native literature appeared in *International Journal of Canadian Studies*. He is currently a lecturer in the Department of English and associate director of the Centre for Education, Research and Culture at Carleton University.

JO-ANN THOM is a Métis woman who was born in Manitoba. She received a BA in English from the Saskatchewan Indian Federated College (1991), an honours certificate (1992) and an MA from the University of Regina (1994). Her thesis is entitled "A Study of Narrative Voice: Discursive Authority and Ideology in the Works of Leslie Marmon Silko." She is on the faculty of the Saskatchewan Indian Federated College, and since 1996 has served as head of the English department.

CLIFFORD E. TRAFZER (Wyandot) is professor of Native American studies and history at the University of California, Riverside, where he is also director of American Indian studies at the Costo Historical and Linguistics Native American Research Center. He has published many books and articles on Native American history and literature, including *Death Stalks the Yakama*, for which he received a Word-craft Circle of Native American Writers and Storytellers Book Award,

Earth Song, Sky Spirit, Blue Dawn, Red Earth, Renegade Tribe, Mourning Dove's Stories, Looking Glass, and others. He is vice-chair of the California Native American Heritage Commission, and a board member of Wordcraft Circle of Native Writers and Storytellers.

GERALD VIZENOR is professor of Native American literature at the University of California, Berkeley. He is author of more than twenty books on Native histories, literature, and critical studies, including *The People Named the Chippewa: Narrative Histories* and *Crossbloods: Bone Courts, Bingo, and Other Reports.* His autobiography, *Interior Landscapes: Autobiographical Myths and Metaphors,* and his first novel, *Bearheart: The Heirship Chronicles,* were published by the University of Minnesota Press. He edited *Narrative Chance,* a collection of essays on Native American literature. *Manifest Manners: Postindian Warriors of Survivance,* critical studies; *The Heirs of Columbus,* a novel; and *Landfill Meditation,* a collection of short stories, were all published by Wesleyan University Press. *Griever: An American Monkey King in China,* his second novel, won an American Book Award. *Dead Voices: Natural Agonies in the New World,* his fifth novel, was published by the University of Oklahoma Press. His recent books include *Shadow Distance: A Gerald Vizenor Reader,* and *Hotline Healers: An Almost Browne Novel,* both published by Wesleyan University Press. He edited *Native American Literature,* an anthology published as part of the Literary Mosaic Series, put out by HarperCollins College Publishers. He is also series editor of American Indian Literature and Critical Studies, published by the University of Oklahoma Press.

RENÉE HULAN teaches Canadian literature at Saint Mary's University in Halifax, Nova Scotia. Her work has been published in *Essays on Canadian Writing, Canadian Literature, Theatre Research in Canada,* and *Echoing Silence: Essays on Arctic Narrative,* edited by John Moss. She is currently completing post-doctoral research on the reception of First Nations writing in Canada.